1

BREAKING THE
SPANISH
BARRIER

LEVEL ONE
BEGINNER

John Conner

Student Edition

BREAKING THE BARRIER, INC.
THE LANGUAGE SERIES WITH ALL THE RULES YOU NEED TO KNOW
THE FASTEST PATH TO TRUE LANGUAGE FLUENCY

For Lisa, Jamie, Hannah, Alexandra and Sarah

ACKNOWLEDGMENTS

Thanks to Guillermo Barnetche for the artistic vision, Barbara Peterson, contributing editor, for her wonderful suggestions, and to Ann Talbot for her stylish layout. A special thanks to Miguel Romá for his brilliant editing.

AN INVITATION

*We invite you to join many of our readers who, over the years, have shared their suggestions for improvements as well as their personal knowledge of the Hispanic world. In doing so, they have become our partners. We are grateful for their invaluable contributions as the evolution of **Breaking the Barrier** belongs, in part, to them.*

BREAKING THE BARRIER, INC.
63 Shirley Road
Groton, MA 01450
Phone: 978-448-0594
Fax: 978-448-1237
E-mail: info@tobreak.com
www.tobreak.com

ISBN: 978-1-955306-00-3

S1SE0421

PREFACE

BREAKING THE **S**PANISH **B**ARRIER is a core text, workbook and handy reference all-in-one. It can stand alone, or complement the multitude of Spanish language resources currently available.

We believe that one of the fastest paths to fluency is built upon a rock-solid understanding of grammar. **BREAKING THE SPANISH BARRIER** provides the essential roadmap for this journey.

In the following twelve lessons, you will find country maps, vocabulary, a review of key grammatical concepts, explanations of new material, many practice exercises, an exciting dialogue series, as well as review tests. Companion audio provides further opportunity to sharpen your Spanish skills — by hearing, modeling, and conversing with native speakers. Sentences throughout the book highlight current people, places and events from the Spanish-speaking world. You will find the tone of these pages informal and conversational — a one-on-one session between teacher and student.

WE LOOK FORWARD TO ACCOMPANYING YOU AS YOU SET OUT TO BREAK THE SPANISH BARRIER.

¡BUENA SUERTE!

JOHN CONNER
Author and Series Editor

⬚An online version of this book is available at www.tobreak.com. It includes audio recordings (new vocabulary, all sample sentences, small group oral practice, action series), interactive exercises, along with video (introduction to chapter, instructional capsules with motion graphics, cultural articles).

⟁⟁ TABLE OF CONTENTS ⟁⟁

FIRST STEPS

*Long before you learned any grammar rules in your native language, you had learned to speak beautifully. As a child, you added vocabulary little by little, figured out how to put sentences together, and discovered how to imitate the sounds of the language. As you begin to **Break the Spanish Barrier**, you will learn — right from the start — some useful vocabulary, expressions, and tips about pronunciation . . . all before you learn any formal grammar rules. For a little bit, you will have to be willing to leave some of your questions unanswered. Never fear, however! By the end of this book, all of your questions will be addressed. These first ten steps will get you speaking Spanish right away.*

STEP ONE — ¿CÓMO SE LLAMA USTED?

> When you want to learn someone's name, you can ask him or her:
>
> 🖥 (Online access offers recordings of all sample sentences.) 🖥
>
> ***Cómo se llama usted?*** (What is your name?)
>   *Me llamo María.* (My name is Mary.)
>   *Me llamo Juan.* (My name is John.)

You can also ask someone to tell you who another person is. Here are some possible questions you might ask:

¿Cómo se llama su profesora? (What's your teacher's name?)
    Mi profesora se llama señora Sánchez. (My teacher's name is Mrs. Sánchez.)

¿Cómo se llama su madre? (What's your mother's name?)
    Mi madre se llama Ana.

¿Cómo se llama su amigo? (What is your friend's name?)
    Mi amigo se llama Andrés.

¿Cómo se llama el presidente? (What is name of the president?)
    El presidente se llama Felipe.

Here are some common Spanish names:

Adela	*Elena*	*Lucía*	*Paco*
Ana	*Gabriel*	*Luis*	*Penélope*
Andrés	*Gisela*	*Lupe*	*Pilar*
Arturo	*Inés*	*Manolo*	*Ramón*
Carlota	*Isabel*	*Marcos*	*Raquel*
Carmen	*Javier*	*María*	*Ricardo*
Chita	*Jorge*	*Miguel*	*Rosaura*
Cristóbal	*Juan*	*Nicolás*	*Tomás*

PRÁCTICA

Answer the following ten questions aloud or on paper.

1) **¿Cómo se llama usted?** Me llamo <u>Ana</u>.

2) **¿Cómo se llama su profesor?** Mi profesor se llama <u>Señora Elena</u>.

3) **¿Cómo se llama su amiga?** Mi amiga se llama <u>Carmen</u>.

4) **¿Cómo se llama su dentista?** <u>Mi dentista se llama Señora macía</u>.

5) **¿Cómo se llama su papá?** <u>Mi papá se llama Ricardo</u>.

6) **¿Cómo se llama su mamá?** <u>Mi mamá se llama Gisela</u>.

7) **¿Cómo se llama usted?** <u>Me llamo Adela</u>.

8) **¿Cómo se llama su amigo?** <u>Mi amigo se llama Jorge</u>.

9) **¿Cómo se llama el presidente?** El presidente se llama <u>Javier</u>.

10) **¿Cómo se llama su profesor de matemáticas?** Mi profesor de

matemáticas <u>se llama Marcos</u>.

PRÁCTICA DE PRONUNCIACIÓN

a, e, i, o, u

Online access has recordings of all words in these pronunciation sections:

The five vowels in Spanish are so important to learn! Fortunately, these sounds don't change from word to word. They are crisp, short sounds, unlike many English vowel sounds that seem to drag on. Oftentimes, English speakers think that Spanish speakers talk so fast. This observation is made, in part, because the sounds of the vowels are shorter.

In order to feel at ease with these new sounds, practice them frequently with the help of your teacher or the CD.

a – This letter sounds like the "a" when you sing the notes "la-la-la."

Repita (repeat!): *casa, bata, mamá, masa, papá, alma, mala, arte, taza, salsa, lata, Nacha*

e – This letter sounds like the "a" in the word "chaos."

bebé, leche, de, té, pele, bese, entender, teme, Enrique

i – This letter sounds like the "ee" in "tee."

sí, misa, pizza, linda, cinta, amiga, chico, di

o – This letter sounds like "o" in the word "nose," but it is actually almost half the sound. You have to try to chop off the last part of the long English "o."

ola, olé, nota, mole, bota, bolo, Lola, onda, chocolate, solo, cola

u – This letter sounds like the "oo" in "soon." Once again, the sound is shorter and crisper.

uno, luna, mucho, cuna, buche, lunes, bambú, fumas, pluma

When you want to find out where someone is from, you can ask him or her:

¿De dónde es usted?   (Where are you from?)
> *Soy de Chicago.*   (I'm from Chicago.)
> *Soy de Santo Domingo.*   (I'm from Santo Domingo.)

You can also ask someone to tell you where someone else is from. Here are some possible questions you might ask:

¿De dónde es su padre?   (Where is your father from?)
> *Mi padre es de Nueva York.*   (My father is from New York.)

¿De dónde es su amiga?   (Where is your friend from?)
> *Mi amiga es de Los Ángeles.*

¿De dónde son los mexicanos?   (Where are Mexicans from?)
> *Los mexicanos son de México.*

¿De dónde son los colombianos?   (Where are Colombians from?)
> *Los colombianos son de Colombia.*

Here are some well-known cities, countries, and geographical locations around the world with Spanish names. How many could you locate on a map?

Amarillo	*España*	*Panamá*
Argentina	*Fresno*	*Paraguay*
Barcelona	*Guatemala*	*Perú*
Bolivia	*Honduras*	*Puerto Rico*
Chile	*Los Andes*	*República Dominicana*
Colombia	*Los Ángeles*	*Río Grande*
Costa Rica	*Madrid*	*San Francisco*
Cuba	*México*	*San Juan*
Ecuador	*Nevada*	*Uruguay*
El Salvador	*Nicaragua*	*Venezuela*

PRÁCTICA

Answer the following ten questions, aloud or on paper, in complete sentences.

1) **¿De dónde es usted?** Soy de Fresno.

2) **¿De dónde es su madre?** Mi madre es de Perú.

3) **¿De dónde es su profesor de español?** Mi profesor de español es de chile.

4) **¿De dónde es su amigo favorito?** Mi amigo es de México.

5) **¿De dónde es Shakira?** Shakira es de Costa Rica.

6) **¿De dónde son los californianos?** Los Californianos Son de California.

7) **¿De dónde son los africanos?** Los africanos Son de África.

8) **¿De dónde son los chilenos?** Los chilenos Son de chile.

9) **¿De dónde es su padre?** Mi padre es de San Juan.

10) **¿De dónde es usted?** Soy de Cuba.

PRÁCTICA DE PRONUNCIACIÓN

y , d

In this section and the remaining ones of First Steps, we will look at Spanish consonants. A number of Spanish consonants are pronounced exactly as in English, while others are completely different. Using your teacher or the CDs as a model, practice and repeat the following:

y – This letter, in fact, has two different sounds — the first is vowel-like, and the other like a consonant. When the letter "y" stands by itself or when it comes at the very end of a word, it sounds just like the "ee" in "tee," except a bit shorter and crisper.

y, ley, buey, ay, hay, Uruguay, Paraguay, soy, muy, hoy

When the letter "y" is found in any other position, it is pronounced just like the "y" sound found in the English word "yes."

ya, yema, yo, cuyo, suya, hoyo, mayo

d – This consonant has different sounds, depending upon where it is placed in a word or sentence. At the beginning of a word or breath group, or following a consonant, it sounds pretty much like the "d" in the word "dentist."

Diego, diablo, dice, doctor, diente, de, dolor, donde, andar, dan, doce, Dalí

Surrounded by vowels, the "d" loses most of its "voiced" sound, and sounds more like the "th" in "lather."

código, lado, helado, comido, aliado, frustrado, modo, Estados Unidos

Finally, at the end of a word, the "d" still sounds like the "th" in "lather," but it is even weaker or "breathier."

comed, edad, ciudad, universidad, facilidad, facultad, id, capacidad

When you want to find out how someone is feeling today, you can ask him or her:

Buenos días. ¿Cómo está usted hoy? (Good morning. How are you today?)
> *Estoy bien.* (I'm well.)
> *Estoy así-así (regular).* (I'm so-so/O.K.)
> *Estoy mal.* (I'm bad, i.e., not feeling well.)

> To add some extra emphasis to your answer, you can add the word *"muy"* meaning "very."
> *Estoy **muy** bien.* (I'm very well.)
> *Estoy **muy** mal.* (I'm very bad.)

You can also ask someone to tell you how another person is doing. Here are some possible questions you might ask:

Buenas tardes. ¿Cómo está su amiga hoy? (Good afternoon. How is your friend today?)
> *Mi amiga está bien.* (My friend is fine.)

¿Cómo está el profesor? (How is the teacher doing?)
> *El profesor está mal.* (The teacher isn't feeling well.)

Buenas noches. ¿Cómo están sus padres? (Good evening. How are your parents?)
> *Mis padres están así-así.* (My parents are so-so/O.K.)

¿Cómo están los animales? (How are the animals?)
> *Los animales están muy bien.* (The animals are very well.)

When you want to say "goodbye" to someone, you could say:

Adiós. Hasta luego. (Goodbye. See you later.)

PRÁCTICA

Answer the following ten questions, aloud or on paper, in complete sentences. Use as many different responses as possible.

1) **Buenos días. ¿Cómo está usted?** Estoy <u>bien</u>.

2) **¿Cómo está su madre?** Mi madre está <u>así-así</u>.

3) **¿Cómo está su padre?** <u>Mi padre Estoy mal</u>.

4) **¿Cómo está su amigo favorito?** <u>Mi amigo favorito está bien</u>.

5) **¿Cómo está Juanes hoy?** <u>Juanes está muy bien hoy</u>.

   _____.

6) **¿Cómo está su profesora de historia hoy?** <u>Mi profesora de historia está muy mal</u>.

7) **Buenas tardes. ¿Cómo están sus amigos hoy?** Mis amigos están <u>bien</u>.

   _____.

8) **¿Cómo están sus padres hoy?** <u>Mis padres están así-así</u>.

   _____.

9) **¿Cómo está su tío (uncle) hoy?** Mi tío <u>Está muy bien</u>.

10) **¿Cómo está usted?** <u>Estoy mal</u>.

PRÁCTICA DE PRONUNCIACIÓN

h, q, s

Here are some more consonants:

h – This letter is <u>completely</u> silent in Spanish. It requires your making no sound at all, no matter what position it is in! Ever!

hotel, historia, hilo, Alhambra, rehén, hielo, hombre, hospital, ahora, hijo

q – This letter is always followed in Spanish by the vowels "ui" or "ue." The "u" in these combinations is silent. The sound of "qu" is like the English "k" in the word "kind."

que, quien, quiero, Raquel, Quito, adquirir, queso, quepo, Querétaro, quiosco

s – This letter sounds like the "s" in the word "song."

sosa, sin, flores, casa, playas, chiste, masa, seta, seis, siete, San Salvador

STEP FOUR — ¿ES USTED NORMAL?

When you want to find out what someone is like, you could ask him or her:

¿Es usted normal? (Are you normal?)
> *Sí, soy normal.* (Yes, I'm normal.)
> *No, no soy normal.* (No, I'm not normal.)

¿Es usted popular? (Are you popular?)
> *Sí, soy popular.*
> *No, no soy popular.*

¿Es usted interesante? (Are you interesting?)
> *Sí, soy interesante.*
> *No, no soy interesante.*

You can also ask someone to tell you what someone else is like. Here are some possible questions you might ask:

¿Es generoso su amigo? (Is your friend generous?)

> *Sí, mi amigo es generoso.* (Yes, my friend is generous.)
> *No, mi amigo no es generoso.* (No, my friend is not generous.)

¿Es sincera su amiga? (Is your friend sincere?)

> *Sí, mi amiga es sincera.* (Yes, my friend is sincere.)
> *No, mi amiga no es sincera.* (No, my friend is not sincere.)

¿Cómo es su amiga? (What is your friend like?)

> *Mi amiga es generosa y popular.* (My friend is generous and popular.)
> *Mi amiga es fantástica.* (My friend is fantastic.)

Adjectives that end in "o" when describing a male change to "a" when describing a female.

¿Es muy diplomático su padre?

> *Sí, mi padre es muy diplomático.*
> *No, mi padre no es muy diplomático.*

¿Es muy diplomática su madre?

> *Sí, mi madre es muy diplomática.*
> *No, mi madre no es muy diplomática.*

The adjectives used so far in this section should sound quite familiar to an English speaker *(normal, popular, interesante, generoso, sincero, fantástico, diplomático)*. It is because these words are <u>cognates</u> — they come from the same Latin roots — that they are easily recognizable. They look and sound quite similar to many English words you know. Here are some other Spanish adjectives whose meanings you could probably guess instantly:

ambicioso/a	*conservador*	*famoso/a*	*paciente*
artístico/a	*cordial*	*importante*	*posible*
atlético/a	*elegante*	*imposible*	*práctico/a*
brillante	*estupendo/a*	*liberal*	*religioso/a*
cómico/a	*estúpido/a*	*maravilloso/a*	*romántico/a*

PRÁCTICA

Using the adjectives that you learned in this section, answer the following ten questions aloud or on paper. Try not to use the same adjective more than once.

1) **¿Es usted normal?** Sí, soy ___normal___ .

2) **¿Cómo es su amigo?** Mi amigo es ___artístico___ .

3) **¿Es liberal su profesor?** ___No, Mi profesor no es liberal___ .

4) **¿Es religiosa su madre?** ___Sí, Mi madre es religiosa___ .

5) **¿Es atlético Rafael Nadal?** ___No, Rafael Nadal no atlético___ .

6) **¿Es atlética Carlota Ciganda?** ___Sí, Carlota Ciganda es atlético___ .

7) **¿Cómo es su amiga?** ___Mi amiga es brillante___ .

8) **¿Es popular su profesor de español?** ___Sí, Mi profesor de español___

___es popular___ .

9) **¿Es romántico Enrique Iglesias?** ___No, Enrique Iglesias No___ .
___romántico.___

10) **¿Cómo es usted?** ___Soy estúpida   No, no es soy estndpú___

PRÁCTICA DE PRONUNCIACIÓN

m, n, ñ

Here are three more consonants:

m – This letter is pronounced just as in English. The Spanish "m" sounds like the "m" in the word "mouse."

mapa, Madrid, Miami, malo, cama, imposible, masa, limpia, mitología, maestro

n – This letter is always pronounced just as in English. The Spanish "n" sounds like the "n" in the word "night."

hermano, piano, nata, Candela, Nicaragua, norte, chimenea, cementerio

ñ – This letter is not found in the English alphabet. However, the same sound exists in English. The "ñ" is just like the "ny" in "canyon" or the "ni" in "onion."

niño, año, caña, cumpleaños, reñir, teñir, viña, mañana, Muñoz

STEP FIVE — ¿QUÉ ES ESTO?

When you want to find out what something is, you could point at it and ask:

¿Qué es esto? (What's this?)
> *Es un libro.* (It's a book.)
> *Es una silla.* (It's a chair.)

The word *un,* meaning "a" or "an," is used before "masculine nouns" — ones that end in "o" and many others, while the word *una* (also meaning "a" and "an") is used before "feminine nouns" — ones that end in "a" and many others.

Here is some useful vocabulary that you can use in the **classroom** or at **home**.

LA CLASE y LA CASA					
(una) alcoba	→	bedroom	*(una) mesa*	→	table
(un) baño	→	bathroom	*(un) papel*	→	paper
(una) cama	→	bed	*(una) pluma*	→	pen
(una) casa	→	house	*(un) profesor*	→	teacher
(un) carro	→	car	*(una) profesora*	→	teacher
(un) coche	→	car (in Spain)	*(una) puerta*	→	door
(una) cocina	→	kitchen	*(un) reloj*	→	watch/clock
(un) comedor	→	dining room	*(una) sala*	→	living room
(una) escuela	→	school	*(una) silla*	→	chair
(un) lápiz	→	pencil	*(una) ventana*	→	window
(un) libro	→	book			

 PRÁCTICA

I. *Study the words carefully that were presented in this section. Once you feel that you have them fairly well memorized, draw a little picture of the five words presented below. Try not to look back at the list as you do this exercise!*

1) una ventana

2) un profesor

3) una casa

4) un lápiz

5) un papel

II. Now answer each question, following the model presented.

Example: *¿Qué es esto?* <u>*Es una pluma.*</u>

1) **¿Qué es esto?** <u>Es una silla</u>

2) **¿Qué es esto?** <u>Es una libro</u>

3) **¿Qué es esto?** <u>Es una escuela</u>

4) **¿Qué es esto?** <u>Es una carro</u>

5) **¿Qué es esto?** <u>Es una reloj</u>

 PRÁCTICA DE PRONUNCIACIÓN

c, ch, p

Here are some more consonants:

c – This consonant has a number of different pronunciations. As in English, before an "a," "o," or "u," this letter sounds like the "c" in "cool."

casa, cama, coche, rica, Cuba, acumular, coco, costa, colina

Again, as in English, when "c" comes before "e" or "i," it is most often pronounced like the "s" in "song." In some parts of Spain, however, the "c" in this position would be pronounced like the "th" in "thin."

celos, cielo, reciente, producir, cinta, cenicero, sinceros, cine

ch – Until recently, this consonant has normally been considered a single letter in the Spanish alphabet, although it certainly looks like two! This "ch" sounds like the "ch" in the word "chocolate."

chica, coche, chiste, chicle, Conchita, Chiapas, rechoncho, relinche

p – This letter is basically like the "p" found in the English word "pizza." At times, the "p" in English "explodes" a little bit, with a fair amount of breath coming out of the speaker's mouth. The Spanish "p" is a little more restrained, but to most people not really distinguishable from the English "p." If you put a candle close to your lips when saying the name "Peter," you might blow out the candle. In Spanish, however, the flame would barely flicker when saying *"Pedro."*

pelo, postal, padre, reportero, ropero, pico, picante, suplicar, aplicado

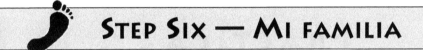

STEP SIX — MI FAMILIA

If you want to learn about someone's family, you might ask him or her:

¿Tiene Ud. (usted) hermanos? (Do you have brothers and sisters?)
> *Sí, tengo un hermano.* (Yes, I have one brother.)
> *Sí, tengo una hermana.* (Yes, I have one sister.)
> *No, no tengo hermanos.* (No, I don't have brothers or sisters.)

¿Tiene Ud. (usted) abuelos? (Do you have grandparents?)
> *Sí, tengo un abuelo.* (Yes, I have one grandfather.)
> *Sí, tengo una abuela.* (Yes, I have one grandmother.)
> *No, no tengo abuelos.* (No, I don't have grandparents.)

You might want to ask someone about another person's family. If so, you could ask:

¿Tiene María hermanos? (Does Mary have brothers and sisters?)
> *Sí, María tiene un hermano.* (Yes, Mary has a brother.)
> *Sí, María tiene una hermana.* (Yes, Mary has a sister.)
> *No, María no tiene hermanos.* (No, Mary doesn't have brothers or sisters.)

¿Tiene su amigo muchos primos? (Does your friend have many cousins?)
> *Sí, mi amigo tiene muchos primos.* (Yes, my friend has many cousins.)
> *No, mi amigo no tiene muchos primos.* (No, my friend doesn't have many cousins.)

The following is a list of useful vocabulary related to the **family**:

LA FAMILIA					
abuela	→	grandmother	*nieta*	→	granddaughter
abuelo	→	grandfather	*nieto*	→	grandson
cuñada	→	sister-in-law	*padre*	→	father
cuñado	→	brother-in-law	*prima*	→	cousin (female)
esposa	→	wife	*primo*	→	cousin (male)
esposo	→	husband	*sobrina*	→	niece
hermana	→	sister	*sobrino*	→	nephew
hermano	→	brother	*suegra*	→	mother-in-law
hija	→	daughter	*suegro*	→	father-in-law
hijo	→	son	*tía*	→	aunt
madre	→	mother	*tío*	→	uncle

 PRÁCTICA

I. *After studying the list of vocabulary about the family, answer the following questions in complete sentences.*

Example: *¿Tiene Ud. primos?* <u>*Sí, tengo primos / No, no tengo primos.*</u>

1) **¿Tiene Ud. (usted) muchos primos?** <u>No, no muchos primos</u>.

2) **¿Tiene Ud. una hermana?** <u>Sí, tengo una hermana</u>.

3) **¿Tiene Ud. un hermano?** <u>Sí, tengo unchermano</u>.

4) **¿Cómo se llama su abuelo?** Mi abuelo se llama <u>Miguel</u>.

5) **¿Cómo se llama su tía? Mi tía** <u>Se llama Ana</u>.

6) **¿Cómo se llama su madre?** <u>Mi madre Se llama Ohita</u>.

7) **¿Tiene Ud. un cuñado?** <u>No, no tengo un cuñado</u>.

8) ¿Tiene muchos primos su amigo? <u>Sí, Mi amigo tiene muchos</u>

<u>primos</u>.

9) ¿Tiene esposo Penélope Cruz? <u>No, no penélope cruz tiene</u>

<u>esposo</u>.

10) ¿Tiene Ud. muchos primos? <u>Sí, Tiene muchos primos</u>.

II. Fill in the following spaces with appropriate vocabulary from this section. One of the sentences has more than one possible answer!

1) **El padre de mi padre es mi** <u>abuelo</u>.

2) **La madre de mi madre es mi** <u>abuela</u>.

3) **El hermano de mi padre es mi** <u>tío</u>.

4) **El hijo de mi hijo es mi** <u>nieto</u>.

5) **La hija de mi tío es mi** <u>prima</u>.

6) **La hija de mi abuela es mi** <u>madre,</u>.

7) **La esposa de mi padre es mi** <u>madre</u>.

8) **El hermano de mi esposa es mi** <u>cuñado</u>.

9) **El hermano de mi prima es mi** <u>primo</u>.

10) **La hermana de mi hijo es mi** <u>hija</u>.

FIRST STEPS **17**

PRÁCTICA DE PRONUNCIACIÓN

z, l, ll

Here are some more consonants:

z – In most of the Spanish-speaking world, this consonant sounds like the "s" in "sailor." In parts of Spain, it sounds like the "th" in "thin."

zapato, zona, lápiz, Zaragoza, azúcar, alzar, realizar, azul, azulejo

l – This consonant is pronounced just as in the English word "lost."

lindo, listo, luego, alto, leal, hotel, loco, lástima, Los Ángeles, líquido, limón

ll – This is another consonant that historically has been considered one letter in the alphabet. In most places in the Spanish speaking world, it is pronounced like the "y" in "yes." In parts of Spain, it resembles the "lli" in "billion," while in Argentina and Uruguay, it sounds like the "Zsa" in the name "Zsa-Zsa."

millón, relleno, callado, calle, valles

STEP SEVEN —
¿LE GUSTA EL ELEFANTE AZUL?
¿HAY TIGRES EN ASIA?

If you want to find out if someone likes something, you could ask him or her:

¿Le gusta el elefante azul? (Do you like the blue elephant?)
  Sí, me gusta el elefante azul. (Yes, I like the blue elephant.)
  No, no me gusta el elefante azul. (No, I don't like the blue elephant.)

¿Le gusta el cocodrilo verde? (Do you like the green crocodile?)
  Sí, me gusta el cocodrilo verde. (Yes, I like the green crocodile.)
  No, no me gusta el cocodrilo verde. (No, I don't like the green crocodile.)

If the thing you like is plural, the sentences will be a little different:

¿Le gustan los elefantes azules? (Do you like [the] blue elephants?)*

> *Sí, me gustan los elefantes azules.* (Yes, I like [the] blue elephants.)
> *No, no me gustan los elefantes azules.* (No, I don't like [the] blue elephants.)

*Note: If the speaker is talking about elephants <u>in general</u>, the English translation would not include the word "the."

¿Le gustan los cocodrilos verdes? (Do you like [the] green crocodiles?)

> *Sí, me gustan los cocodrilos verdes.* (Yes, I like [the] green crocodiles.)
> *No, no me gustan los cocodrilos verdes.* (No, I don't like [the] green crocodiles.)

If you want to find out if someone else likes something, you could ask:

¿Le gusta el elefante azul? (Does she/he like the blue elephant?)

> *Sí, le gusta el elefante azul.* (Yes, she/he likes the blue elephant.)
> *No, no le gusta el elefante azul.* (No, she/he doesn't like the blue elephant.)

¿Le gustan los cocodrilos verdes? (Does she/he like [the] green crocodiles?)

> *Sí, le gustan los cocodrilos verdes.* (Yes, she/he likes [the] green crocodiles.)
> *No, no le gustan los cocodrilos verdes.* (No, she/he doesn't like [the] green crocodiles.)

Helpful Tip: Do you notice that these questions all start with the word *"le"*? *"¿Le gusta(n)?"* can mean either *"Do you like?," "Does he like?"* or *"Does she like?"*

Here is a list of names of **common animals** in Spanish. (The corresponding definite article — "the" — is written in parentheses before each word . . . *el* is used for masculine nouns and *la* is used for feminine ones.)

LOS ANIMALES			
(la) ballena	→ whale	*(el) pájaro*	→ bird
(el) caballo	→ horse	*(el) perro*	→ dog
(la) cebra	→ zebra	*(el) pez*	→ fish
(el) gato	→ cat	*(la) rana*	→ frog
(la) jirafa	→ giraffe	*(el) ratón*	→ mouse
(el) león	→ lion	*(la) serpiente*	→ snake
(el) llama	→ llama	*(el) tigre*	→ tiger
(el) oso	→ bear	*(la) vaca*	→ cow

Helpful Tip: A handy word to learn now is *"hay."* It means "there is" and "there are." *¿Hay tigres en Asia? ¿Hay un perro en la casa?¿Hay una llama en el parque?* (Are there tigers in Asia? Is there a dog in the house? Is there a llama in the park?)

This next list has the names of **common colors**. (You may have noticed that these adjectives are placed after the nouns that they modify . . . e.g., *elefante rosado, cocodrilo verde*.)

LOS COLORES			
amarillo/a → yellow		*morado/a* → purple	
anaranjado/a → orange		*negro/a* → black	
azul → blue		*rojo/a* → red	
blanco/a → white		*rosado/a* → pink	
gris → gray		*verde* → green	
marrón (café) → brown			

PRÁCTICA

I. *Answer the following questions in complete sentences.*

1) **¿Le gustan los gatos amarillos?** Sí, me gustan los gatos amarillos

   _____.

2) **¿Le gustan los perros negros?** No, no gustan los perros

   negros _____.

3) **¿Le gusta su casa?** Sí, me gusta mi casa _____

4) **¿Le gusta su escuela?** Sí, Me gusta mi escuela _____.

5) **¿Le gustan las casas verdes?** No, no gustan las casas

   verdes _____.

6) **¿Le gusta más (more) Nueva York o Chicago?** Me gusta más

   Chicago _____.

7) ¿Le gustan más los perros o los gatos? *me gustan más los gatos* .

8) ¿Le gustan más los caballos grises o los caballos negros?

me gustan más los caballos negros .

9) ¿Le gusta su casa? *No, no gusta mi casa* .

10) ¿Qué animal le gusta más? *me gusta más el perro*

.

11) ¿Hay una serpiente en la casa? *No, no hay una serpiente*

en la casa .

12) ¿Hay perros en la escuela? *Si, hay perros en la escuela* .

II. Fill in the following paragraph with names of colors and animals from this section.

En mi casa tengo un *gato* . El color de mi

gato es *anaranjado* . Mi amiga Elena tiene una

ratón . No es blanca; es *gris* . Mi

gato se llama Fido y su *ratón* se llama

Kermit. ¡Son animales fantásticos!

PRÁCTICA DE PRONUNCIACIÓN

b , v

The consonants in this section — "b" and "v" — are pronounced exactly the same way!

b and **v** – At the beginning of a word or following another consonant, the "b" and "v" sound just like the "b" in "buffalo."

bello, bola, barco, barba, béisbol, Bogotá, bilingüe, bizcocho, verde, vamos, vértigo, Venezuela, voz, votamos, invierno, valle

If a "b" or "v" is found between vowels, however, the sound is different. You start to say the "b" sound as in "buffalo," but you don't close your lips all the way. You'll have to practice this one a bit. You can try placing a thin pencil lengthwise between your lips to prevent them from closing during the sound.

abuelo, cubo, sabemos, labio, nubes, caminaban, cabido, nueve, ave, lívido, uvas, tuvimos, llave, caverna, Oviedo

 ## STEP EIGHT — UNO, DOS, TRES . . .

In this section, you will learn to count from one to thirty-one. Here is the vocabulary that you will need:

LOS NÚMEROS (1-20)			
uno	→ one	*once*	→ eleven
dos	→ two	*doce*	→ twelve
tres	→ three	*trece*	→ thirteen
cuatro	→ four	*catorce*	→ fourteen
cinco	→ five	*quince*	→ fifteen
seis	→ six	*dieciséis (diez y seis)*	→ sixteen
siete	→ seven	*diecisiete (diez y siete)*	→ seventeen
ocho	→ eight	*dieciocho (diez y ocho)*	→ eighteen
nueve	→ nine	*diecinueve (diez y nueve)*	→ nineteen
diez	→ ten	*veinte*	→ twenty

Note: Did you notice that the numbers 16–19 can be written either as one word or as three? The one word version, however, is preferred in modern Spanish.

This list will take you through to thirty-one:

LOS NÚMEROS (21-31)		
veintiuno	→	twenty-one
veintidós	→	twenty-two
veintitrés	→	twenty-three
veinticuatro	→	twenty-four
veinticinco	→	twenty-five
veintiséis	→	twenty-six
veintisiete	→	twenty-seven
veintiocho	→	twenty-eight
veintinueve	→	twenty-nine
treinta	→	thirty
treinta y uno	→	thirty-one

PRÁCTICA

I. *After studying the numbers in this section, fill in the following spaces with the appropriate number to complete the sequence.*

1) uno, dos, __tres__, cuatro, cinco

2) dos, cuatro, seis, __ocho__

(handwritten above: 2 4 6)

3) diez, once, doce, __trece__, catorce, quince

4) cinco, diez, quince, veinte, __veinticinco__, treinta

5) nueve, ocho, __siete__, seis, cinco

6) __uno__, tres, cinco, siete, nueve, once

7) dos, cuatro, __cinco, siete__, ocho, diez, doce

8) uno, once, dos, doce, tres, _trece_____, cuatro, catorce

9) veintiuno, veinticuatro, _veintisiete_____, treinta

10) veintinueve, _veinticinco_____, veintiuno, diecisiete

II. In the following exercise, first read the mathematical equations aloud, and then write them out. Follow these models:

$1 + 1 = 2$ _uno y uno son dos_____

$5 - 2 = 3$ _cinco menos dos son tres_____

$2 \times 5 = 10$ _dos por cinco son diez_____

1) $2 + 4 = 6$ _dos y cuatro son seis_____

2) $9 - 3 = 6$ _nueve menos tres son seis_____

3) $2 \times 2 = 4$ _dos por dos son cuatro_____

4) $5 + 5 = 10$ _cinco y cinco son diez_____

5) $14 + 4 = 18$ _catorce y cuatro son dieciocho_____

6) $7 \times 4 = 28$ _siete por cuatro son veintiocho_____

7) $12 - 4 = 8$ _doce menos cuatro son ocho_____

8) $1 + 1 = 2$ _uno y uno son dos_____

III. Write the corresponding number next to the figures.

1) _cuatro_____

2) <u>nueve</u>

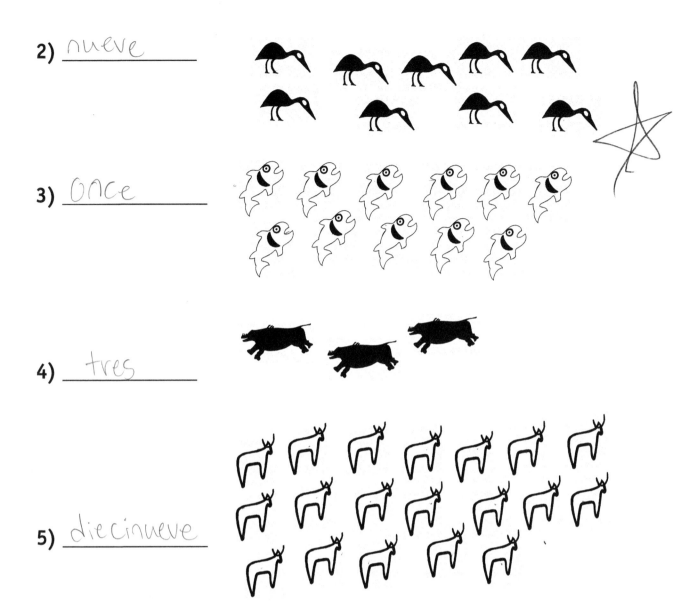

3) <u>once</u>

4) <u>tres</u>

5) <u>diecinueve</u>

r , rr

Here are two more consonants:

r – The Spanish "r" is different from the English "r." It is a "rolled" r . . . it sounds as though you were imitating the sound of a motor of an airplane. A number of years back, a famous advertisement for *"Ruffles"* potato chips presented this "r" sound with the line *"Ruffles* have ridges." Some have learned this sound by repeating the

word "butter" or "kitty" ten times in a row as fast as possible. The rolled "r" sound starts to come to life. You will have to practice this one with your teacher and CD.

caro, pero, hablar, comer, irse, arte, comercio, carta, puerta

rr – The "rr" is also considered a single consonant in Spanish. It is almost like the "r" sound, but it has even more force and roll.

perro, carro, barrera, carrera, correo, errar, errante, zorro

Note: A single "r" is pronounced like the "rr" when it is the first letter of the word (e.g., *ramo, rosa, reloj*).

 # STEP NINE — ¿QUÉ DÍA ES HOY? . . . ¿QUÉ TIEMPO HACE HOY?

In this section, you will first learn to find out what day, month and season it is. You will then learn how to talk about the weather.

When you want to find out what day it is, you can ask someone:

¿Qué día es hoy? (What day is it?)
> *Hoy es lunes.* (Today is Monday.)
> *Hoy es martes.* (Today is Tuesday.)

When you want to find out what day tomorrow is, you could ask:

¿Qué día es mañana? (What day is tomorrow?)
> *Mañana es jueves.* (Tomorrow is Thursday.)
> *Mañana es viernes.* (Tomorrow is Friday.)

Here is a list of the days of the week:

LOS DÍAS DE LA SEMANA					
lunes	→	Monday	*viernes*	→	Friday
martes	→	Tuesday	*sábado*	→	Saturday
miércoles	→	Wednesday	*domingo*	→	Sunday
jueves	→	Thursday			

If you want to find out in what month someone's birthday falls, you could ask:

¿En qué mes es su cumpleaños? (In what month is your birthday?)

    Mi cumpleaños es en agosto. (My birthday is in August.)
    Mi cumpleaños es en noviembre. (My birthday is in November.)

Here is a list of the months of the year:

LOS MESES DEL AÑO					
enero	→	January	*julio*	→	July
febrero	→	February	*agosto*	→	August
marzo	→	March	*septiembre*	→	September
abril	→	April	*octubre*	→	October
mayo	→	May	*noviembre*	→	November
junio	→	June	*diciembre*	→	December

If you want to ask someone which season is his or her favorite, you could ask:

¿Qué estación le gusta más? (What season do you like best?)

    Me gusta más la primavera. (I like the spring best.)
    Me gusta más el verano. (I like the summer best.)
    Me gusta más el otoño. (I like the fall most.)
    Me gusta más el invierno. (I like the winter most.)

When you want to find out what the weather is like, you can ask someone:

¿Qué tiempo hace hoy? (How's the weather today?)

    Hace frío. (It's cold.)
    Hace calor. (It's hot.)

If it is particularly hot or cold, a person might respond:

    Hace mucho frío. (It's very cold.)
    Hace mucho calor. (It's very hot.)

Here are a few common expressions that describe the weather:

EL TIEMPO					
Hace calor.	→	It's hot.	*Hace viento.*	→	It's windy.
Hace frío.	→	It's cold.	*Llueve.*	→	It's raining.
Hace sol.	→	It's sunny.	*Nieva.*	→	It's snowing.

PRÁCTICA

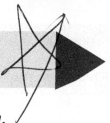

I. Answer the following questions using vocabulary from this section.

1) **¿Qué tiempo hace hoy?** hace calor.

2) **¿Qué día es hoy?** hoy es miércoles.

3) **¿Qué tiempo hace en diciembre en Minnesota?** hace mucho frío.

4) **¿Hace mucho viento en Chicago?** Sí, en chicago hace mucho viento.

5) **¿Qué estación le gusta más?** Me gusta más el ootoño.

6) **¿En qué mes es su cumpleaños?** Mi cumpleaños es en octubre.

7) **¿Le gustan más los lunes o los sábados?** Me gustan más los sábados.

8) **¿Cuántos (How many) meses hay en un año?** hay doce meses en un año.

9) **¿Cuántos días hay en una semana?** Hay siete días en una semana.

10) **¿Qué tiempo hace en San Juan, Puerto Rico?** Hace calor en Puerto Rico.

II. Complete the following lists using vocabulary from this section.

1) **lunes, martes, miércoles, jueves,** <u>Viernes</u> **, sábado**

2) **enero, marzo, mayo,** <u>julio</u> **, septiembre**

3) **sí-no, día-noche, frío-** <u>calor</u>

4) **primavera, verano, otoño,** <u>invierno</u>

5) **lunes, el veintidós de octubre; miércoles, el veinticuatro de octubre;**

<u>Viernes, el veintiséis de octubre</u>

 # PRÁCTICA DE PRONUNCIACIÓN

j, g

Here are two more consonants:

j – The Spanish "j" has a rather harsh sound, kind of like an English "h" that got caught in the back of your throat. At times, it sounds as if one were clearing one's throat.

jota, jamón, rojo, reloj, jaca, lejos, junio, julio, jarabe, justos

g – The "g" is pronounced in two different ways. As in English, when a "g" comes before an "a," "o," or "u," it sounds just like the "g" in "goose."

gota, gozar, lago, Gutiérrez, gato, lúgubre, Galicia, gobierno

Note: The groupings "gui" and "gue" are pronounced in Spanish in a special way. The "u" sound in both of these combinations is completely silent. The purpose of the silent "u" is to make the "g" sound like the one in "goose."

guitarra, guerra, guisar, llegue, merengue, guisado, guiñar, sigue

When a "g" is before an "e" or an "i," however, it sounds just like the "j" described above.

gente, gitano, gesto, girar, ágil, generoso, general

In this final "**STEP**" section, you will learn to tell time.

When you want to find out what time it is, you can ask someone:

¿Qué hora es?

> *Es la una.* (It's one o'clock.)
> *Son las dos.* (It's two o'clock.)
> *Son las tres.* (It's three o'clock.)

Here are some other useful constructions to use when talking about time:

> *Es la una y cuarto.* (It's quarter after one.)
> *Son las dos y cuarto.* (It's quarter after two.)

> *Es la una y media.* (It's one-thirty.)
> *Son las cinco y media.* (It's five-thirty.)

> *Es la una menos cuarto.* (It's quarter of one.)
> *Son las nueve menos cuarto.* (It's quarter of nine.)

> *Es la una en punto.* (It's one o'clock sharp.)
> *Son las once en punto.* (It's eleven o'clock sharp.)

> *Es la una y veinte.* (It's one-twenty.)
> *Son las nueve y veinte.* (It's nine-twenty.)

> *Es (el) mediodía.* (It's noon.)
> *Es (la) medianoche.* (It's midnight.)

Here are some possible questions you might ask when you want to find out when an event is taking place:

¿A qué hora es la clase de español? ([At] what time is the Spanish class?)

> *La clase de español es a las diez.* (The Spanish class is at ten.)

¿A qué hora es el partido de fútbol? ([At] what time is the soccer game?)

> *El partido de fútbol es a las tres.* (The soccer game is at three.)

¿A qué hora es la fiesta? ([At] what time is the party?)

> *La fiesta es a las ocho.* (The party is at eight.)

PRÁCTICA

I. Answer the following questions in complete sentences.

1) **¿Qué hora es?** Es la una .

2) **¿A qué hora es su clase de español? Mi clase de español es a**

   las tres .

3) **¿A qué hora es su clase de historia?**

   Mi clase de historia es a las dos .

4) **¿A qué hora es su programa favorito* de televisión?**

   Mi programa favorito de televisión es a las ocho

   ¿◆❓ Why does *"favorito"* end with "o" when *"programa"* ends with "a"? Good question! *"Programa"* is an exception — it's a "masculine" noun!

5) **¿A qué hora hace mucho sol?**

   Hace mucho sol a las doce .

6) **Son las cinco ahora. ¿Qué hora es en treinta minutos?**

   Son las cinco y media .

7) Son las cuatro menos cuarto. En veinte minutos, ¿qué hora es?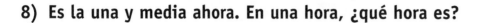

Son las cuatro y cinco _____.

8) Es la una y media ahora. En una hora, ¿qué hora es?

Son las dos y media _____.

II. Using the following clock faces, tell what time it is.

 1)

Son las tres _____

2)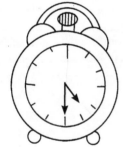

Son llas cuatro y media _____

3)

Es la una menos cuarto _____

4)    Son las seis y cuatro

5)    Son las siete

6)    Son las nueve y diez

7)    Son las once menos cuarto

8)    Son las cinco y media

f, t, x

Here are the last three consonants!

f – Here is an easy one. This consonant sounds like the "f" in "finger."

fe, fiel, café, filosofía, farol, alfabeto, Rafael, física, fideos

t – This consonant is similar to the English "t" in "toss," except that it has a bit softer sound. There is not the same explosion of breath, however, that follows the English "t." If you put a candle close to your lips when saying "Tom," you might blow out the candle. In Spanish, the flame will barely flicker when saying *"Tomás."*

taco, tentar, té, coyote, atleta, tío, temperatura, tostado, tela, timbre, Tomás

x – Depending on its position, the "x" has different sounds. Between vowels, it sounds like the "x" in the English word "exactly."

examen, exigir, éxito, exactamente, exacto

When the "x" comes before a consonant, however, it can sound like the "s" in "soap" or like the "x" in "exactly."

extraño, extraordinario, experimental, extraterrestre, explicación

Note: The words *"Texas"* and *"México"* are pronounced "Tejas" and "Méjico."

MÉXICO

MÉXICO

CAPITAL:	La Ciudad de México (México, D.F.)
POBLACIÓN:	129.800.000
GOBIERNO:	república federal
PRESIDENTE:	Andrés Manuel López Obrador
DINERO ($):	peso mexicano
PRODUCTOS:	industria, petróleo, plata, telenovelas
MÚSICA, BAILE:	corridos, mariachi, rancheras
SITIOS DE INTERÉS:	Baja California, Cancún, Oaxaca, Querétaro, ruinas de los aztecas y de los mayas
COMIDA TÍPICA:	frijoles, guacamole, huevos rancheros, mole poblano, quesadillas, tacos, tamales, tequila, tortillas

MEXICANOS FAMOSOS:

Gael García Bernal (ACTOR)

Cantinflas (ACTOR)

Sor Juana Inés de la Cruz (POETA)

Salma Hayek (ACTRIZ)

Benito Juárez (HÉROE NACIONAL)

Frida Kahlo (ARTISTA)

José Clemente Orozco (MURALISTA)

Octavio Paz (POETA)

Diego Rivera (ARTISTA)

Hugo Sánchez (ATLETA)

Pancho Villa (HÉROE NACIONAL)

THEME WORDS: "PEOPLE"

la *amiga*	friend
el *amigo*	friend
el *bebé*	baby
la *chica*	girl
el *chico*	boy
el *hombre*	man
la *mujer*	woman
la *niña*	(small) girl
el *niño*	(small) boy

OTHER NOUNS

la *clase*	class
el *día*	day
la *escuela*	school
la *fiesta*	party
el *libro*	book
la *noche*	night
el *reloj*	clock, watch

ADJECTIVES

bueno/a	good
grande	big
guapo/a	good-looking
interesante	interesting
malo/a	bad
pequeño/a	small
rígido/a	rigid
simpático/a	nice

VERBS

admitir	to admit
aprender	to learn
bailar	to dance
beber	to drink
caminar	to walk
comer	to eat
comprar	to buy
correr	to run
enseñar	to teach
escribir	to write
ganar	to win, to earn
hablar	to talk, to speak
leer	to read
limpiar	to clean
preparar	to prepare
trabajar	to work
vender	to sell
vivir	to live

MISCELLANEOUS

a	at, to
allí	there
aquí	here
con	with
después	after
en	in, on
mucho	a lot
no	no
poco	a little
sí	yes
sin	without
también	also
y	and

LECCIÓN UNO

KEY GRAMMAR CONCEPTS

A) VERBS IN THE PRESENT TENSE → *Los verbos en el presente*

B) SUBJECT PRONOUNS → *Los pronombres pronominales*

C) INTERROGATIVES → *Los interrogativos*

 A) VERBS IN THE PRESENT TENSE

Verbs are the words in a sentence that narrate the action; they tell you what is going on. Unlike in English, the letters at the end of a verb in Spanish let you know who the subject is. Once you learn these endings, you will be ready to speak complete Spanish sentences!

The infinitive of a verb is its simplest form, the starting place before it is conjugated or changed to correspond to a specific person. All Spanish infinitives end in the letters **-AR**, **-ER**, or **-IR**.

The **present tense** describes actions that are happening now, reports current conditions or traits, describes customary events, and also announces what may be happening in the immediate future.

Here are the full conjugations of three common verbs in the present tense:

	HABLAR (to speak)	**COMER** (to eat)	**VIVIR** (to live)
I	hablo	como	vivo
you (familiar)	hablas	comes	vives
he/she/you (formal)	habla	come	vive
we	hablamos	comemos	vivimos
you all (familiar)	habláis	coméis	vivís
they/you all (formal)	hablan	comen	viven

Helpful Tip: Did you notice that **-AR**, **-ER**, and **-IR** verbs share some common endings but have different ones as well? Study the <u>endings</u> of the verbs carefully. They provide a clue to help you figure out who the subject is.

✳ EXAMPLES: *Cristina **habla** mucho.*
Cristina speaks a lot.

***Como** chocolate en febrero.*
I eat chocolate in February.

***Vivimos** en Chihuahua, México.*
We live in Chihuahua, Mexico.

*¿**Come** Miguel Vázquez mucha pizza?*
Does Miguel Vázquez eat a lot of pizza?

*¿**Viven** los tigres en Asia?*
Do tigers live in Asia?

You may have noticed that the subject is sometimes mentioned *(Cristina habla . . .)* and at other times not *(Como chocolate . . .)*. Because the ending of the verb helps to identify the subject, the subject is normally only mentioned for **clarification** or **emphasis**. In a statement in which the subject is mentioned, it is usually placed before the verb; in a question, however, it will follow the verb.

The following list contains some of the most frequently used verbs in the Spanish language. All of these verbs follow the conjugation patterns presented on the previous page. Although you do not need to know the meanings of all these words just yet, you will be noticing them throughout this book. In time, they will all become old friends.

Here is a list of some "high frequency" verbs:

-AR		-ER	-IR
andar (to walk)	*estudiar* (to study)	*aprender* (to learn)	*abrir* (to open)
apagar (to turn off)	*ganar* (to earn, win)	*beber* (to drink)	*admitir* (to admit)
bailar (to dance)	*lavar* (to wash)	*comer* (to eat)	*descubrir* (to discover)
bajar (to go down)	*limpiar* (to clean)	*comprender*	*escribir* (to write)
caminar (to walk)	*llamar* (to call)	(to understand)	*ocurrir* (to occur)
cantar (to sing)	*llegar* (to arrive)	*correr* (to run)	*permitir* (to permit)
cocinar (to cook)	*llorar* (to cry)	*leer* (to read)	*subir* (to go up)
contestar (to answer)	*mirar* (to look at)	*romper* (to break)	*vivir* (to live)
entrar (to enter)	*pasar* (to spend time, to happen)	*vender* (to sell)	
escapar (to escape)	*preguntar* (to ask)		
escuchar (to listen to)	*preparar* (to prepare)		
esperar (to wait for)	*trabajar* (to work)		

✳ EXAMPLES: *Mi papá **prepara** tacos en el restaurante.*
My dad prepares tacos in the restaurant.

*¿**Venden** los artistas mucho arte?*
Do the artists sell a lot of art?

*¿**Escribe** el profesor mucho en julio?*
Does the teacher write a lot in July?

*Bailamos **la salsa con la música de Marc Anthony.***
We dance the salsa to the music of Marc Anthony.

 # PRACTICE EXERCISES

1. **Conjugate these verbs fully in the present tense using the models presented earlier:**

   i don't understand

   cantar (to sing)   **vender** (to sell)   **permitir** (to permit)

   _____ _____ _____ _____ _____ _____

   _____ _____ _____ _____ _____ _____

   _____ _____ _____ _____ _____ _____

2. **Now write the correct form of the indicated verb in the spaces provided:**

   a. Celine Dion ____canta____ la canción al final de *Titanic.* (cantar)

   b. (We) ____vivimos____ en Oaxaca, México. (Vivir)

   c. (I) ____vendo____ limonada deliciosa. (Vender)

   d. Mi mamá y mi papá ____trabajan____ en un hospital. (trabajar)

   e. (You, familiar) No ____admites____ tus errores. (admitir)

   f. (You all) ____Leen____ *People en español* en el taxi. (Leer)

   g. El actor Diego Luna ____aprende____ mucho en Hollywood. (aprender)

   h. Megan Rapinoe ____gana____ muchos trofeos de fútbol. (ganar)

   i. (I) ____practico____ la música con mi profesora. (Practicar)

   j. (We) ____escribimos____ poemas interesantes. (Escribir)

Pronouns are words that can take the place of nouns. Nouns are people, animals, places, things or ideas. A subject pronoun can serve as the main actor of a sentence. In English, we use subject pronouns all the time. In Spanish, however, **subject pronouns** are only used for emphasis or clarity.

Here are the subject pronouns in Spanish and their English equivalents:

yo →	I
tú →	you (familiar)
él →	he
ella →	she
usted (Ud.) →	you (formal)
nosotros/nosotras →	we
vosotros/vosotras* →	you all (familiar)
(*used only in Spain!*)	
ellos →	they (masculine)
ellas →	they (feminine)
ustedes (Uds.) →	you all

Helpful Tips: **1)** You may have noticed that Spanish expresses "you" in two different ways: *tú* and *usted* (commonly abbreviated *Ud.*).
2) *Tú* is used when a person directly addresses a friend or peer. It is a familiar, friendly pronoun.
3) *Ud.* also means "you," but it is reserved for addressing a stranger, an acquaintance, someone whose title you use (Dr., Professor), or someone older than you. It is a formal, respectful greeting. When in doubt, it is wise to use *Ud.*

There are also two ways to say "you all": *vosotros/vosotras* and *ustedes (Uds.)*. In most of Spain, *vosotros/vosotras* is the familiar plural form used when addressing friends. *Vosotros* is used when speaking to a group of male friends or to a group of male and female friends; *vosotras* is used only when addressing female friends. However, in all other areas of the Spanish-speaking world, *Uds.* is used to mean "you all," whether speaking to friends or strangers, to men or women.

EXAMPLES: *Yo hablo con Chayanne, pero **tú** cantas con Shakira.*
I talk with Chayanne, but you sing with Shakira.

*¿Miguel, Isabel? –¡**Nosotros** estamos aquí!*
Miguel, Isabel? –We're here!

***Ellas** no comen hamburguesas en la cafetería.*
They don't eat hamburgers in the cafeteria.

Uds. no limpian el sofá.
You all don't clean the sofa.

Vosotros vivís en Guadalajara, ¿no?
You all live in Guadalajara, don't you?

Ramón y Mercedes son amigos; **él** *es de México y* **ella** *es de Venezuela.**
Ramón and Mercedes are friends; he is from Mexico, and she is from Venezuela.

*Note: In this sentence, the listener would be confused without *"él"* and *"ella."*

PRACTICE EXERCISES

1. Translate the following English pronouns into Spanish:

a. I _____yo_____

e. we (2 ways) _____nosotros_____

b. you (familiar) _____usted_____

f. you all (familiar) (in Spain, 2 ways) _____vosotros_____

c. they (feminine) _____ellas_____

g. she _____ella_____

d. he _____él_____

h. you all (formal) _____ustedes_____

2. The speakers of the following sentences want to emphasize the subject. Provide a proper subject pronoun. Remember, you'll know the subject by looking at the verb ending:

a. _____Tú_____ escuchas la música de David Guetta.

b. _____Nosotros_____ aprendemos mucho en la clase de física.

c. Marco lee día y noche; _____él_____ es muy inteligente.

d. Tú y _____yo_____ caminamos por el parque bonito.

e. _____Tú_____ escuchas la música de Alejandro Fernández en el autobús.

f. Mi mamá y mi abuela enseñan español en una escuela de niñas; _____ellas_____ son profesoras.

g. ¿Cantan _____Uds_____ normalmente en la clase? –Sí, cantamos allí.

h. _____Vosotras_____ vivís en Madrid, ¿no? –Sí, vivimos en Madrid.

i. Ana no permite distracciones; _____ella_____ es muy rígida.

j. _____Yo_____ corro en el Maratón de Nueva York.

3. The following paragraph contains five verbal errors. Underline each error and write the correct word above it:

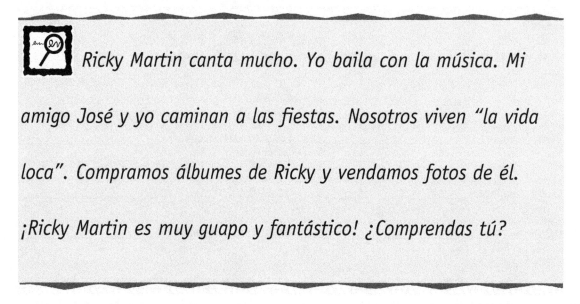

Ricky Martin canta mucho. Yo baila con la música. Mi

amigo José y yo caminan a las fiestas. Nosotros viven "la vida

loca". Compramos álbumes de Ricky y vendamos fotos de él.

¡Ricky Martin es muy guapo y fantástico! ¿Comprendas tú?

C) INTERROGATIVES

Interrogatives are words that ask questions. These words help you zero in on the answer you want. In Spanish, these interrogative words always carry a written accent mark.

Here are the most common interrogative words:

¿Quién?/¿Quiénes?	→	Who?	*¿Por qué?* → Why?	
¿Qué?	→	What?	*¿Cuándo?* → When?	
¿Cuál?/¿Cuáles?	→	Which?/What?	*¿Cuánto?/¿Cuánta?* → How much?	
¿Dónde?	→	Where?	*¿Cuántos?/¿Cuántas?* → How many?	
			¿Cómo? → How?	

¡CUIDADO! *"Porque"* means "because" when it is written as one word with no accent.

EXAMPLES:

¿Quién admite sus errores?
Who admits his/her errors?

¿Quiénes bailan ahora?
Who are dancing now?

¿Qué libro lees en el hotel?
What book are you reading in the hotel?

Vendo pizza y tacos. ¿Cuál compra Ud. hoy?
I sell pizza and tacos. Which are you buying today?

¿Dónde viven tus amigas?
Where do your friends live?

¿Por qué no miramos The Voice*?*
Why don't we watch *The Voice*?

¿Cuándo es la fiesta de San Valentín?
When is the St. Valentine's party?

¿Cuánto dinero ganan los políticos?
How much money do politicians earn?

¿Cuántos bebés hay en la familia?
How many babies are there in the family?

¿Cómo está Ud., señor Chávez? –Bien, gracias.
How are you, Mr. Chávez? –Fine, thanks.

PRACTICE EXERCISES

1. Insert the appropriate interrogative word in the sentences below:

a. ¿_____Cuándo_____ es el examen de historia? –Mañana.

b. ¿_____Dónde_____ viven los leones? –Viven en África.

c. ¿_____Quién_____ es el actor en *Che*? –Benicio del Toro.

d. ¿_____Qué_____ libro prefieres leer? –*Don Quijote.*

e. Yo bebo mucha Coca-Cola y Pepsi. –¿_____cuál_____ prefieres tú?

f. ¿_____Por qué_____ no abren la puerta los niños? –Porque hace mucho frío.

g. ¿_____Cuántas_____ personas hay en la clase? –16.

2. The following dialogue contains four errors related to interrogative words. Underline each error and write the correct word above it:

–Hola, Marcos. ¿Quién es el chico?

–Se llama José.

Dónde
–¿~~Cuando~~ vive?

–Vive en Los Ángeles.

–¿Qué come José?

–Come enchiladas y tacos.

Cuál
–¿~~Qué~~ de los dos come más?

–José come más tacos.

–¿Cuántos tacos come?

–Come diez.

–¡Caramba!

ORAL PRACTICE
PREGUNTAS EN GRUPOS DE DOS

(Online access offers audio recordings of these questions.)

These two sets of questions use grammatical structures and vocabulary from this lesson. Working with a partner, alternate asking and answering each question. Even though you are working with a classmate, some of the questions will use the familiar "tú" form and others will use the more formal "Ud." When you get to the bottom of each list, start over at the top, switching roles. As a variation, write out the answers in complete sentences.

A) ¿Hablas español en la clase?

¿Comes mucho chocolate?

¿Le gusta caminar en el parque?

¿Cómo se llama tu libro favorito?

¿De dónde es usted?

¿Cómo estás hoy?

¿Es grande o pequeño un bebé?

B) ¿Bailas mucho en las fiestas?

¿Dónde vives?

¿Es bueno o malo escribir en los libros?

¿Bebes Coca-Cola o Pepsi?

¿Quién trabaja en una escuela?

¿Cuándo hablas con tus amigos?

¿Cómo se llama un actor muy guapo?

DIALOGUE

The following dialogue contains grammar and vocabulary that you've seen in this lesson and in the introductory section. After listening to the dialogue, read it aloud, alone or with friends. Afterwards, try to answer the questions that follow either aloud or in written form.

LAS AVENTURAS DE RAFAEL, ELISA Y "EL TIGRE"
ESCENA UNO
(Online access offers recordings of this adventure series.)

Rafael y "El Tigre" hablan en el parque. Son de Washington, D.C.

Rafael: ¿Cómo estás, Tigre?

El Tigre: Muy bien, Rafael, pero hace mucho calor hoy.

Rafael: Sí, vivimos en Washington donde siempre hace mucho calor.

El Tigre: Es verdad, pero no me gusta el calor.

Rafael: ¿Por qué no caminamos a la fiesta de mi prima?

El Tigre: ¿Quién es tu prima?

Rafael: Es Elisa . . . Elisa Montesinos.

El Tigre: Ella es muy inteligente y muy guapa. ¡Vamos! (Let's go!).

Rafael y "El Tigre" entran en la casa de Elisa.

Rafael: Hola, Elisa. Te presento a mi amigo, El Tigre.

Elisa: Hola, Tigre. Me llamo Elisa. ¿Te gusta la música?

El Tigre: Sí, mucho. Me gusta mucho el disco compacto de Carlos Santana, *Supernatural.* ¡Es lo máximo!

Elisa: Es divino. La canción *"María, María"* es sensacional.

El Tigre: ¿Bailamos un poco?

Elisa: ¿Por qué no?

Rafael come muchos Doritos y bebe Fanta de limón.

Elisa: ¡Bailas muy bien!

El Tigre: Gracias, Elisa.

Elisa: Rafael, tu amigo es muy simpático.

Rafael: Es verdad. Elisa, El Tigre y yo preparamos un viaje a Nueva York en una semana. ¿Te gusta Nueva York?

Elisa: Sí, mucho, pero mis padres son muy estrictos. No me permiten viajar.

El Tigre: No te preocupes, Elisa. Tenemos un plan excelente.

PREGUNTAS

1) ¿De dónde son Rafael y El Tigre?

_____

2) ¿Qué tiempo hace normalmente en Washington, D.C.?

_____

3) ¿Cómo se llama la prima de Rafael?

_____

4) ¿Cómo es Elisa Montesinos?

_____

5) ¿Cómo se llama el disco compacto que escuchan?

_____

6) ¿Quiénes bailan?

_____

7) ¿Qué come Rafael?

_____

8) ¿Adónde van Rafael y El Tigre en una semana?

_____

9) ¿Puede ir Elisa, también?

_____

10) ¿Cómo son los padres de Elisa?

_____

PRUEBA DE REPASO

1. Answer in complete sentences:

a. ¿Habla Ud. mucho en la clase?

_____

b. ¿Dónde lees los libros?

_____

c. ¿Come su hermano muchos tacos?

_____

d. ¿Bailan Uds. en la discoteca?

_____

e. ¿Cuándo es la clase de español?

_____

2. Conjugate the following six verbs fully in the present tense:

hablar (to speak)   **comer** (to eat)   **vivir** (to live)

_____ _____   _____ _____   _____ _____

_____ _____   _____ _____   _____ _____

_____ _____   _____ _____   _____ _____

limpiar (to clean)   **leer** (to read)   **admitir** (to admit)

_____ _____   _____ _____   _____ _____

_____ _____   _____ _____   _____ _____

_____ _____   _____ _____   _____ _____

3. **Write the correct form of each verb in the spaces provided:**

   a. Yo _____ la mesa todos los días. (limpiar)

   b. Nosotras _____ mucho dinero en Las Vegas. (ganar)

   c. Ud. no _____ bien las lecciones. (preparar)

   d. Penélope y Javier _____ a la fiesta. (correr)

   e. Tú _____ muchos productos buenos. (vender)

   f. Los chicos guapos de Pentatonix no _____ en el día.
   (trabajar)

   g. Tú y ella no _____ en Cancún. (vivir)

   h. La profesora de mi clase de inglés _____ muy bien la
   materia. (enseñar)

   i. Mi primo no _____ sus errores. (admitir)

   j. Ud. y yo _____ mucho en la escuela. (aprender)

4. **Write all possible subject pronouns in front of each of these conjugated verbs:**

   a. _____ aprendes

   b. _____ ganan

   c. _____ leo

   d. _____ preparamos

   e. _____ vivís

   f. _____ baila

   g. _____ trabajo

   h. _____ corres

   i. _____ vende

5. Write an appropriate interrogative word in the spaces provided:

a. ¿_____ es la fiesta? –El viernes.

b. ¿_____ de los libros le gusta más? –Me gusta más
Don Quijote.

c. ¿_____ es el presidente de México? –Andrés Manuel López
Obrador.

d. ¿_____ comes muchos tacos? –Como muchos tacos porque
me gustan.

e. ¿_____ hablan español? –Hablan español en México,
Colombia y Puerto Rico.

f. ¿_____ hora es? –Son las seis y media.

g. ¿_____ personas hay en la clase de español? –Veinte.

h. ¿_____ está Ud.? –Muy bien, gracias.

6. Translate the following sentences into Spanish:

a. She works with a friend in the park.

_____

b. Who is the small boy with the book?

_____

c. My brother and I run a lot, also.

_____

d. Yes, I dance with them at the party.

_____

7. The following paragraph contains **seven** errors. Underline each error and write the correct word above it. ¡CUIDADO! Be on the lookout for verb errors and agreement errors:

Buenos días. Mi amiga y yo caminemos mucho en el parque. El parque no es grande; es pequeña. Después mi amiga y yo comamos en un restaurante. ¿Por que? La pizza es bueno. Los tacos son deliciosos. Mi amiga beba Sprite y yo beba té con limón. Adiós.

ESPAÑA

Océano Atlántico

FRANCIA

PORTUGAL

La Coruña
Santiago de Compostela
LA CORDILLERA CANTÁBRICA
Bilbao
LOS PIRINEOS
Valladolid
Salamanca
Segovia
Zaragoza
Barcelona
Madrid ★
RÍO TAJO
Toledo
ESPAÑA
Valencia
GOLFO DE VALENCIA
Córdoba
SIERRA MORENA
Alicante
Mar Mediterráneo
GOLFO DE CÁDIZ
Sevilla
ANDALUCÍA
Cádiz
Málaga
Granada
SIERRA NEVADA

ESPAÑOLES FAMOSOS:

Pedro Almodóvar (DIRECTOR DE CINE)

Antonio Banderas (ACTOR)

Emilia Pardo Bazán (ESCRITORA)

Montserrat Caballé (CANTANTE DE ÓPERA)

Pablo Casals (MÚSICO)

Miguel de Cervantes (AUTOR DE DON QUIJOTE)

Penélope Cruz (ACTRIZ)

Salvador Dalí (ARTISTA)

Plácido Domingo (CANTANTE)

Generalísimo Francisco Franco (DICTADOR)

Pau Gasol (JUGADOR DE BALONCESTO)

Antoni Gaudí (ARQUITECTO)

Francisco Goya (ARTISTA)

El Greco (ARTISTA)

Miguel Induráin (CICLISTA)

Ana María Matute (ESCRITORA)

Rafael Nadal (TENISTA)

Pablo Picasso (ARTISTA)

Andrés Segovia (MÚSICO)

Miguel de Unamuno (ESCRITOR Y FILÓSOFO)

Diego Velázquez (PINTOR)

ESPAÑA

CAPITAL: Madrid
POBLACIÓN: 47.400.000
GOBIERNO: monarquía parlamentaria
JEFE DEL ESTADO: El rey don Felipe VI
PRESIDENTE DEL
GOBIERNO: Pedro Sánchez
DINERO ($):   euro
PRODUCTOS: aceite de oliva, naranjas, vino
MÚSICA, BAILE: flamenco, sevillanas
SITIOS DE INTERÉS: Acueducto (Segovia), La Alhambra
                       (Granada), La Mezquita (Córdoba),
                       Museo del Prado (Madrid), Museo
                       Guggenheim (Bilbao), Parque Güell
                       (Barcelona)
COMIDA TÍPICA: cochinillo, cordero, gazpacho, paella,
                       sangría, tapas, tortilla española, vino

Practice this vocabulary with our mobile app! Visit tobreak.com/app for more details.

VOCABULARIO
LECCIÓN DOS

THEME WORDS: "TRANSPORTATION"

el *autobús*	bus
el *avión*	airplane
el *barco*	boat
la *bicicleta*	bicycle
el *camión*	truck
el *coche* - el *carro*	car
la *moto(cicleta)*	motorcycle
el *taxi*	taxi
el *tren*	train

OTHER NOUNS

el *amor*	love
la *ciudad*	city
la *cosa*	thing
el *dinero*	money
el *disco compacto*	compact disc (CD)
la *fecha*	date
el *premio*	prize
el *pueblo*	town, village

ADJECTIVES

alto/a	tall
atestado/a	crowded
bajo/a	short
caro/a	expensive
difícil	difficult
especial	special
fácil	easy
frío/a	cold
nuevo/a	new
pobre	poor
rico/a	rich
viejo/a	old

VERBS

abrir	to open
cerrar (ie)*	to close
comenzar (ie) / *empezar (ie)*	to begin
creer	to believe
jugar (ue)*	to play
llegar	to arrive
mirar	to look at
mover (ue)	to move
mudar	to move (location)
poder (ue)	to be able to
preferir (ie)	to prefer
recibir	to receive
recordar (ue)	to remember
servir (i)*	to serve
viajar	to travel
volver (ue)	to return

MISCELLANEOUS

ahora	now
frecuentemente	frequently
gracias	thanks
más	more
menos	less
que	that, which
siempre	always

***Note:** The letters *"ie," "ue,"* and *"i"* in parentheses will indicate a "boot" verb, explained on page 55.

LECCIÓN DOS

KEY GRAMMAR
CONCEPTS

A) "BOOT" VERBS IN THE PRESENT TENSE → *Los verbos de "bota" en el presente*

B) CONJUNCTIONS → *Las conjunciones*

C) NOUNS: SINGULAR AND PLURAL FORMS → *Los sustantivos: las formas singulares y plurales*

D) ADJECTIVES AND THE IDEA OF AGREEMENT → *Los adjetivos y el concepto de concordancia*

A) "BOOT" VERBS IN THE PRESENT TENSE

The regular verbs presented in *Lección Uno* share the same stem for all six conjugations. When you conjugate certain other verbs, however, it is necessary to make changes in some of the stems, that is, in the vowel found in the next to last syllable of the infinitive. You will find three kinds of **stem changes**:

1 e→ ie

2 o→ ue

3 e→ i

These changes only take place in the singular forms and in the 3rd person plural.

Let's take a look at three model verbs that illustrate these types of stem change:

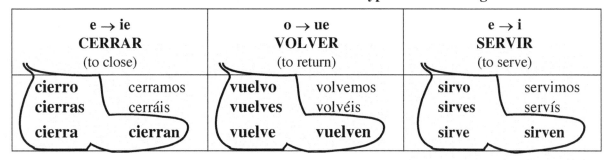

e → ie CERRAR (to close)		o → ue VOLVER (to return)		e → i SERVIR (to serve)	
cierro	cerramos	**vuelvo**	volvemos	**sirvo**	servimos
cierras	cerráis	**vuelves**	volvéis	**sirves**	servís
cierra	**cierran**	**vuelve**	**vuelven**	**sirve**	**sirven**

Helpful Tip: Can you figure out why these verbs have traditionally been called "boot" verbs? The forms that change seem to make a boot shape.

The following is a list of the most common "boot" verbs. You will notice that there are **-AR**, **-ER**, and **-IR** verbs represented in different categories.

Here are common "boot" verbs:

e → ie	o → ue	e → i
cerrar (to close)	*contar* (to count, to tell)	*competir* (to compete)
comenzar (to begin)	*costar* (to cost)	*conseguir** (to obtain)
empezar (to begin)	*devolver* (to return something)	*corregir** (to correct)
entender (to understand)	*dormir* (to sleep)	*elegir** (to elect)
pensar (to think)	*encontrar* (to find)	*pedir* (to ask for)
perder (to lose)	*jugar** (to play)	*reír** (to laugh)
preferir (to prefer)	*morir* (to die)	*repetir* (to repeat)
querer (to want, to love)	*mostrar* (to show)	*seguir** (to follow)
sentar (to seat)	*mover* (to move)	*servir* (to serve)
sentir (to feel)	*poder* (to be able to)	
	recordar (to remember)	
	volver (to return)	

*This verb is a little different:

u → ue

Note: The five asterisked verbs in this list are, in fact, "boot" verbs. In addition, however, there are some other unusual spelling changes in certain forms, which will be illustrated next lesson.

✳ **EXAMPLES:** *¿Por qué **cierras** la puerta de mi casa?*
    Why are you closing the door of my house?

*Eva Longoria no **duerme** mucho cuando viaja.*
    Eva Longoria doesn't sleep a lot when she travels.

*Los profesores **corrigen** los errores en los exámenes.*
    The teachers correct the errors on the tests.

*¿Cuándo **comienza** el invierno?*
    When does the winter start?

*Yo **vuelvo** a Cádiz con el actor William Levy el lunes.*
    I'm returning to Cádiz with the actor William Levy on Monday.

¡CUIDADO! Remember, the changes in these "boot" verbs only occur <u>inside</u> the boot. The *nosotros/as* and *vosotros/as* forms have <u>no</u> change.

✳ **EXAMPLE:** *No **pedimos** dinero; **queremos** amor.*
        We don't ask for money; we want love.

PRACTICE EXERCISES

1. Conjugate these verbs fully in the present tense using the models presented earlier:

comenzar (to begin) **mostrar** (to show) **pedir** (to ask for)

_____ _____ _____ _____ _____ _____

_____ _____ _____ _____ _____ _____

_____ _____ _____ _____ _____ _____

2. In the spaces provided, conjugate the infinitives in the present tense. Be sure that the subject of the sentence agrees with the verb:

a. Mi amigo _____ mucho por la noche. (dormir)

b. La futbolista Marta _____ muy bien con otras atletas profesionales. (competir)

c. Ellos _____ que la canción de Maroon 5 es fantástica. (pensar)

d. Nosotras siempre _____ mucho dinero en Las Vegas. (perder)

e. ¿Cuánto _____ el nuevo iPhone de Apple? (costar)

f. Tú y ella no _____ el día de la fiesta en el barco. (recordar)

g. Yo _____ aprender todo el vocabulario del libro. (poder)

h. Mis plantas _____ cuando no tienen mucho sol. (morir)

i. Mis amigas _____ leer _El País_ en el avión. (preferir)

j. Tú no _____ los conceptos complicados de matemáticas. (entender)

k. Mi amiga siempre _____ los libros a la biblioteca. (devolver)

3. The following paragraph contains five verbal errors. Underline each error and write the correction above it:

Mi amiga Silvia no dorme muchas horas. Ella no volve a su casa hasta la una de la mañana. Ella y yo prefieremos bailar en las discotecas con chicos guapos. Silvia baila como Shakira. Ella no quere hablar con su mamá y papá. Pensa que ellos no comprenden la situación. ¡Silvia es normal!

 B) CONJUNCTIONS

Conjunctions are words that join parts of sentences or even entire sentences. They are connecting words such as "and," "or/either," "nor/neither," "but."

Here are some common conjunctions in Spanish:

Conjunctions
y → and
o → or, either
ni → nor, neither
pero → but

 EXAMPLES: *Marc Anthony **y** Enrique Iglesias cantan en español.*
 Marc Anthony and Enrique Iglesias sing in Spanish.

 *Normalmente duermo ocho **o** nueve horas.*
 I normally sleep eight or nine hours.

 *No queremos **ni** pizza **ni** tamales.**
 We don't want either pizza or tamales.

 *Note: To avoid what is considered a "double negative" in English, we translate *"ni, ni"* in the above sentence as "either, or." Spanish sentences often have a double negative. More on this concept in a later lesson!

 *José pierde mucho, **pero** yo gano frecuentemente.*
 José loses a lot, but I win frequently.

*Sergio García y Camilo Villegas compiten en el torneo de golf, **pero** yo prefiero ver* America Idol.

Sergio García and Camilo Villegas are competing in the golf tournament, but I prefer to watch *American Idol.*

 PRACTICE EXERCISES

1. Place one of these conjunctions *(y, o, ni, pero)* in the sentences below:

a. Salma Hayek _____ Antonio Banderas trabajan en Hollywood.

b. La profesora ni repite _____ recuerda las instrucciones.

c. No puedo decidir cuál es mi número favorito: el cuatro _____ el cinco.

d. Ni Marco Rubio _____ Nancy Pelosi son de Washington, D.C.

e. Dos _____ dos son cuatro.

f. Normalmente como dos tortillas, _____ hoy prefiero comer tres.

g. _____ Nicki Minaj _____ Bruno Mars va a cantar primero en los Premios Grammy.

h. Hannah habla español, _____ Alexandra y Sarah hablan inglés.

i. Mi hermano juega bien al tenis, _____ ¡no es Rafael Nadal!

j. Bernie _____ Ted hablan mucho de política.

2. The following paragraph contains four errors related to conjunctions. Underline each error and write the correction above it:

Mi amigo Diego duerme mucho. Normalmente duerme nueve ni diez horas. Un día Diego no puede dormir. Quiere visitar el hospital, perro no encuentra su motocicleta. No quiere tomar ni su bicicleta o un taxi. Corre al hospital o habla con el médico. Ahora está bien.

 ## C) NOUNS: SINGULAR AND PLURAL FORMS

A **noun** is a word that represents a person, place, thing, or concept.

Here is a list of some common nouns:

Common Nouns		
(la) casa → house	*(la) mesa* → table	
(el) coche → car	*(el) momento* → moment	
(la) lección → lesson	*(el) papel* → paper	
(la) libertad → liberty	*(el) pueblo* → town	
(el) libro → book	*(la) silla* → chair	
(la) madre → mother	*(el) tren* → train	

All of the words in the list above are singular. To make most nouns plural in Spanish, simply add an "s" if the word ends in a vowel (a, e, i, o, u). However, if the word ends in a consonant (any letter other than a, e, i, o, u), add "es."

Let's look at the plural forms of all the words listed above:

Common Nouns (plural form)		
(las) casas → houses	*(las) mesas* → tables	
(los) coches → cars	*(los) momentos* → moments	
(las) lecciones → lessons	*(los) papeles* → papers	
(las) libertades → liberties	*(los) pueblos* → towns	
(los) libros → books	*(las) sillas* → chairs	
(las) madres → mothers	*(los) trenes* → trains	

Helpful Tips: 1) Did you notice that the small accent mark on the word *lección* disappeared on the plural form *lecciones*?

2) On most words that <u>end</u> with a syllable having a written accent mark, the accent mark drops off in the plural form. Another example of a word like this is *huracán* (hurricane). The plural form is *huracanes* (hurricanes).

 ¡CUIDADO! There is one unusual spelling change that occurs in the plural form of some nouns (and adjectives!). If a noun (or adjective) ends with the letter "z," the "z" must become "c" when in the plural form.

 EXAMPLES:

capaz (capable)	*capaces* (capable)
(el) juez (judge)	*(los) jueces* (judges)
(el) lápiz (pencil)	*(los) lápices* (pencils)
(la) nuez (nut)	*(las) nueces* (nuts)
(el) pez (fish)	*(los) peces* (fish)

A Special Noun Ending

The endings *"-ito"* and *"-ita"* can be used with most nouns . . . this ending may signal affection or diminutive size.

 EXAMPLES: *Juan → Juanito* (Johnny)   *casa → casita* (little house)
                            perro → perrito (little dog)   *Ana → Anita* (Annie)

 # PRACTICE EXERCISES

1. **Write the plural forms of the following ten nouns, being careful to remember the special rules about accent marks and nouns ending with the letter "z":**

   a. abrigo _____

   b. pluma _____

   c. papel _____

   d. padre _____

   e. nuez _____

   f. lección _____

   g. ciudad _____

   h. capitán _____

   i. ventana_____

   j. camión _____

2. Write the "-ito" or "-ita" form of these nouns. Follow the models illustrated on the previous page.

a. papel _____

b. mesa _____

c. perro _____

d. vaso _____

e. Lola _____

f. Ana _____

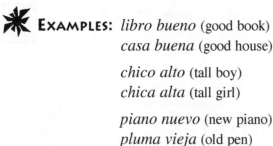

D) ADJECTIVES AND THE IDEA OF AGREEMENT

An **adjective** is a word that describes a noun. Often an adjective helps to distinguish one noun from another, e.g., *tacos buenos, tacos malos* (good tacos, bad tacos).

Spanish adjectives are different from English adjectives in two important ways:

1 Spanish adjectives generally <u>follow</u> the nouns they modify.

2 Spanish adjectives must agree in gender and number with the nouns they modify.

What does this all mean? Let's look at few examples:

EXAMPLES: *libro bueno* (good book)
casa buena (good house)

chico alto (tall boy)
chica alta (tall girl)

piano nuevo (new piano)
pluma vieja (old pen)

_____

Helpful Tips: **1)** Did you notice that some of the nouns above end in "o" and some in "a"?
2) In general, nouns that end in "o" are considered "masculine," and the ones that end in "a" are considered "feminine."
3) Did you also notice that the adjectives associated with those nouns followed the pattern (ending either with "o" or "a")?
_____

As we learned in the previous section, nouns can also be plural. Look what happens when we make the previous nouns plural:

EXAMPLES: *libros buenos* (good books)
casas buenas (good houses)

 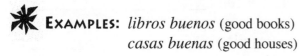

chicos altos (tall boys)

chicas altas (tall girls)

pianos nuevos (new pianos)

plumas viejas (old pens)

As you can see, the adjectives became plural to agree with the nouns.

◆ What happens if a noun doesn't end in an *"o"* or an *"a"*? These nouns will still be either masculine or feminine; you just might not be able to know by looking at the word. You must memorize the gender (whether it's masculine or feminine) of these nouns.

Here are a few examples of nouns with modifying adjectives. You can tell if they are masculine or feminine by looking at the adjective ending:

✳ EXAMPLES: *leche fría* (cold milk)   *ciudad atestada* (crowded city)

hotel caro (expensive hotel)   *lápices nuevos* (new pencils)

◆ Sometimes, adjectives end with a consonant or with a vowel other than "o" or "a." These adjectives don't change endings when modifying nouns of different genders. For example, *grande* (big) can modify either *río* (river) or *casa* (house): *río grande* or *casa grande*. Here are some more examples:

✳ EXAMPLES: *libro fácil* (easy book)   *chica cortés* (polite girl)

prueba fácil (easy quiz)   *hombres pobres* (poor men)

chico cortés (polite boy)   *mujeres pobres* (poor women)

◆ A few adjectives ending with consonants <u>do</u> change when modifying masculine or feminine nouns. When certain adjectives of nationality end with a consonant, the letter *"a"* (or letters *"as"* for plural) is added to make the feminine form.

✳ EXAMPLES: *chico inglés* (English boy)

chica inglesa (English girl)

chicos ingleses (English boys)

chicas inglesas (English girls)

queso francés (French cheese)

torta francesa (French cake)

vino español (Spanish wine)

tortilla española (Spanish omelette)

coches japoneses (Japanese cars)

banderas japonesas (Japanese flags)

Helpful Tip: Do you notice that the accent mark dropped off of *inglés* and *francés* in the feminine forms *(inglesa, francesa)*?

PRACTICE EXERCISES

1. **Write the appropriate form of the adjective in parentheses to agree with each noun:**

   a. silla _____ (rojo)

   b. guitarra _____ (eléctrico)

   c. amigos _____ (inglés)

   d. padre _____ (generoso)

   e. teléfono _____ (celular)

   f. diccionarios _____ (fácil)

   g. novelas _____ (exótico)

   h. planta _____ (japonés)

   i. oficinas _____ (grande)

   j. chicos _____ (cómico)

2. **The following paragraph contains many errors related to adjectives and nouns. Underline each error you find, and write the correction above it:**

   Mis padres trabajan en La Casa Blanco. Preparan comida delicioso para el presidente y su familia. Cocinan tortillas españoles, tacos mexicano y ensalada francés. Ganan mucho dinero, pero prefieren tomar más días de vacaciones. Mi hermano cómica ayuda un poco en la cocina y mi hermana come los platos especialas. ¡Me gusta mucho la vida loco en la Casa Blanca!

ORAL PRACTICE
PREGUNTAS EN GRUPOS DE DOS

These two sets of questions use grammatical structures and vocabulary from this lesson. Working with a partner, alternate asking and answering each question. When you get to the bottom of each list, start over at the top, switching roles. As a variation, write out the answers in complete sentences.

A) ¿Quién cierra la puerta en la clase normalmente?

¿A qué hora vuelves a tu casa?

¿Recibes muchos discos compactos?

¿A qué hora comienza la clase de español?

¿Prefieres las ciudades grandes o los pueblos pequeños?

¿Dónde juegas al béisbol con tus amigos favoritos?

¿Es fácil o difícil recordar la fecha?

B) ¿Le gusta la comida francesa?

¿Prefiere Ud. los autobuses o los taxis? ¿Por qué?

¿Juegan Uds. (tus amigos y tú) con las bicicletas?

¿Cuánto cuesta un disco compacto nuevo?

¿Prefieres lecciones fáciles o lecciones difíciles?

¿Qué tiempo hace hoy?

¿Siempre recibes premios en la escuela?

PRUEBA DE REPASO

1. Answer in complete sentences:

a. ¿Cierra Ud. la ventana en la clase?

_____

b. ¿A qué hora vuelves de la escuela?

_____

c. ¿Quién juega al tenis en esta clase?

_____

d. ¿Comes paella frecuentemente?

_____

e. ¿Mueves los brazos (your arms) cuando bailas?

_____

2. Conjugate the following six verbs fully in the present tense:

cerrar (to close)   **volver** (to return)   **servir** (to serve)

_____ _____   _____ _____   _____ _____

_____ _____   _____ _____   _____ _____

_____ _____   _____ _____   _____ _____

recordar (to remember)   **mover** (to move)   **pedir** (to ask for)

_____ _____   _____ _____   _____ _____

_____ _____   _____ _____   _____ _____

_____ _____   _____ _____   _____ _____

3. Write the correct form of each verb in the spaces provided:

a. Mi madre _____ la puerta todas las noches. (cerrar)

b. Tú y yo _____ de Sevilla el domingo. (volver)

c. Eva Longoria _____ comer la comida caliente. (preferir)

d. Tú siempre _____ qué día es hoy. (recordar)

e. Mi hermano _____ frecuentemente a mi abuela en su silla preferida. (sentar)

f. Mis amigos no _____ ver *MTV* porque sus padres prefieren un programa de Disney. (poder)

g. Rafael Nadal siempre _____ muy bien con su raqueta en Wimbledon. (competir)

h. Yo _____ la paciencia cuando camino por una ciudad atestada. (perder)

i. ¿Cuánto _____ un coche nuevo? (costar)

j. Mi madre _____ perfectamente del uno al diez en italiano. (contar)

4. In the following exercise, if a word is singular, make it plural. However, if the word is plural, make it singular:

a. casa _____

b. papel _____

c. lección _____

d. viejas _____

e. corteses _____

f. españoles _____

g. pluma _____

h. lápiz _____

i. libertades _____

5. Write an appropriate conjunction in the space provided:

a. Dos _____ dos son cuatro.

b. No puedo decidir cuál es mi sabor favorito de Ben & Jerry's: chocolate

_____ vainilla.

c. Ni mi padre _____ mi madre quieren viajar ahora a Alicante.

d. O mi madre _____ mi padre puede hablar con la profesora.

e. Normalmente me gusta escuchar la música de Calle 13, _____ ahora deseo escuchar mi álbum nuevo de Selena Gómez.

f. Marcos, Roberto _____ Elisa comienzan a estudiar en el Instituto de Segovia.

g. Mi amiga es inteligente, _____ su hermano no comprende mucho.

h. Ni Carlota Ciganda _____ Sergio García juegan al golf cuando nieva.

i. En Chicago hace mucho frío _____ hace viento también.

6. Translate the following sentences into Spanish:

a. They are returning to the city, but Johnny prefers the village.

_____

b. Ramón and Rosa always close the door.

_____

c. The Spanish kids begin the homework at three.

_____

d. Enrique Iglesias and Anna Kournikova look at the train.

_____

7. The following paragraph contains six errors. Underline each error and write the correct word above it:

Pablo conta su dinero frecuentemente. Pablo es pobre, perro no es muy pobre. Le gusta la música. Prefiere comprar álbumes nuevo de Juanes. También le gustan los músicos españols, especialmente Mecano, Miguel Bosé y David Bisbal. Comenza a contar su dinero a las ocho de la mañana. Es muy fácil porque sólo tiene diez dólares. Un día o su madre ni su padre compra un disco compacto muy especial para él.

COLOMBIA

COLOMBIA

CAPITAL:	Bogotá
POBLACIÓN:	50.400.000
GOBIERNO:	república
PRESIDENTE:	Iván Duque Márquez
DINERO ($):	peso colombiano
PRODUCTOS:	azúcar, café, fruta, petróleo
MÚSICA, BAILE:	cumbia, influencia afro-caribeña, salsa
SITIOS DE INTERÉS:	el bosque de lluvia, Cali, Cartagena, Ciudad Perdida, Medellín, San Andrés, Villa de Leiva
COMIDA TÍPICA:	ajiaco, arroz con pollo, canasta de coco, guayaba, mazamorra, sancocho, tamales

COLOMBIANOS FAMOSOS:

Fernando Botero
(ARTISTA)

Gabriel García Márquez
(ESCRITOR)

Cecilia Herrera
(ARTISTA)

Juanes
(CANTANTE)

Juan Pablo Montoya
(ATLETA)

Mariana Pajón
(ATLETA)

Shakira
(CANTANTE)

José Asunción Silva
(POETA)

Camilo Villegas
(ARTISTA)

Practice this vocabulary with our mobile app! Visit tobreak.com/app for more details.

VOCABULARIO
LECCIÓN TRES

THEME WORDS:
"BODY PARTS"

la	boca	mouth
el	brazo	arm
el	dedo	finger
el	diente	tooth
la	mano	hand
la	nariz	nose
el	ojo	eye
la	oreja, el oído	ear
el	pelo	hair
el	pie	foot
la	pierna	leg

OTHER NOUNS

la	bebida	drink
el	cuero/ la piel (Sp.)	leather
la	foto(grafía)	photo(graph)
los	jóvenes	youth, youngsters
la	luna	moon
la	madera	wood
el	plástico	plastic
el	problema*	problem
la	verdad	truth

ADJECTIVES

bonito/a, bello/a	pretty
enfermo/a	sick
extraño/a (raro/a)	strange

*Although *"problema"* ends in "a," it's a <u>masculine</u> noun!

feo/a	ugly
frustrado/a	frustrated
íntimo/a	intimate, close
típico/a	typical
único/a	only, unique

VERBS

conocer	to know (a person or place)
dar	to give
decir (i)	to say, to tell
ir	to go
odiar	to hate
oír	to hear
saber	to know (a fact)
seguir (i)	to follow
tocar	to play (an instrument), to touch
traer	to bring
ver	to see

MISCELLANEOUS

a la derecha	to the right
a la izquierda	to the left
algo	something
antes (de)	before
cerca (de)	near
después (de)	after
lejos (de)	far
nunca	never
porque	because

LECCIÓN TRES

KEY GRAMMAR CONCEPTS

A) IRREGULAR VERBS IN THE PRESENT TENSE → *Los verbos irregulares en el presente*

B) THE VERBS "SER" AND "ESTAR" → *"Ser" y "estar"*

C) DEFINITE AND INDEFINITE ARTICLES → *Los artículos definidos y indefinidos*

D) NEGATIVE SENTENCES → *Las frases negativas*

 ## A) IRREGULAR VERBS IN THE PRESENT TENSE

The following chart features verbs that are among the most common in the Spanish language. As they are used so frequently, it would be wise to master them now.

caber (to fit)		**caer** (to fall)		**coger** (to grab)		**conocer** (to know)	
quepo	cabemos	**caigo**	caemos	**cojo**	cogemos	**conozco**	conocemos
cabes	cabéis	caes	caéis	coges	cogéis	conoces	conocéis
cabe	caben	cae	caen	coge	cogen	conoce	conocen

construir (to build)		**dar** (to give)		**decir** (to say)		**estar** (to be)	
construyo	construimos	**doy**	damos	**digo**	decimos	**estoy**	estamos
construyes	construís	das	**dais**	**dices**	decís	**estás**	estáis
construye	**construyen**	da	dan	**dice**	**dicen**	**está**	**están**

hacer (to do, make)		**ir** (to go)		**oír** (to hear)		**poner** (to put)	
hago	hacemos	**voy**	**vamos**	**oigo**	**oímos**	**pongo**	ponemos
haces	hacéis	**vas**	**vais**	**oyes**	oís	pones	ponéis
hace	hacen	**va**	**van**	**oye**	**oyen**	pone	ponen

saber (to know)		**salir** (to leave)		**seguir** (to follow)		**ser** (to be)	
sé	sabemos	**salgo**	salimos	**sigo**	seguimos	**soy**	**somos**
sabes	sabéis	sales	salís	**sigues**	seguís	**eres**	**sois**
sabe	saben	sale	salen	**sigue**	**siguen**	es	son

tener (to have)		**traer** (to bring)		**valer** (to be worth)		**venir** (to come)	
tengo	tenemos	**traigo**	traemos	**valgo**	valemos	**vengo**	venimos
tienes	tenéis	traes	traéis	vales	valéis	**vienes**	venís
tiene	**tienen**	trae	traen	vale	valen	**viene**	**vienen**

ver (to see)	
veo	vemos
ves	**veis**
ve	ven

Note: The forms in **boldface** indicate something a little out of the ordinary: a spelling change, a stem change, an accent mark or lack thereof.

¡CUIDADO! Some verbs have conjugations that can't be predicted easily. Some have special changes in the 1st person form only; others have special changes in every form. In this section, you will need to spend a fair amount of time memorizing the verbs presented.

Helpful Tips: **1)** You undoubtedly noticed that some verbs are irregular only in the *yo* form (e.g., *caber, caer, coger, conocer, hacer, poner, saber, salir, traer, valer*).
2) Other verbs are different only in the *yo* form and in the *vosotros/vosotras* form where there is no written accent (e.g., *dar, ver*).
3) The other verbs are irregular in more than one form.

EXAMPLES: *Alejandro Fernández y Luis Miguel **tienen** mucho talento.*
    Alejandro Fernández and Luis Miguel have a lot of talent.

*No **pongo** mis libros nuevos en la mesa.*
    I don't put my new books on the table.

***Sé** que dos y dos **son** cuatro.*
    I know that two and two are four.

*Mi profesora inteligente **dice** que Bogotá es bonita.*
    My intelligent teacher says that Bogotá is pretty.

*Mis hermanos **construyen** casas grandes de cartón.*
    My brothers are building big cardboard houses.

*Yo no **quepo** en la silla pequeña.*
    I don't fit in the small seat.

*Sócrates **es** mi filósofo favorito.*
    Socrates is my favorite philosopher.

***Oigo** la música, pero no **veo** la trompeta.*
    I hear the music, but I don't see the trumpet.

*Mi prima **tiene** las manos pequeñas, los pies normales y una boca muy grande.*
    My cousin has small hands, normal feet, and a very big mouth.

PRACTICE EXERCISES

1. **Study the list of irregular verbs carefully. Now conjugate the following six verbs fully without looking at the lists. Then check your answers carefully and correct any errors:**

   conocer (to know)   **decir** (to say)   **ir** (to go)

   _____ _____ _____ _____ _____ _____

   _____ _____ _____ _____ _____ _____

   _____ _____ _____ _____ _____ _____

   poner (to put)   **ser** (to be)   **ver** (to see)

   _____ _____ _____ _____ _____ _____

   _____ _____ _____ _____ _____ _____

   _____ _____ _____ _____ _____ _____

2. **Complete the following sentences in the present tense using the correct form of the verb in parentheses:**

   a. Nosotros _____ estudiantes aplicados. (ser)

   b. Mi amiga Lucía _____ el nuevo disco de Kings of Leon. (tener)

   c. Ellos no _____ la verdad. (decir)

   d. Julia Louis-Dreyfus _____ la vicepresidenta en el programa de televisión *Veep*. (ser)

   e. Yo no _____ mi tarea todas las noches porque prefiero jugar con mis amigos. (hacer)

   f. Mi hermana _____ los secretos íntimos de mis padres. (oír)

   g. Cuando no estudias, tu mamá _____ muy frustrada. (estar)

   h. Mis fotos de Elvis _____ mucho dinero. (valer)

i. Soledad O'Brien no _____ a ver más partidos de béisbol este año. (ir)

j. Mi madre coge un lápiz para escribir, pero yo _____ una pluma. (coger)

3. The following dialogue contains eight errors. Underline each error and write the correct word above it:

Raúl: Vamos a salir.

Lucía: No, yo no salo. No teno dinero.

Raúl: Tengo diez dólares. Vamos.

Lucía: Pero, yo no cabo en el taxi.

Raúl: Estas loca. ¡Sí, cabes!

Lucía: Pero, yo no esto contenta.

Raúl: ¿Por qué?

Lucía: Porque yo no conoco Bogotá.

Raúl: ¿De dónde eres?

Lucía: So de Medellín.

Raúl: Caramba, ¿vienes?

Lucía: Sí, vo.

B) THE VERBS "SER" AND "ESTAR"

Spanish has two different verbs that mean "to be." Not only are their conjugations irregular, but they are also used in different situations. Here are the main uses of each verb:

1) THE USES OF "SER"

a) To identify a defining characteristic

EXAMPLES: *Los ojos de mi hijo **son** azules.*
My son's eyes are blue.

The Voice ***es** mi programa de televisión favorito.*
The Voice is my favorite television program.

b) To tell where someone or something is from; to indicate origin

EXAMPLES: *Camilo Villegas **es** de Colombia.*
Camilo Villegas is from Colombia.

*Mi vestido **es** de Guatemala.*
My dress is from Guatemala.

c) To tell time or give a date

EXAMPLES: ***Son** las siete y cinco.*
It is five after seven.

*Hoy **es** el veintidós de octubre.*
Today is the twenty-second of October.

d) To indicate possession

EXAMPLES: *La guitarra **es** de Shakira.*
The guitar is Shakira's.

*La pelota de baloncesto **es** de Ricky Rubio.*
The basketball is Ricky Rubio's.

e) To indicate profession, nationality, religion, or political affiliation

EXAMPLES: *Mi abuelo **es** colombiano.*
My grandfather is Colombian.

*Joaquín Castro **es** político y Geraldo Rivera **es** periodista.*
Joaquín Castro is a politician, and Geraldo Rivera is a journalist.

f) To tell when or where an event is taking place

✳ **EXAMPLES:** *El concierto de Nicky Jam es a las seis.*
Nicky Jam's concert is at six.

La fiesta de Año Nuevo es en Times Square.
The New Year's party is in Times Square.

g) To tell what something is made of

✳ **EXAMPLES:** *Mi casa es de madera.*
My house is made out of wood.

Los pantalones de Ricky Martin son de cuero.
Ricky Martin's pants are made of leather.

h) For mathematical calculations

✳ **EXAMPLES:** *Tres y uno son cuatro.*
Three plus one is four.

Cuatro por tres son doce.
Four times three is twelve.

2) THE USES OF "ESTAR" ═══════════════════

a) To express a condition, as opposed to a defining characteristic

✳ **EXAMPLES:** *Estoy enferma y voy al hospital.*
I'm sick, and I'm going to the hospital.

Estamos tristes porque no tenemos entradas para el concierto de Pitbull.
We are sad because we don't have tickets for the Pitbull concert.

b) To identify location (though <u>not</u> of an event!)

✳ **EXAMPLES:** *Mis amigos están en la cocina ahora.*
My friends are in the kitchen now.

Santo Domingo está en la República Dominicana.
Santo Domingo is in the Dominican Republic.

¿ ◆ ? Did you notice that the location may be temporary or permanent?

---

c) **To indicate a change from the norm or to emphasize the special state or nature of something**

 EXAMPLES: *¡Estás muy guapo hoy!*
You look great today!

(The idea here is that you have gotten all dressed up, your hair looks great, etc. By using *estar,* the speaker emphasizes that you look especially good today!)

Enrique, ¡estás flaquísimo!
Enrique, you look so thin!

(The speaker is emphasizing that Enrique looks especially thin — maybe he has lost weight or his clothes make him look slimmer than usual.)

d) **To talk about certain weather conditions**

 EXAMPLES: *Está nublado ahora en Barranquilla.*
It is cloudy now in Barranquilla.

Está soleado esta tarde en la playa.
It's sunny this afternoon on the beach.

PRACTICE EXERCISES ▶

1. **Insert the correct present tense of either the verb "ser" or "estar" in the following sentences. Write the reason (2b, 1e, etc.) in the margin to the right:**

a. Rihanna _____ muy enferma hoy y no puede cantar en el concierto. ____

b. Nosotros _____ de Cartagena, Colombia. ____

c. Tú _____ un profesor muy inteligente. ____

d. Alec Martínez _____ uno de los pocos jugadores latinos de la Liga Nacional de Hockey. ____

e. Disney World _____ en Orlando, Florida. ____

f. _____ las cuatro de la tarde . . . ¡comienza el programa *Cristina!* ____

g. No podemos ver la Luna porque _____ muy nublado ahora. ____

h. La guitarra bonita _____ de Juan Luis Guerra. ____

i. Ramona, ¡_____ muy bonita hoy . . . tu camisa es preciosa!   ____

j. Los libros _____ de papel.   ____

**2. The following paragraph contains seven errors of *"ser"* and *"estar."*
Underline each error and write the correction above it:**

*Voy a Nueva York. Está una ciudad fantástica. Mis padres están
de Phoenix, pero ahora son en Nueva York. Mi padre es dentista y mi
madre está actriz. Están las tres y media y a las cuatro comienza una
producción con mi madre. Hoy mi madre es un poco enferma, pero yo
no soy nervioso. Ella tiene mucho talento.*

C) DEFINITE AND INDEFINITE ARTICLES

Articles are adjectives that help to identify nouns. In English, we have only one **definite
article** — "the," which refers to a specific thing or things, e.g., "the afternoon, the cars."
We also have **indefinite articles** — "a, an, some" which refer to one or a few, of those
things, e.g., "an afternoon, some cars."

1) DEFINITE ARTICLES

Spanish has four definite articles. Remember, because they are a type of adjective,
they have to agree with the masculine or feminine nouns they modify. They will also
be singular or plural!

Here are the Spanish definite articles:

Definite Articles	
el (masculine, singular)	*los* (masculine, plural)
la (feminine, singular)	*las* (feminine, plural)

 **EXAMPLES:** *El chico que tiene **el** brazo roto es mi primo Ernesto.*
The boy with the broken arm is my cousin Ernesto.

*"**La** persona del siglo" es Albert Einstein, dice la revista* Time.
"The Person of the Century" is Albert Einstein, says *Time* magazine.

*Como **los** chocolates en mi cama.*
I eat the chocolates in my bed.

***Las** bebidas están muy frías.*
The drinks are very cold.

2) INDEFINITE ARTICLES

Indefinite articles also have four forms, which correspond to the gender and number of the noun they modify.

Here are the Spanish indefinite articles:

Indefinite Articles	
un (masculine, singular)	*unos* (masculine, plural)
una (feminine, singular)	*unas* (feminine, plural)

 **EXAMPLES:** *Normalmente leo **un** libro con mi amiga.*
I normally read a book with my friend.

*Fanny Lú es **una** cantante famosa.*
Fanny Lú is a famous singer.

*Tengo **unos** amigos que viven en Bucaramanga, Colombia.*
I have some friends who live in Bucaramanga, Colombia.

***Unas** personas misteriosas viven aquí en el hotel.*
Some mysterious people live here in the hotel.

Helpful Tip: Did you notice that both definite and indefinite articles come <u>before</u> the nouns that they modify? In this way, they are different from the descriptive adjectives that we saw earlier.

PRACTICE EXERCISES

1. Fill in the blanks with the correct definite article:

a. _____ libros

b. _____ pierna

c. _____ madre

d. _____ profesores

e. _____ japonesas

f. _____ narices

g. _____ padres

h. _____ lápiz

i. _____ libertad

j. _____ cucarachas

2. Now fill in the blanks with the correct indefinite article:

a. _____ puertas

b. _____ abuelo

c. _____ guitarra

d. _____ españoles

e. _____ camisas

f. _____ dedo

g. _____ luna

h. _____ momentos

i. _____ oportunidades

j. _____ coche

3. The following paragraph contains seven errors related to definite and indefinite articles. Underline each error and write the correction above it:

Los amigas de mi hermano Pepito están locas. Un amiga es Natalia. Tiene una frutas en su coche. Los frutas no son buenas . . . Un amiga es Nacha. Tiene uno guitarra eléctrica, pero su música es mala. Un día voy a decir: "Pepito, los amigas que tienes son raras".

D) NEGATIVE SENTENCES

As you may have noticed in the **FIRST STEPS** section of this text, if you answer a question negatively, a negative word must come <u>before</u> the verb.

Here is a list of some negative words that will come in handy right now:

Common Negative Words
nada → nothing
nadie → no one
ni → neither, nor
no → no, not
nunca → never

EXAMPLES: *¿Vas al concierto de Selena Gómez? –**No, no** voy.*
Are you going to the Selena Gómez concert? –No, I'm not going.

*¿Tienes mucho dinero aquí? –**No, no** tengo mucho.*
Do you have much money here? –No, I don't have much.

*¿Escuchas la música de Christian Daniel? –**No, nunca** escucho su música. (**No, no** escucho su música **nunca**.)*
Do you listen to the music of Christian Daniel? –I never listen to his music.

*¿Quién va a mi restaurante favorito? –**No** va **nadie**. (**Nadie** va.)*
Who is going to my favorite restaurant? –No one is going.

*¿Hay mucha comida en el refrigerador? –**No, no** hay **nada**.*
Is there a lot of food in the refrigerator? –No, there is nothing.

*¿Va Pepe o Luisa al restaurante? –**No, ni** Pepe **ni** Luisa van.*
Is Pepe or Luisa going to the restaurant? –No, neither Pepe nor Luisa is going.

*¿Tienes algo? –**No, no** tengo **nada**.**

Do you have something? –No, I don't have anything.

*Note: You could <u>not</u> say: *"No, no tengo algo." Once a negative indicator is placed before the verb, words that follow <u>must</u> take a negative form.

PRACTICE EXERCISES

1. **Answer the following questions negatively, being sure to place a negative word before the verb in your answer. Use at least one of the following four negative words in each complete sentence** *(nada, nadie, nunca, ni)*:

a. ¿Tienes siempre mucha tarea en tu clase de matemáticas?

_____

b. ¿Quién va a la fiesta el sábado?

_____

c. ¿Vas frecuentemente a la discoteca con Mick Jagger?

_____

d. ¿Tienes algo?

_____

e. ¿Cuáles de tus amigos tienen dientes bonitos?

_____

f. ¿Hablas portugués, italiano y francés?

_____

g. ¿Cuándo ves *The Bachelor* y *World News Tonight*?

_____

2. Correct the errors that you spot in the following job interview. Be on the lookout for "negative" errors!

Sra. Ortega: *Buenos días. ¿Es Ud. Roberto Gómez?*

Luis Gómez: *Soy no Roberto; soy Luis.*

Sra.: *Sí, sí. ¿Desea Ud. un trabajo?*

Luis: *Sí, pero tengo no experiencia.*

Sra.: *Pero, ¿habla Ud. bien el español?*

Luis: *Sí, señora.*

Sra.: *¿Con quién habla Ud.?*

Luis: *Hablo con nadie, pero veo la televisión.*

Sra.: *¿Qué programas?*

Luis: American Idol *y* The Voice.

Sra.: *Pero, son no programas en español.*

Luis: *Es verdad.*

Sra.: *¿Ud. cree que soy idiota?*

Luis: *No . . . sí . . . no . . . no sé.*

Sra.: *Adiós, Sr. Gómez.*

Luis: *¡Voy a volver nunca aquí!*

ORAL PRACTICE
PREGUNTAS EN GRUPOS DE DOS

These two sets of questions use grammatical structures and vocabulary from this lesson. Working with a partner, alternate asking and answering each question. When you get to the bottom of each list, start over at the top, switching roles. As a variation, write out the answers in complete sentences.

A) ¿Siempre dices la verdad?

¿Dónde pones los libros en la clase? (*silla* – chair, *suelo* – floor)

¿Vas a la escuela los domingos?

¿Eres americano/a?

¿Tienes muchos amigos íntimos con pelo bonito?

¿Puedes ver la luna donde vives?

¿Sabes qué hora es?

B) ¿Cómo estás hoy?

¿De qué material es tu casa? (*madera* – wood, *piedra* – stone)

¿Cuándo estás muy triste?

¿Tocas la guitarra o el piano?

¿Hay bebidas frías en la cafetería de la escuela?

¿Cuál es tu favorita banda de música?

¿Siempre escuchas la música de Enrique Iglesias?

DIALOGUE

The following dialogue contains grammar and vocabulary that you've seen in this lesson and in the introductory section. After listening to the dialogue, read it aloud, alone or with friends. Afterwards, try to answer the questions that follow either aloud or in written form.

LAS AVENTURAS DE RAFAEL, ELISA Y "EL TIGRE"

ESCENA DOS

Rafael, "El Tigre" y Elisa hablan en un restaurante en Georgetown. Es martes.

Rafael:	Sí, Tigre. No hay problema. Tengo el dinero.
El Tigre:	Pero cuesta mucho viajar a Nueva York.
Rafael:	Viajamos en tren, no en taxi. No cuesta mucho.
El Tigre:	¿Estás nerviosa, Elisa?
Elisa:	Sí, un poco. Mis padres creen que voy a un campamento de tenis en las montañas de New Hampshire por una semana.
Rafael:	Exactamente. Tus padres son muy buenos, pero un poco estúpidos.
El Tigre:	Rafael, no es bueno insultar a los padres de Elisa.
Rafael:	Pero, son mis tíos. ¿No recuerdas? Soy el primo de Elisa. Es mi familia. Amo muchísimo a mi tío José y a mi tía Sarita.

Entra una camarera.

Camarera:	Buenas tardes.
Elisa:	Hola. Para mí, un café con leche.
El Tigre:	Dos, por favor.
Rafael:	Prefiero una Fanta de limón.

La camarera sale y vuelve en un momento con las bebidas.

El Tigre:	Muchas gracias, señorita.
Elisa:	¿A qué hora nos reunimos (do we meet) mañana en la estación de tren?
Rafael:	A las nueve en punto.
El Tigre:	El viaje a Nueva York sólo es de cinco horas.
Elisa:	Fantástico. ¿Es posible mañana caminar un poco en el famoso Parque Central?
Rafael:	Claro, Elisa. Y hay caballos para los turistas.
El Tigre:	Bueno, hasta mañana, Elisa y Rafael. Vuelvo a mi casa.
Elisa:	Rafael y yo volvemos a nuestras casas, también.
Rafael:	Hasta mañana.

PREGUNTAS

1) ¿Dónde hablan Elisa, Rafael y El Tigre?

_____

2) ¿Cómo viajan los jóvenes a Nueva York?

_____

3) ¿Está nerviosa Elisa? ¿Por qué?

_____

4) ¿Insulta Rafael a los padres de Elisa?

_____

5) ¿Qué beben los tres amigos?

_____

6) ¿Dónde se reúnen los chicos mañana?

_____

7) ¿Cuántas horas es el viaje a Nueva York?

_____

8) ¿Cómo se llama el famoso parque de Nueva York?

_____

9) ¿Qué animales hay en el parque?

_____

10) ¿Adónde van todos al final de la escena?

_____

PRUEBA DE REPASO

1. Answer in complete sentences:

a. ¿Dónde estás?

_____

b. ¿Dices siempre la verdad en la clase?

_____

c. ¿A qué hora vas a la escuela?

_____

d. ¿Tienes una guitarra eléctrica?

_____

e. ¿Oyes música ahora?

_____

2. Conjugate the following six verbs fully in the present tense:

salir (to leave)   **ser** (to be)   **seguir** (to follow)

_____ _____   _____ _____   _____ _____

_____ _____   _____ _____   _____ _____

_____ _____   _____ _____   _____ _____

oír (to hear)   **estar** (to be)   **ir** (to go)

_____ _____   _____ _____   _____ _____

_____ _____   _____ _____   _____ _____

_____ _____   _____ _____   _____ _____

PRUEBA DE REPASO (side tab)

3. Write the correct present tense of each verb in the spaces provided:

a. Tengo los ojos cerrados. No _____ nada. (ver)

b. ¿Cuánto _____ una cámara nueva de Canon? (valer)

c. Uds. _____ de Colombia y yo soy de Uruguay. (ser)

d. Yo _____ en la clase del señor Álvarez. (estar)

e. Yo no _____ bien la ciudad de Cali. (conocer)

f. Nosotros _____ la ropa nueva en la mesa. (poner)

g. Tú no _____ la música porque hablas mucho. (oír)

h. Yo me _____ en diciembre cuando nieva mucho. (caer)

i. Yo no _____ en la silla pequeña. (caber)

j. La actriz Sofía Vergara dice: "Yo siempre les _____ las gracias a todos mis amigos". (dar)

4. Write the correct definite or indefinite article as indicated:

definite article

a. _____ madre

b. _____ amigos

c. _____ persona

d. _____ chico

e. _____ trompeta

f. _____ españoles

g. _____ camisa

h. _____ piano

indefinite article

a. _____ bebida

b. _____ brazo

c. _____ foto

d. _____ trenes

e. _____ jóvenes

f. _____ cosa

g. _____ premios

h. _____ bicicleta

5. Write the correct form of the present tense of *"ser"* or *"estar"*:

a. Mi tía _____ alta.

b. Nosotras _____ muy frustradas ahora.

c. _____ las siete y media.

d. _____ muy nublado ahora y no podemos ver el sol.

e. La casa _____ de madera.

f. Mi padre no _____ aquí.

g. El piano _____ de Pepe Aguilar.

h. Mi abuelo _____ muy rico.

i. El concierto de Cher_____ en Madison Square Garden.

j. ¡José, _____ muy guapo hoy! Me gusta tu camisa nueva.

k. En mi opinión, la lámpara _____ muy fea.

6. Translate the following sentences into Spanish:

a. I am from Bogotá, but I am in San Francisco.

_____

b. Alejandro is going to his uncle's school.

_____

c. We never put the old wood near the house.

_____

7. The following paragraph contains six errors related to verbs, adjectives and spelling. Underline each error and write the correction above it:

 Buenos días. Están las seis de la mañana y es muy nublado.

¡Hoy no teno escuela! Mi amigo y yo vamas al parque. Vamos a comprar

comida delicioso. Posiblemente vamos a estudiar un poco las leccions en

el parque porque el lunes hay un examen, pero, primero, voy a comer

cereal y beber leche fría. Adiós.

ARGENTINA

ARGENTINA

CAPITAL:	Buenos Aires
POBLACIÓN:	44.900.000
GOBIERNO:	república federal representativa
PRESIDENTE:	Alberto Fernández
DINERO ($):	peso argentino
PRODUCTOS:	agricultura, carne, petróleo
MÚSICA, BAILE:	milonga, tango, zamba
SITIOS DE INTERÉS:	Los Andes, la Casa Rosada, las Cataratas del Iguazú, La Pampa, Patagonia
COMIDA TÍPICA:	arroz con pollo, churrasco, empanadas, locro, mate, parrillada

ARGENTINOS FAMOSOS:

Jorge Mario Bergoglio
(PAPA FRANCISCO)

Jorge Luis Borges
(ESCRITOR)

Julio Cortázar
(ESCRITOR)

Raquel Forner
(ARTISTA)

Manu Ginóbili
(ATLETA)

Diego Maradona
(FUTBOLISTA)

Lionel Messi
(FUTBOLISTA)

Juan y Evita Perón
(POLÍTICOS)

Manuel Puig
(ESCRITOR)

Gabriela Sabatini
(TENISTA)

Practice this vocabulary with our mobile app! Visit tobreak.com/app for more details.

VOCABULARIO LECCIÓN CUATRO

THEME WORDS: "IN TOWN""

el *aeropuerto*	airport
la *biblioteca*	library
la *calle*	street
la *cárcel*	jail
el *cine*	movie theater
la *estación de tren*	train station
la *gasolinera*	gas station
la *iglesia*	church
el *parque*	park
el *restaurante*	restaurant
la *sinagoga*	synagogue
el *supermercado*	supermarket
el *teatro*	theater
la *tienda*	store

OTHER NOUNS

el *año*	year
la *canción*	song
la *carta*	letter
el *chicle*	gum
el *continente*	continent
el *equipo*	team
la *limonada*	lemonade
el *mes*	month
la *montaña*	mountain
la *novia*	girlfriend
el *novio*	boyfriend
el *oso*	bear
el *país*	country
la *playa*	beach
el *río*	river

el *secreto*	secret
la *tarea*	homework, task
el *zapato*	shoe

ADJECTIVES

débil	weak
fuerte	strong
otro/a	another, other
último/a	past, last

VERBS

bajar	to go down
descubrir	to discover
*elegir (i)**	to elect, to choose
llorar	to cry
necesitar	to need
subir	to go up

*This verb is conjugated: *elijo, eliges, elige, elegimos, elegís, eligen.*

MISCELLANEOUS

anoche	last night
ayer	yesterday
de la mañana	A.M. (in the morning)
de la tarde/noche	P.M. (in the afternoon/evening)
durante	during
esta mañana	this morning
esta noche	tonight
esta tarde	this afternoon
luego	later
rápidamente	quickly
¿verdad?	isn't that so?

LECCIÓN CUATRO

KEY GRAMMAR
CONCEPTS

A) THE PRETERITE (PAST) TENSE OF REGULAR VERBS →
El pretérito de los verbos regulares

B) PREPOSITIONS → *Las preposiciones*

C) PRONOUNS AFTER PREPOSITIONS → *Los pronombres
después de preposiciones*

A) THE PRETERITE (PAST) TENSE OF REGULAR VERBS

The **preterite** is one of many tenses used in Spanish to describe events that occurred in the past. The preterite talks about <u>completed</u> actions. These actions have a clear ending point (as opposed to habits or descriptions, which have a more ongoing, continuous feeling). The preterite emphasizes the conclusion or ending point of an event or narrative.

Here are the conjugations of three regular verbs in the preterite:

HABLAR		COMER		VIVIR	
hablé	hablamos	comí	comimos	viví	vivimos
hablaste	hablasteis	comiste	comisteis	viviste	vivisteis
habló	hablaron	comió	comieron	vivió	vivieron

Helpful Tips: **1)** Did you notice that there are accents on the *yo* and *Ud./él/ella* forms?
2) You can see that the *nosotros* form of *hablar* is *hablamos* and of *vivir* is *vivimos* — the preterite and present have identical *nosotros* forms for **-AR** and **-IR** verbs! It is only through context that you can know which tense the speaker intended.
3) Do you see the similarities between the *tú* and *vosotros/as* forms? Just add "is" to the *tú* form!

 EXAMPLES: ***Comí*** *en un restaurante cubano, "Victor's Café", en Nueva York.*
I ate in a Cuban restaurant, "Victor's Café," in New York.

*Anoche **preparamos** la tarea en la biblioteca.*
We prepared the homework in the library last night.

*Coldplay **escribió** una canción excelente:* "Viva la vida".
Coldplay wrote an excellent song: *"Viva la vida."*

Vendiste el libro de español en la escuela, ¿verdad?
You sold the Spanish book in school, right?

Mis amigos nunca lavaron sus chaquetas de Patagonia.
My friends never washed their Patagonia jackets.

El año pasado, Carolina Herrera y yo abrimos una tienda nueva en Buenos Aires.
Last year, Carolina Herrera and I opened a new store in Buenos Aires.

Whenever you tell how long an event lasted, you will choose the preterite tense. By saying, for example, that a person studied for a year or rested for a number of hours, you convey an ending point. This ending point, indicating a <u>completed</u> action, is a signal for the preterite.

 **EXAMPLES:** *Estudié por tres horas anoche.*
I studied last night for three hours.

Vivimos en Buenos Aires por un año.
We lived in Buenos Aires for one year.

Ayer Rafael Nadal jugó al tenis con Juan Martín del Potro por tres horas.
Rafael Nadal played tennis with Juan Martín del Potro for three hours yesterday.

 # PRACTICE EXERCISES

1. Conjugate the following verbs fully into the preterite:

llorar (to cry)   **correr** (to run)   **permitir** (to permit)

_____ _____   _____ _____   _____ _____

_____ _____   _____ _____   _____ _____

_____ _____   _____ _____   _____ _____

esperar (to wait for)   **romper** (to break)   **escribir** (to write)

_____ _____   _____ _____   _____ _____

_____ _____   _____ _____   _____ _____

_____ _____   _____ _____   _____ _____

2. **Complete the following sentences using the appropriate form of the preterite tense:**

   a. Mi prima _____ rápidamente al río. (correr)

   b. Los Buccaneers _____ el Super Bowl en 2021. (ganar)

   c. Thalía y Enrique Iglesias _____ juntos por unos minutos durante el programa de televisión. (bailar)

   d. Rigoberta Menchú _____ el Premio Nobel de la Paz en 1992. (recibir)

   e. Yo _____ la puerta grande para mi abuelo. (abrir)

   f. Nosotros _____ montañas muy altas en Perú para ver Machu Picchu, la famosa ciudad de los incas. (subir)

   g. La estudiante inteligente _____ muchas preguntas difíciles. (contestar)

   h. No comprendo por qué tú no _____ la limonada. (beber)

   i. Cuando el equipo perdió, ellas _____ por unos minutos. (llorar)

   j. ¿Por qué nunca _____ Uds. chicle en la iglesia? (permitir)

   k. Nosotros _____ primero a la derecha y después a la izquierda,

   pero nunca _____ la salida. (caminar/encontrar)

3. **The following paragraph contains five misconjugated verbs. Underline each mistaken verb and write the correct word above it:**

   Elián González llegió a Florida desde la isla de Cuba. Su madre y él escapieron de allí. Muchas personas desaparecieran cuando su barco se hundió en el agua. Elián vivó con familiares en Miami por muchos meses y luego volvó a Cuba donde vive su papá. El chico es muy fuerte y a veces hay programas en la televisión sobre él.

B) PREPOSITIONS

Prepositions are words in a sentence that join with nouns and pronouns to form phrases (e.g., *in the forest; with him*). These words help to establish relationships between words.

The forms of the prepositions never change; they are the same no matter what words are nearby.

Here is a list of ten of the most common prepositions in Spanish:

Common Prepositions	
a → at, to	*en* → in, on
antes de → before	*hasta* → until
con → with	*para* → by, for, in order to
de → of, from	*por* → by, for, through
después de → after	*sin* → without

 **EXAMPLES:** *Vamos **a** la casa de la cantante Esperanza Spaulding.*
We are going to the home of the singer Esperanza Spaulding.

*Gael García Bernal es el actor principal **en** la película* Diarios de motocicleta.
Gael García Bernal is the main actor in the movie *Motorcycle Diaries*.

*En junio, el presidente boliviano, Evo Morales, habló **con** la presidenta chilena, Michelle Bachelet.*
In June, the Bolivian president, Evo Morales, spoke with the Chilean president, Michelle Bachelet.

*Voy a leer muchos cuentos de Jorge Luis Borges **antes de** junio.*
I'm going to read many stories by Jorge Luis Borges before June.

*Siempre dejo una carta y muchas galletas **para** Santa Claus.*
I always leave a letter and many cookies for Santa Claus.

*Hoy voy a trabajar **hasta** las diez **de** la noche.*
I'm going to work today until 10 P.M.

The prepositions *"a"* and *"de"* form contractions when they are followed by the definite article *"el."* These two contractions are the only ones used in the Spanish language. They are obligatory! When *"a"* or *"de"* is followed by *"el,"* you <u>must</u> make the following contractions:

a + el = al	*de + el = del*

Helpful Tip: Be aware that *"a"* + *él* (he, him) is not contracted!

Here are some sentences that use these contractions:

 **EXAMPLES:** *La bicicleta nueva es **del** chico, no de la chica.*
The new bicycle is the boy's, not the girl's.

*Cuando mis amigos van **al** parque, nunca me invitan.*
When my friends go to the park, they never invite me.

*Nunca vamos a revelar el secreto **del** robo nocturno.*
We will never reveal the secret of the nighttime robbery.

*Kelly Ripa y Mark Consuelos fueron primero **al** hotel y después a la playa.*
Kelly Ripa and Mark Consuelos first went to the hotel and afterwards to the beach.

❓ ◆ ❓ Did you notice that there are no contractions with *a la, a los, a las,* nor with *de la, de los,* or *de las?*

Certain verbs are followed by the preposition "a" when an infinitive follows:

aprender → to learn	*empezar (ie)* → to begin
comenzar (ie) → to begin	*ir* → to go

 EXAMPLES: *Aprendemos **a** esquiar en New Hampshire.*
We're learning to ski in New Hampshire.

*Comienzas **a** bailar.*
You are beginning to dance.

*Empiezan **a** pintar.*
They are beginning to paint.

*Voy **a** estudiar.*
I'm going to study.

PRACTICE EXERCISES

1. **Place one of these prepositions** *(a, antes de, con, de, después de, en, hasta, para, por, sin)* **in the following sentences. Make the appropriate contraction "del" or "al" when necessary. For a few sentences, there may be more than one correct answer:**

a. Mi plato favorito en este restaurante es el chili _____ carne.

b. Cuando estoy en la clase de español, siempre me siento _____ mi silla favorita.

c. No quiero ir al supermercado _____ María; ella necesita ir también.

d. Voy _____ el hospital ahora porque mi abuelita está enferma.

e. ¡Rápido! Sólo quedan cinco minutos _____ el comienzo de la película de Almodóvar, *Dolor y Gloria*.

f. Si tienes tiempo, ¿quieres ir a mi casa _____ la conferencia?

g. _____ aprender a hablar bien el español, es necesario estudiar muchas horas.

h. Mi hermano siempre corre en la calle _____ llegar rápidamente; yo prefiero caminar.

i. Son las ocho _____ la noche; ahora empieza mi programa favorito, *Doña Bárbara*.

j. Me gusta mucho caminar _____ la playa _____ zapatos.

2. **The following letter contains six errors; a few errors are based on prepositions, the others are verbal in nature. Find them and make appropriate corrections:**

Mariana:

Salí hoy de el hotel y descubré que mi novio, Jorge, salió can otra chica, Luisa. Llegaron a un restaurante a las dos de la tarde. Después de diez minutos yo entre en el restaurante. Pregunté: "Jorge, ¿vas a salir de aquí con ella o sino ella?" Jorge no es estúpido. Él saló inmediatamente con su novia favorita: yo.

Silvia

 ## C) PRONOUNS AFTER PREPOSITIONS

You undoubtedly remember the subject pronouns we first learned in *Lección Uno: yo, tú, él, ella, Ud., nosotros/nosotras, vosotros/vosotras, ellos, ellas,* and *Uds.* These pronouns serve as the main actors or "stars" (subjects!) of a sentence. What happens, however, when a **pronoun follows a preposition**? This lesson will teach you what to do.

Here is the list of pronouns that follow a preposition:

mí	*nosotros, nosotras*
ti	*vosotros, vosotras*
él, ella, Ud.	*ellos, ellas, Uds.*

Helpful Tips: **1)** Did you notice that this list is almost identical to the subject pronoun list? The only differences are seen in the 1st person singular *(mí)* and 2nd person singular *(ti).*
2) *Ti* does <u>not</u> have an accent (ever!), although many beginning Spanish students can't seem to resist adding one!

✳ **EXAMPLES:** *Para mí, el mejor cantante es Juanes.*
For me, the best singer is Juanes.

*No vamos al concierto **sin ellos**.*
We aren't going to the concert without them.

*No sólo pienso **en mí**; pienso **en ti**, también.*
I don't only think about myself; I think of you, too.

*Podemos ir **con ella**, pero prefiero caminar sola.*
We can go with her, but I prefer to walk alone.

*Creo que Gaby Espino y Jencarlos Canela son muy guapos. ¿Qué opinión tienes **de ellos**?*
I believe that Gaby Espino and Jencarlos Canela are very good-looking. What do you think of them?

*Uds. no van a oír mucho **de mí** en el futuro porque me voy a otro país.*
You all are not going to hear much of me in the future because I am going to another country.

¡CUIDADO! After the preposition *"con,"* however, you must use these special forms:

> *conmigo* → with me
> *contigo* → with you (familiar)

✳ **EXAMPLES:** *Mi amiga no viene **conmigo** hoy porque sale con su novio, el gaucho.*
My friend isn't coming with me today because she is going out with her boyfriend, the cowboy.

*Madonna no puede hablar **contigo** ahora porque está con Jesús Luz.*
Madonna can't speak with you now because she is with Jesús Luz.

*No hablo con él ni con ella; hablo **contigo**.*
I'm not talking with him, nor with her; I'm talking with you.

1. Translate the pronouns in parentheses:

a. El nuevo video de Disney es para _____. (me)

b. Nunca tengo tiempo de hacer las camas para _____. (them)

c. Mi oso de peluche siempre va con_____ cuando viajo en tren. (me)

d. Lionel Messi, el futbolista, es una inspiración para _____. (us)

e. Es verdad que mis padres no saben nada de _____. (you, familiar)

f. _____ tienen mucha familia en las pampas de Argentina, ¿verdad? (You all)

g. Voy a hablar con _____ después de la clase. (you, formal)

h. ¿Qué piensas de _____? (her)

i. Esta motocicleta nueva es para _____. (him)

j. Voy a leer *La vida es sueño* con_____, mi amor. (you, familiar)

2. Try to write one long sentence that uses the following five words and phrases:

después de	*en*	*conmigo*	*de ella*	*al*

_____

_____

ORAL PRACTICE
PREGUNTAS EN GRUPOS DE DOS

These two sets of questions use grammatical structures and vocabulary from this lesson. Working with a partner, alternate asking and answering each question. When you get to the bottom of each list, start over at the top, switching roles. As a variation, write out the answers in complete sentences.

A) ¿Qué comiste anoche?

¿Quién cerró la puerta en la clase hoy?

¿Escribiste una carta esta mañana?

¿Compraste zapatos nuevos en agosto?

¿Caminaron tus amigos en las montañas en el verano?

¿Preparaste una sorpresa (surprise) con tus hermanos ayer?

¿Corriste en un maratón el año pasado?

B) ¿Tienes una carta para mí?

¿Quieres oír un secreto?

¿Cuál es tu aeropuerto favorito?

¿Es muy fuerte un oso?

¿Te gusta cantar en el baño?

¿Es la limonada de la chica o del chico?

¿Vendiste tu otro coche esta tarde?

PRUEBA DE REPASO

1. Answer in complete sentences, paying close attention to whether the present or preterite is used:

a. ¿Hablaste mucho español ayer?

____

b. ¿Escribiste muchas cartas el verano pasado?

____

c. ¿Tienes información nueva para mí?

____

d. ¿Estudiaron Uds. mucho el domingo?

____

e. ¿Prefieres hablar conmigo o con Cristiano Ronaldo, el futbolista?

____

2. Conjugate the following six verbs fully in the preterite tense:

hablar (to speak)		**comer** (to eat)		**vivir** (to live)	
________	________	________	________	________	________
________	________	________	________	________	________
________	________	________	________	________	________

necesitar (to need)		**vender** (to sell)		**escribir** (to write)	
________	________	________	________	________	________
________	________	________	________	________	________
________	________	________	________	________	________

3. **Write the correct form of the preterite in the spaces provided:**

   a. Sean _____ rápidamente para ganar la competición en *Survivor*. (correr)

   b. Nosotros _____ hablar con el director de la escuela. (necesitar)

   c. En la tienda ellos _____ chicle delicioso. (vender)

   d. Diego Luna _____ con Jennifer Lawrence por cinco minutos. (hablar)

   e. Uds. _____ en el restaurante cerca de la playa. (comer)

   f. Mi suegra _____ en Córdoba por dos años. (vivir)

   g. Antonio Banderas no _____ una carta ayer. (escribir)

   h. Tú _____ una comida fantástica anoche. (cocinar)

   i. Yo no _____ la silla pequeña; ¡tú y yo

   _____ la silla grande! (romper/romper)

   j. El sargento no _____ secretos en su clase. (permitir)

4. **Write one of these prepositions in the sentences that follow** *(a, antes de, con, de, después de, en, hasta, para, por, sin)***:**

   a. No voy a la playa antes de las doce; voy _____ las doce.

   b. No corro con mis amigos; corro _____ ellos.

   c. Voy _____ la cárcel para visitar a tus padres.

   d. Vamos a estar en Los Andes _____ el fin del mes.

   e. ¿Dejas muchas galletas y una carta _____ Santa Claus?

   f. Hay seis gatos que viven _____ la casa.

   g. "Me gustan las pizzas _____ mucho queso", confesó Tom Brady.

h. Vamos a pasar _____ el parque ahora.

i. Primero caminamos a la tienda y después vamos _____ el banco.

j. Enero es _____ febrero.

5. Translate the pronouns in parentheses:

a. Siempre bailo el tango con_____, mi amor. (you)

b. La canción no es para _____; es para mi novio. (him)

c. ¿Qué opinión tienes de _____? (her)

d. Señor, estos platos exquisitos son para _____. (you)

e. Mis amigos no saben nada de _____. (you, familiar)

f. El café de Starbucks no es demasiado fuerte para _____. (us)

g. La semana pasada mi novia necesitó hablar con_____ en la estación de tren. (me)

h. La tarea no es para _____; es para _____. (them/you, familiar)

i. Durante la fiesta, hay chicle y limonada para _____. (you all)

j. Los zapatos no son para ellos; son para _____. (me)

6. Translate the following sentences into Spanish:

a. They needed to run to the other gas station.

_____

b. The letters are for him.

_____

c. During the meeting last night, I sold my new song.

_____

7. The following paragraph contains six errors. Underline each error and write the correction above it:

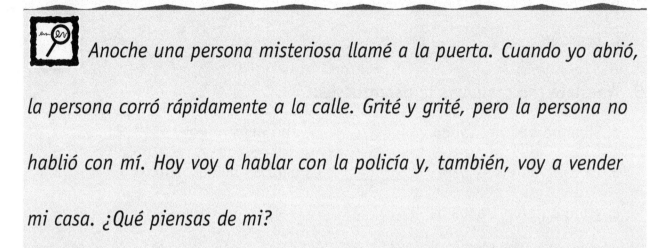

Anoche una persona misteriosa llamé a la puerta. Cuando yo abrió, la persona corró rápidamente a la calle. Grité y grité, pero la persona no hablió con mí. Hoy voy a hablar con la policía y, también, voy a vender mi casa. ¿Qué piensas de mi?

ESTADOS UNIDOS

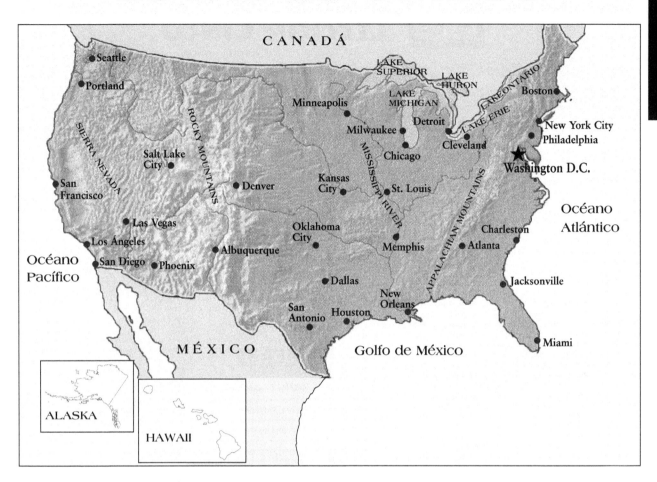

ESTADOS UNIDOS

CAPITAL:	Washington, D.C.
POBLACIÓN:	332.300.000
GOBIERNO:	república constitucional
PRESIDENTE:	Joseph Biden
DINERO ($):	dólar
PRODUCTOS:	agricultura, tecnología
MÚSICA, BAILE:	"bluegrass," country, jazz, rap, "square dance"
SITIOS DE INTERÉS:	las Cataratas del Niágara, el Gran Cañón del Colorado, Yosemite
COMIDA TÍPICA:	carne, hamburguesas, maíz, panqueques, pavo asado, perros calientes, pizza, tarta de manzana

ESTADOUNIDENSES FAMOSOS:

César Chávez
(ACTIVISTA)

Rosa Gumataotao Ríos
(TESORERA)

Scott Gómez
(ATLETA)

Ellen Ochoa
(ASTRONAUTA)

Bill Richardson
(POLÍTICO)

Marco Rubio
(POLÍTICO)

Loretta y Silvia Sánchez
(POLÍTICAS)

Sonia Sotomayor
(JUEZ DEL TRIBUNAL SUPREMO)

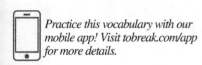

VOCABULARIO
LECCIÓN CINCO

THEME WORDS: "FOOD AND DRINK"

el agua (f.)	water
el arroz	rice
el/la azúcar	sugar
el café	coffee
la carne	meat
la ensalada	salad
la hamburguesa	hamburger
el helado	ice cream
el huevo	egg
la mantequilla	butter
la manzana	apple
la naranja	orange
el pan	bread
el pescado	fish
el pollo	chicken
el queso	cheese
la sopa	soup
el té	tea
el tomate	tomato
el vino	wine
la zanahoria	carrot

OTHER NOUNS

el bigote	mustache
la botella	bottle
el chiste, la broma	joke
el cumpleaños	birthday
el regalo	present
la reunión	meeting, reunion
el vaso	glass

ADJECTIVES

abierto/a	open
cerrado/a	closed
eléctrico/a	electric
feliz	happy
original	original
tarde	late
temprano/a	early

VERBS

amar, querer	to love
conseguir (i) / obtener	to get, to obtain
dormir (ue)	to sleep
esperar	to hope, to wait
insultar	to insult
llevar	to take, to carry
morir (ue)	to die
pedir (i)	to ask for, to order (food)
poner	to put
quedar	to remain
sentir (ie)	to feel, to regret

MISCELLANEOUS

a veces	at times, sometimes
aunque	although, even though
dos veces	twice
sólo	only
una vez	once

LECCIÓN CINCO

KEY GRAMMAR CONCEPTS

A) **THE PRETERITE OF "BOOT" VERBS** → *El pretérito de verbos de bota*

B) **DIRECT OBJECT PRONOUNS (DOPs)** → *Los pronombres complementos (directos)*

C) **THE PERSONAL "A"** → *El uso de la "a" personal*

D) **IDIOMATIC EXPRESSIONS THAT USE "TENER"** → *Expresiones idiomáticas con "tener"*

A) THE PRETERITE OF "BOOT" VERBS

What happens to "boot" verbs in the preterite tense? Do all of the stem changes continue?

1) -AR AND -ER "BOOT" VERBS

There are no stem changes at all for **-AR** and **-ER** "boot" verbs! Hooray! Their preterite forms follow the exact pattern that you learned in the last lesson for regular **-AR** and **-ER** verbs.

Here are four -AR and -ER "boot" verbs in the preterite tense:

CERRAR (to close)		PERDER (to lose)	
cerré	cerramos	perdí	perdimos
cerraste	cerrasteis	perdiste	perdisteis
cerró	cerraron	perdió	perdieron

CONTAR (to count)		VOLVER (to return)	
conté	contamos	volví	volvimos
contaste	contasteis	volviste	volvisteis
contó	contaron	volvió	volvieron

Helpful Tip: As you can see, the vowels in the stem remain unchanged from the infinitive, with no variation in any form.

EXAMPLES: *Goldilocks **cerró** la puerta después de entrar en la casa de los osos.*
Goldilocks shut the door after entering the bears' house.

***Volviste** a casa muy tarde porque bailaste por tres horas.*
You returned home very late because you danced for three hours.

*Michelle Obama y yo **nos sentamos** en la misma mesa en la Casa Blanca.*
Michelle Obama and I sat down at the same table at the White House.

2) -IR "BOOT" VERBS

The **-IR** "boot" verbs, however, are different. They have a special change, found only in the 3rd person singular and 3rd person plural of the preterite: **e → i** or **o → u**. It's only the sole (bottom) of the boot that changes. It now looks more like a slipper!

Here are four -IR "boot" verbs in the preterite tense:

PEDIR (to ask for)		DORMIR (to sleep)	
pedí	pedimos	dormí	dormimos
pediste	pedisteis	dormiste	dormisteis
pidió	pidieron	durmió	durmieron
SENTIR (to feel)		**MORIR (to die)**	
sentí	sentimos	morí	morimos
sentiste	sentisteis	moriste	moristeis
sintió	sintieron	murió	murieron

Helpful Tip: Obviously, it is important that you remember which **-IR** verbs are stem-changers and which are not. It is a good idea to review the list of those verbs presented in *Lección Dos* (page 56).

EXAMPLES: *Anoche Miguel Cabrera **durmió** nueve horas.*
Miguel Cabrera slept nine hours last night.

*Mis hermanos me **pidieron** el nuevo álbum de Calle 13.*
My brothers asked me for the new Calle 13 album.

*Cuando Fernando Verdasco **sirvió** muy fuerte, tú serviste muy mal.*
When Fernando Verdasco served very strongly, you served poorly.

*Jenni Rivera **murió** en 2012.*
Jenni Rivera died in 2012.

*Ayer mi tía **repitió** el mismo chiste dos veces.*
My aunt repeated the same joke twice yesterday.

¿ ◆ ? Once again, did you notice that it is only the 3rd person singular and plural forms of **-IR** verbs that change in the preterite?

PRACTICE EXERCISES

1. **Conjugate the following "boot" verbs fully into the preterite:**

   perder (to lose)   **competir** (to compete)   **morir** (to die)

   _____ _____   _____ _____   _____ _____

   _____ _____   _____ _____   _____ _____

   _____ _____   _____ _____   _____ _____

   sentar (to seat)   **pedir** (to ask for)   **dormir** (to sleep)

   _____ _____   _____ _____   _____ _____

   _____ _____   _____ _____   _____ _____

   _____ _____   _____ _____   _____ _____

2. **Complete the following sentences using the appropriate form of the preterite tense. Some, but not all, are "boot" verbs:**

   a. Serena Williams _____ muy bien cuando ganó el Open de Francia en junio. (servir)

   b. Mi hermana _____ mucho chicle para su cumpleaños. (pedir)

   c. Taylor Swift _____ a Nashville después de su concierto en Dallas. (volver)

   d. Tú _____ muchos regalos para tu cumpleaños. (pedir)

   e. Los chicos del club _____ un nuevo presidente ayer. (elegir)

   f. ¿Cuántas horas _____ el hombre anoche? (dormir)

   g. Mi abuela _____ mucho dinero cuando visitó ese casino en Atlantic City. (perder)

h. Cuando ganó su Grammy por el álbum *25,* Adele se

_____ muy feliz. (sentir)

i. Mis abuelos no _____ la película *Vicky Cristina Barcelona.* (entender)

j. El sargento _____ las instrucciones tres veces. (repetir)

3. **Change these verbs from the present tense to the corresponding form of the preterite:**

a. muestra → _____

b. sirven → _____

c. pierdes → _____

d. mostramos → _____

e. duerme → _____

f. sigue → _____

g. mueren → _____

h. muevo → _____

i. recuerdan → _____

j. repite → _____

4. **The following letter contains seven verbal errors. Underline each mistaken verb and write the correction above it:**

Estimado señor Presley:

Ayer Ud. vuelvió a Memphis. Cantó muy bien en el concierto. Soy la

chica con la blusa roja y la guitarra eléctrica que esperió dos horas cerca

de su coche. Ud. pedió la guitarra, pero no la conseguió. No duermí bien

después. Me sientí terrible. ¿Duermió Ud. bien? Mañana voy a poner mi

guitarra en su coche.

Silvia

B) DIRECT OBJECT PRONOUNS (DOPs)

In *Lección Uno,* we learned that pronouns can take the place of nouns. That lesson presented a list of subject pronouns that could serve as the main actor of a sentence. In *Lección Cuatro,* we learned about pronouns that followed prepositions. In this section, we will look at a special list of pronouns that have a different use.

Direct object pronouns (DOPs) are used in place of nouns that get "acted upon" by verbs directly. For example, in the sentence "Elvis found the guitar," the word "guitar" is the direct object because the guitar is what was found. In the related sentence "Elvis found it," the word "it," is the <u>direct object pronoun</u> ("it" stands for the guitar).

Let's look at another example. In the sentence "Silvia saw Elvis," "Elvis" is the direct object, because he directly received the action of the verb, i.e., <u>he</u> was seen. In the sentence, "Silvia saw him," "him" is the <u>direct object pronoun</u>.

Here is the list of direct object pronouns in Spanish:

Direct Object Pronouns	
me	nos
te	os
lo, la*	los, las*

*Note: The object pronouns *le* and *les* are often used as **masculine** direct object pronouns in Spain. In this book, however, we will use *lo, la, los, las* exclusively as the direct object pronouns.

"Lo" is used in place of a singular, masculine noun, while *"la"* is used in place of a singular, feminine noun. The plural forms *"los"* and *"las"* correspond to masculine and feminine plural nouns.

WHERE DO YOU PLACE DOPs?

Direct object pronouns generally come <u>before</u> conjugated verbs in Spanish. The word order may seem peculiar to a speaker of English, who places all object pronouns after verbs. Let's look at some sentences to see these direct object pronouns in action.

 EXAMPLES: *Mi hermana comprende el libro, pero yo no **lo** comprendo.*
My sister understands the book, but I don't understand it.

*Lucía **me** ama, pero yo no **la** amo.*
Lucy loves me, but I don't love her.

*¿Los pantalones? –No **los** limpiamos.*
The pants? –We didn't clean them.

*No **te** insulté, Rosaura; ¿no **me** crees?*
I didn't insult you, Rosaura; don't you believe me?

*No **te** oí, Lola; ¿puedes repetir las instrucciones?*
I didn't hear you, Lola; can you repeat the instructions?

*¿Tienes las botellas de Coca-Cola? –Claro, **las** tengo.*
Do you have the bottles of Coke? –Of course, I have them.

*Los Lonely Boys nunca **nos** ven cuando cantan.*
Los Lonely Boys never see us when they sing.

In certain cases, direct object pronouns may be <u>attached</u> to the end of a verb. For example, they may be attached to infinitives. You will see in the examples below that you may choose to put a direct object pronoun before the first verb, or attach it directly to the infinitive. In later lessons, we will also see them after affirmative commands and following present participles.

 **EXAMPLES:** *¿La canción* Shake It Off*? Taylor Swift va a cantar**la** ahora.*
*(Taylor Swift **la** va a cantar ahora.)*
The song *Shake It Off*? Taylor Swift is going to sing it now.

*Necesito las cartas; voy a pedir**las** en la reunión. (. . . **las** voy a pedir en la reunión).*
I need the letters; I'm going to ask for them in the meeting.

*Julia, no puedes entender**me** siempre. (Julia, no **me** puedes entender siempre.)*
Julia, you can't understand me always.

 # PRACTICE EXERCISES

1. **Rewrite the following questions, replacing the underlined direct object with the appropriate direct object pronoun:**

Example: ¿Dónde compras <u>pizza</u>? **<u>¿Dónde la compras?</u>**_____

a. ¿Dónde pones <u>tus libros</u>? _____

b. ¿Ves <u>muchos perros</u> en el parque? _____

c. ¿Tienes <u>la tarea</u> aquí? _____

d. ¿Comprendes <u>el cuento</u>? _____

e. ¿Vas a comprar <u>los discos compactos nuevos</u>? (two ways)

_____   _____

f. ¿Sabes hablar <u>español</u>? (two ways)

_____   _____

g. ¿Vas a repetir <u>las palabras</u>? (two ways)

_____   _____

h. ¿Quieres preparar <u>la ensalada de tomate</u>? (two ways)

_____   _____

2. **Now <u>answer</u> the following questions, replacing the underlined word(s) with the appropriate direct object pronoun:**

Example: ¿Dónde compras <u>pizza</u>? **La compro en Pizzeria Uno.** _____

   a. ¿Dónde pones <u>tus libros</u>? _____

   b. ¿<u>Me</u> amas?   _____

   c. ¿<u>Te</u> entiendo siempre?   _____

   d. ¿Comprendes <u>el cuento</u>?   _____

   e. ¿Vas a comprar <u>los discos compactos nuevos</u>? (two ways)

_____   _____

   f. ¿Sabes hablar <u>italiano</u>? (two ways)

_____   _____

   g. ¿Vas a repetir <u>los cuentos</u>? (two ways)

_____   _____

   h. ¿Quieres cocinar <u>las hamburguesas</u>? (two ways)

_____   _____

3. Translate the following sentences into Spanish:

a. The doors? I closed them yesterday.

_____

b. The apples and oranges? I counted them with my brother.

_____

c. The test? I am going to correct it tomorrow.

_____

d. I remember you. And you, do you remember me?

_____

e. Jorge Ramos sees me, but he doesn't see you.

_____

4. The following paragraph contains five errors related to object pronouns. Underline each error and write the correction above it:

Ayer mi hermana y yo compramos el CD de Carlos Santana, Supernatural. _La escuchamos muchas veces. Mi primo comentó que la música no es original, pero no la creemos; mi primo nunca dice la verdad. Los discos de Carlos Santana son fantásticos; tenemos diez y siempre ponemos los en la mesa al lado de la cama. Sólo hay un disco de él que no tenemos; mañana vamos a lo comprar en la tienda. Nuestros padres dicen que la música es muy buena también; ellos escuchan la todo el tiempo. ¡Bravo, Carlos Santana!_

C) THE PERSONAL "A"

In Spanish, the word *"a"* is usually placed between a verb and a direct object when that object is a person. This *"a"* does not translate into English. It's almost as if this word *"a"* protected or buffered the direct object from the force of the verb. Because we do not have anything comparable in English, it may take a little while to get the hang of this idea. Let's look at a few examples:

EXAMPLES: *Quiero **a** Lucy, pero ella no me quiere.*
   I love Lucy, but she doesn't love me.

   *Veo **a** dos chicos en la puerta, pero no veo mi pizza.*
   (Because pizza is not a person, there is no *"a"* between it and the verb *"veo."*)
   I see two boys at the door, but I don't see my pizza.

   *Miramos **a** los jóvenes en la playa; ¡no llevan ropa!*
   We are looking at the young people on the beach; they aren't wearing any clothes!

   *¿Esperas **a** tu novia otra vez? ¡Siempre llega tarde!*
   Are you waiting for your girlfriend again? She always arrives late!

¡CUIDADO! After the verb *"tener,"* however, the personal *"a"* is not normally used.

EXAMPLES: *Tengo dos hermanos y una hermana.*
   I have two brothers and a sister.

   Tenemos una profesora de español fantástica.
   We have a fantastic Spanish teacher.

 # PRACTICE EXERCISE

Translate the following sentences into Spanish:

a. I see Sarah in church.

_____

b. We have many cousins, uncles and friends.

_____

c. You are waiting for your teacher, right?

_____

d. They know Hope Solo very well.

_____

D) IDIOMATIC EXPRESSIONS THAT USE "TENER"

The Spanish word _"tener,"_ meaning "to have," combines with many other words to form common expressions that you'll hear all the time. The expressions, when translated literally, may seem somewhat unusual to a speaker of English. For example, "I am thirsty" is expressed in Spanish as _"Tengo sed,"_ which literally means "I have thirst."

Here is a list of the most common _"tener"_ expressions. You will notice they are listed here in the _"yo"_ form. They, of course, can be conjugated in any form:

Common _"Tener"_ Expressions	
tengo (diez) años → I am (ten) years old	_tengo prisa_ → I am in a hurry
tengo (mucho) calor → I am (very) hot	_tengo razón_ → I am right
tengo frío → I am cold	_tengo sed_ → I am thirsty
tengo (mucha) hambre → I am (very) hungry	_tengo sueño_ → I am sleepy
tengo miedo → I am scared	_tengo suerte_ → I am lucky

All of these expressions use the Spanish word meaning "to have" along with a noun (heat, cold, hunger, fear, thirst, etc.).

There is another expression formed with a conjugation of _"tener"_ along with the word _"que"_ and an infinitive:

tengo que (bailar, dormir, estudiar, etc.) → I have to (dance, sleep, study, etc.)

Let's look at all of these *"tener"* expressions in sentences:

EXAMPLES: ***Tenemos suerte;*** *la película* Frozen *comienza en cinco minutos.*
We are lucky; the movie *Frozen* starts in five minutes.

Cuando ***tengo sed****, siempre bebo limonada o té con hielo.*
When I'm thirsty, I always drink lemonade or iced tea.

En verano mis abuelos siempre ***tienen calor*** *en la playa; no sé por qué no se quedan en casa.*
In the summer, my grandparents are always hot on the beach; I don't know why they don't stay at home.

Tienes que escuchar *la canción de Carlos Santana,* Smooth. *¡Es increíble!*
You have to listen to the Carlos Santana song, *Smooth*. It's incredible!

¡Tengo razón! *Cuando nieva, todos* ***tienen frío*** *en las montañas.*
I'm right! When it snows, everyone is cold in the mountains.

Los perros ***tienen mucha hambre****; necesitan comer ahorita.*
The dogs are very hungry; they need to eat right now.

En mi clase de español nunca ***tenemos sueño*** *porque todo es superinteresante.*
In my Spanish class, we are never sleepy because everything is very interesting.

Nunca ***tengo miedo*** *cuando camino solo en el parque; soy muy fuerte y otras personas* ***tienen miedo*** *de mí.*
I am never scared when I walk alone in the park; I am very strong, and other people are afraid of me.

Michael Jordan ***tiene*** *más de* ***cincuenta años.***
Michael Jordan is older than fifty.

*"****¡Tengo prisa!*** *El tren sale a las ocho", dijo Gael García Bernal.*
"I'm in a hurry! The train leaves at eight," said Gael García Bernal.

Tengo que estudiar *mucho porque hay un examen mañana.*
I have to study a lot because there is a test tomorrow.

1. **Fill in the following spaces with a *"tener"* expression, being certain to conjugate *"tener"* properly to agree with the subject:**

   a. LeBron James no _____ de nadie; es muy inteligente y muy fuerte.

   b. Cuando mis padres _____, siempre van o a Burger King para comer un Whopper o a Ben y Jerry's para tomar un helado.

   c. Yo _____ ahora; necesito dormir dos o tres horas más.

   d. En el espacio los astronautas nunca _____ porque tienen ropa muy especial.

   e. ¡Yo _____ aquí! Hace mucho sol y el acondicionador de aire no funciona bien.

   f. Cuando mi tío va a Las Vegas, nunca _____; siempre pierde todo el dinero.

   g. El embajador _____ ir hoy a Bolivia para hablar con el nuevo presidente.

   h. Es bueno beber mucha agua si tú _____ durante un maratón.

   i. Mi padre duerme en el sofá cuando _____.

   j. No hace sol y nieva mucho ahora; por eso, yo _____.

2. **Translate the following sentences into Spanish, being certain to use a *"tener"* expression:**

   a. She is sleepy because she slept only three hours last night.

   _____

b. My uncle normally isn't lucky, but he won a lot of money in November.

_____

c. We have to buy a new chair because the old chair is ugly.

_____

d. I'm hungry, thirsty and cold. Where is there a Taco Bell?

_____

e. Nelson Cruz is never scared when he plays baseball.

_____

3. **The following paragraph contains six errors in total: two preterite errors, two direct object pronoun errors, and two mistakes related to _"tener"_ expressions. Find each error and correct it:**

Hoy es el veinticinco de diciembre y son las seis de la mañana.

Yo estoy sueño, pero voy a ver si Santa Claus llegó anoche. Caramba, ¡la

puerta está abierta! Santa Claus no la cierró bien cuando salió. Hay

muchos regalos. Lo voy a contar ahora. ¡Ay! Tiengo mucha suerte . . .

hay cinco regalos perfectos para mí. Sólo hay un regalo grande para

mi hermano, pero él pedió dos. ¿Qué pasó? ¿Es un error? Santa nunca

va a lo admitir, pero creo que es posible.

These two sets of questions use grammatical structures and vocabulary from this lesson. Working with a partner, alternate asking and answering each question. When you get to the bottom of each list, start over at the top, switching roles. As a variation, write out the answers in complete sentences.

A) ¿A qué hora volviste a casa anoche?

¿Quién cerró la puerta de tu casa hoy?

¿Cuántas horas durmió tu amigo anoche?

¿Qué persona famosa murió recientemente?

¿Normalmente insultas a tus amigos?

¿Compras pantalones nuevos una vez o dos veces al año?

¿Tienes que pedir más pan frecuentemente en la cafetería?

B) ¿Conoces personalmente a Barack Obama?

¿Bebes café con azúcar cuando tienes sed?

Tu guitarra eléctrica . . . ¿la tienes aquí hoy?

Tu cumpleaños . . . ¿lo celebraste este mes?

Un regalo para mí . . . ¿lo compraste ayer?

¿Qué persona tiene mucha suerte en tu opinión?

¿Están abiertos o cerrados los bancos hoy?

DIALOGUE

The following dialogue contains grammar and vocabulary that you've seen in this lesson and in the introductory section. After listening to the dialogue, read it aloud, alone or with friends. Afterwards, try to answer the questions that follow either aloud or in written form.

LAS AVENTURAS DE RAFAEL, ELISA Y "EL TIGRE"

ESCENA TRES

Rafael, "El Tigre" y Elisa están en un tren de Amtrak. Sus mochilas están a sus pies y los tres jóvenes hablan animadamente.

El Tigre: ¿Cuándo vamos a llegar a Nueva York, Rafael?

Rafael: En quince minutos, Tigre. ¡No te preocupes!

El Tigre: Es un viaje bien largo.

Rafael: Tranquilo, miren; ¿pueden Uds. ver los edificios muy altos a la distancia?

El Tigre: Yo no veo nada.

Rafael: Abre los ojos, Tigre, ¿no ves el Empire State Building allí?

El Tigre: Sí, ahora yo lo veo. Elisa, no dices nada. ¿Por qué?

Elisa: Pues, estoy muy emocionada. Y muy nerviosa. Y me siento culpable (guilty) también. Mis padres creen que estoy en New Hampshire ahora. Voy a llamarlos esta noche con mi teléfono celular. ¡No van a saber que estoy en Nueva York!

Un hombre alto y misterioso pasa por el vagón (train car). Tiene bigote y lleva una chaqueta que dice "NY Mets". No dice nada mientras pasa cerca de ellos.

Rafael: Pronto llegamos a Penn Station. Tomamos un taxi a Central Park. Tengo un amigo, Javier, que vive muy cerca. Podemos pasar la noche en su apartamento.

El Tigre: Pero un taxi cuesta muchísimo dinero. Yo prefiero caminar.

Elisa: Yo, también. Rafael, ¿es simpático tu amigo?

Rafael: Claro, es supersimpático. Y sus padres no están en casa hoy porque están de viaje. Su prima, Marisela, se queda en casa con él. Ella sólo tiene veintitrés años y es muy simpática.

Elisa: Me alegro. Y otra chica es buena para nuestro grupo. Pero tengo hambre. ¿Tienes más chicle, Tigre?

El Tigre: Claro.

"El Tigre" busca su mochila. Mira debajo de los asientos, encima de ellos y por todos lados.

Rafael: Llegamos ya. Aquí estamos.

El tren se detiene (stops). *Se oye un anuncio* (An announcement is heard).

Voz: Llegamos ahora a Penn Station en la ciudad de Nueva York. Todos los pasajeros tienen que bajar aquí. Gracias.

El Tigre: ¡Caramba! Elisa, Rafael. ¿Dónde está mi mochila?

Elisa: No sé. ¿No está debajo del asiento?

El Tigre: No, no está.

Rafael: Siempre pierdes tus cosas, Tigre.

Elisa: Pero, un momento. ¿De qué color es tu mochila?

El Tigre: Verde.

Elisa: Claro. No recuerdas, ese hombre con el bigote. Creo que ahora él tiene tu mochila.

Rafael: ¡Miren! Creo que lo veo en el andén. ¡Vamos!

Elisa: ¡Vamos!

El Tigre: ¡Vamos!

Los tres amigos salen rápidamente. Hay muchas personas y es muy difícil ver. En la distancia, una mujer vestida de blanco observa la escena con un telescopio.

PREGUNTAS

1) ¿Qué tipo de transportación usan los jóvenes en su viaje a Nueva York?

_____

2) ¿Qué edificio famoso ven a la distancia?

_____

3) ¿Cómo se siente Elisa ahora?

_____

4) ¿Qué palabras tiene el hombre misterioso en su chaqueta?

_____

5) ¿Dónde van a pasar la noche los tres amigos?

_____

6) ¿Por qué está alegre Elisa con la noticia sobre Marisela?

_____

7) ¿Qué quiere Elisa? ¿Por qué?

_____

8) ¿Qué busca El Tigre?

_____

9) ¿Quién tiene probablemente la mochila?

_____

10) ¿Quién observa la escena al final?

_____

1. Answer in complete sentences:

a. ¿Durmió Ud. bien o mal anoche?

_____

b. ¿Quién sirvió la comida ayer en tu casa?

_____

c. ¿Conoces a Antonio Villaraigosa, el exalcalde de Los Ángeles?

_____

d. ¿Qué cantante famoso/a murió recientemente?

_____

e. ¿Pidieron Uds. muchos favores esta semana?

_____

2. Conjugate the following six verbs fully in the preterite tense:

cerrar (to close)	**volver** (to return)	**pedir** (to ask for)
_____ _____	_____ _____	_____ _____
_____ _____	_____ _____	_____ _____
_____ _____	_____ _____	_____ _____

contar (to count)	**entender** (to understand)	**dormir** (to sleep)
_____ _____	_____ _____	_____ _____
_____ _____	_____ _____	_____ _____
_____ _____	_____ _____	_____ _____

3. Write the correct form of the preterite in the spaces provided:

a. Los chicos _____ del uno al diez y después corrieron a la reunión. (contar)

b. Mis amigos _____ tres pizzas con salchicha y tres botellas grandes de Coca-Cola. (pedir)

c. Alejandro Sanz _____ a su amiga en la primera fila del concierto. (sentar)

d. Avni Yildirim no se _____ muy bien cuando perdió la corona contra Canelo Álvarez. (sentir)

e. Los chicos que tienen los ojos rojos no _____ bien anoche. (dormir)

f. Lucero _____ su talento cuando presentó las nominaciones a los Grammy Latinos. (mostrar)

g. Mi nieta _____ no hablar conmigo después del incidente. (preferir)

h. Miguel Cabrera _____ que el clima de Detroit es magnífico. (pensar)

i. Aunque Bernie Sanders _____ las elecciones, ganó muchos votos. (perder)

j. Los perros me _____ de la playa a mi casa. (seguir)

4. Answer the following questions, replacing the underlined words with the correct direct object pronoun *(me, te, lo, la, nos, os, los, las)*:

a. ¿Compraste <u>la botella de vino</u> aquí?

_____

b. ¿Comió tu amigo <u>una hamburguesa</u> hoy?

_____

c. ¿Dónde compró Chayanne <u>sus pantalones de cuero nuevos</u>?

_____

d. ¿Comiste <u>pavo asado</u> la semana pasada?

_____

e. ¿Puedes poner <u>los papeles</u> en la mesa? (two ways)

_____   _____

f. ¿Vas a limpiar <u>las blusas nuevas</u>? (two ways)

_____   _____

g. ¿Vas a comprar <u>los regalos</u> en la tienda? (two ways)

_____   _____

h. ¿Insultaste a <u>María</u>?

_____

5. **Insert a personal _"a"_ in the following sentences when needed:**

   a. Amo mucho _____ mi novia porque es muy cariñosa.

   b. Queremos _____ los nuevos libros de Julia Álvarez.

   c. Nunca veo _____ Lili Estefan en la televisión.

   d. Tengo _____ tres primos y cinco sobrinos.

   e. Esperamos _____ Aarón Díaz; siempre llega tarde.

6. **Insert a common _"tener"_ expression into the following spaces:**

   a. Yo _____ en Las Vegas porque siempre gano dinero.

   b. Nosotros _____; vamos a beber muchísima agua.

c. Cuando nieva y no tengo mi ropa caliente, yo _____.

d. Cuando mi hermana ve películas de terror siempre _____.

e. Tú _____, ¿verdad? ¿Quieres comer más pescado, una ensalada con queso o una tarta de manzana con helado?

7. **Find the errors in the following list of things to do. There's one error in each line:**

1) Tengo que lavo la ropa.

2) Tengo que invitar mi primo Lorenzo a la fiesta.

3) Los regalos — tengo que los comprar en la tienda.

4) Tengo que correr en el parque con mis amigos favorito.

5) Las chicas durmieron en casa anoche.

6) ¿La sopa? No lo comí ayer.

7) No veo a la zanahoria en la ensalada.

8) Tengo muy frío en diciembre.

PERÚ

PERÚ

CAPITAL: Lima
POBLACIÓN: 32.800.000
GOBIERNO: república presidencialista
PRESIDENTE: Francisco Sagasti Hochhausler
DINERO ($): nuevo sol
PRODUCTOS: algodón, azúcar, metales, pescado
MÚSICA, BAILE: "El cóndor pasa", huaylas, marinera norteña, zampoña
SITIOS DE INTERÉS: Arequipa, Cuzco, lago Titicaca, Machu Picchu (templo de los incas), Parque Nacional del Manu
COMIDA TÍPICA: ceviche, mazamorra morada, papas a la huancaína, pisco

PERUANOS FAMOSOS:

Eva Ayllón
(CANTANTE)

Chabuca Granda
(CANTAUTORA)

Javier Pérez de Cuéllar
(DIPLOMÁTICO)

César Vallejo
(POETA)

Mario Vargas Llosa
(ESCRITOR)

Practice this vocabulary with our mobile app! Visit tobreak.com/app for more details.

VOCABULARIO
LECCIÓN SEIS

THEME WORDS: "SPORTS"

el	básquetbol/ el baloncesto (Sp.)	basketball
el	béisbol	baseball
el	deporte	sport
el	equipo	team
el	esquí	skiing
el	fútbol	soccer
el	fútbol americano	football
el	hockey sobre hielo	ice hockey
la	natación	swimming
el	remo	rowing
el	tenis	tennis
la	vela	sailing

OTHER NOUNS

el	buzón	mailbox
el/la	camarero/a, (mesero/a)	waiter
el	cartel	poster
el	clima	climate
la	cuenta	bill
el	cuento, la historia	story, tale
la	década	decade
el	empleo	job
la	entrevista	interview
la	misa	mass, church service
la	película	film (used in a camera), movie
el	precio	price
el	recibo	receipt
la	revista	magazine

la	sorpresa	surprise
la	toalla	towel

ADJECTIVES

ancho/a	wide
divino/a	divine
estrecho/a	narrow
furioso/a	furious, very mad
libre	free
mejor	better, best
orgulloso/a	proud
peor	worse, worst

VERBS

ayudar	to help
besar	to kiss
caber	to fit
cambiar	to change
contar, decir	to tell
cortar	to cut
detener	to detain, to stop
disfrutar	to enjoy
gritar	to shout
lastimar, dañar	to hurt
matar	to kill
pagar	to pay
preparar	to prepare
secar	to dry
susurrar	to whisper

MISCELLANEOUS

como	as, since, like
enfrente de	in front of
en voz alta	aloud
ir de compras	to go shopping
sobre	over, about

LECCIÓN SEIS

KEY GRAMMAR
CONCEPTS

A) THE PRETERITE OF IRREGULAR VERBS → *El pretérito de verbos irregulares*

B) POSSESSIVE ADJECTIVES → *Los adjetivos posesivos*

C) INDIRECT OBJECT PRONOUNS (IDOPs) → *Los pronombres complementos (indirectos)*

D) THE VERB "GUSTAR" → *El verbo "gustar"*

A) THE PRETERITE OF IRREGULAR VERBS

In *Lección Cuatro,* we saw the preterite conjugations for regular verbs in Spanish.

In *Lección Cinco,* we learned that **-AR** and **-ER** stem-changing verbs are also regular in the preterite, while the **-IR** verbs have a special vowel change in the 3rd person singular and plural.

This lesson will take a final look at preterite verbs. The eighteen verbs that you will see on the following page are <u>irregular</u> in the preterite. They have conjugations that you simply must memorize. Because these verbs are among the most commonly used in the Spanish language, you should be sure to study them thoroughly.

You will notice a number of interesting features of these conjugations:

◆ There are no written accents marks in any form!

◆ Once you memorize the *"yo"* form for each verb, the rest of the conjugations will follow a familiar pattern.

◆ The letter *"i"* drops out after the *"j"* in the 3rd person singular and 3rd person plural of verbs that end with *"-cir"* (e.g., *conducir, decir, producir*) as well as in the verb *"traer."*

◆ You will see that the conjugations of *"ir"* and *"ser"* are absolutely identical in the preterite. Because of this fact, you will need to rely on the context of the sentence to know which verb the speaker is using.

andar (to walk)		**caber** (to fit)		**conducir** (to drive)	
anduve	anduvimos	cupe	cupimos	conduje	condujimos
anduviste	anduvisteis	cupiste	cupisteis	condujiste	condujisteis
anduvo	anduvieron	cupo	cupieron	condujo	condujeron
dar (to give)		**decir** (to say, to tell)		**estar** (to be)	
di	dimos	dije	dijimos	estuve	estuvimos
diste	disteis	dijiste	dijisteis	estuviste	estuvisteis
dio	dieron	dijo	dijeron	estuvo	estuvieron
hacer (to do, to make)		**ir** (to go)		**poder** (to be able to)	
hice	hicimos	fui	fuimos	pude	pudimos
hiciste	hicisteis	fuiste	fuisteis	pudiste	pudisteis
hizo	hicieron	fue	fueron	pudo	pudieron
poner (to put)		**producir** (to produce)		**querer** (to want, to wish)	
puse	pusimos	produje	produjimos	quise	quisimos
pusiste	pusisteis	produjiste	produjisteis	quisiste	quisisteis
puso	pusieron	produjo	produjeron	quiso	quisieron
saber (to know)		**ser** (to be)		**tener** (to have)	
supe	supimos	fui	fuimos	tuve	tuvimos
supiste	supisteis	fuiste	fuisteis	tuviste	tuvisteis
supo	supieron	fue	fueron	tuvo	tuvieron
traer (to bring)		**venir** (to come)		**ver** (to see)	
traje	trajimos	vine	vinimos	vi	vimos
trajiste	trajisteis	viniste	vinisteis	viste	visteis
trajo	trajeron	vino	vinieron	vio	vieron

Let's take a look at a number of these verbs in the preterite:

✳ EXAMPLES: *Anduve a la escuela esta mañana porque me gusta el aire fresco.*
I walked to school this morning because I like fresh air.

*Mi amiga **dijo** que Alfredo Palacio ya no es el presidente de Ecuador.*
My friend said that Alfredo Palacio is no longer the president of Ecuador.

*Cuando **pusiste** la rana en la silla de la profesora, ella comenzó a gritar.*
When you put the frog on the teacher's chair, she began to scream.

*Salma Hayek **vino** con François-Henri Pinault a la fiesta en Soho.*
Salma Hayek came with François-Henri Pinault to the party in Soho.

*Cuando el profesor nos **vio** en la cafetería, **tuvimos** que salir de allí.*
When the teacher saw us in the cafeteria, we had to leave.

*Mis amigas **fueron** al concierto de Tommy Torres.*
My friends went to the *Tommy Torres* concert.

***Conduje** el coche muy rápido y ahora estoy en la cárcel.*
I drove the car very fast, and now I'm in jail.

*Mi amiga me **trajo** un cartel de David Bisbal.*
My friend brought me a David Bisbal poster.

*Anoche nadie **pudo** ir al partido de baloncesto para ver a Manu Ginóbili por el examen de hoy.*
No one could go to the basketball game last night to see Manu Ginóbili because of the test today.

There are also some verbs that are irregular in a few conjugations only. The irregularities are found in consonants and in vowels, which change or are added to preserve a sound that is found in the infinitive. We'll fully conjugate four such verbs here, but you will also see some additional infinitives that follow the same pattern.

COMENZAR / empezar (to begin/to begin)		LEER / creer (to read/to believe)	
comencé	comenzamos	leí	leímos
comenzaste	comenzasteis	leíste	leísteis
comenzó	comenzaron	**leyó**	**leyeron**
PAGAR / colgar, llegar (to pay/to hang up/to arrive)		TOCAR / buscar, sacar (to play/to look for/to take out)	
pagué	pagamos	**toqué**	tocamos
pagaste	pagasteis	tocaste	tocasteis
pagó	pagaron	tocó	tocaron

In the verbs above, the special changes have been highlighted in **boldface**. Unlike the other irregular verbs in this section, only one or two of the forms are irregular.

✳ EXAMPLES: *Cuando yo **pagué** la cuenta, mi papá dijo: "Gracias".*
When I paid the bill, my dad said: "Thanks."

*Yo **toqué** el piano por cinco minutos, pero Eddie Palmieri tocó por una hora.*
I played the piano for five minutes, but Eddie Palmieri played for an hour.

*Mis amigos **leyeron** un artículo interesante sobre el actor César Romero en una revista.*
My friends read an interesting article about the actor César Romero in a magazine.

*Cuando **comencé** a lavar los platos, mi madre me dio un beso.*
When I began to wash the dishes, my mom kissed me.

PRACTICE EXERCISES

1. Conjugate the following verbs fully into the preterite:

   estar (to be)   **ser** (to be)   **decir** (to say)

   _____ _____   _____ _____   _____ _____

   _____ _____   _____ _____   _____ _____

   _____ _____   _____ _____   _____ _____

   venir (to come)   **comenzar** (to begin)   **pagar** (to pay)

   _____ _____   _____ _____   _____ _____

   _____ _____   _____ _____   _____ _____

   _____ _____   _____ _____   _____ _____

2. Now change each of the following verbs from the present tense to the corresponding form of the preterite:

   Examples: van → **fueron** _____   puede → **pudo** _____

   a. dice   → _____   **f.** hacéis → _____

   b. estás   → _____   **g.** cabe   → _____

   c. comienzo   → _____   **h.** hago   → _____

   d. traemos   → _____   **i.** tienes → _____

   e. andan   → _____   **j.** vienen → _____

3. Complete the following sentences using the appropriate form of the preterite tense:

   a. Jennifer López no _____ anoche; por eso canté yo. (venir)

   b. Robert Rodríguez _____ a la playa solo. (andar)

c. Ayer mis primos _____ el coche nuevo de mi tía. (conducir)

d. Nosotros _____ la guitarra enfrente de la casa. (poner)

e. Benjamín Bratt y Talisa Soto _____ sólo unos minutos en el restaurante peruano. (estar)

f. Tú _____ a Machu Picchu sin mí el verano pasado. (ir)

g. Como mi amigo nunca tiene dinero, yo _____ la cuenta en el restaurante anoche. (pagar)

h. Mi novia dijo que ella comenzó la discusión, pero no es verdad: yo la

_____. (comenzar)

i. El pobre elefante no _____ en el cuarto estrecho. (caber)

j. "No robé el banco", _____ en voz alta cuando la policía me detuvo. (decir)

4. The following paragraph contains seven errors related to preterite verbs. Underline each error and write the correct word above it:

Mi hermano condució su moto a la playa. Estoy furioso porque yo

andé sola con todas las toallas y bebidas. Cuando llegé, vi a mi hermano,

Raúl, con sus amigos. Él me vió, pero no hició nada. Vi la pizza en las

manos de sus amigos, pero ellos no me daron nada. Lloré por unos

minutos y luego yo fue a casa en la moto que tomé de mi hermano.

¡Y me llevé todas las toallas y bebidas!

B) POSSESSIVE ADJECTIVES

Possessive adjectives are words that let people know to whom or to what something belongs. Unlike most other adjectives, possessive adjectives are placed <u>before</u> the nouns they modify. Remember, because these words are adjectives, they must correspond in gender and number to the nouns they describe.

Here are the Spanish possessive adjectives:

mi/mis	*nuestro/nuestra/nuestros/nuestras*
tu/tus	*vuestro/vuestra/vuestros/vuestras*
su/sus	*su/sus*

Here are their equivalents in English:

my	our
your (familiar)	your all's (familiar)
his, her, your (formal)	their, your all's (formal)

 **EXAMPLES:** *"**Mi** bisabuela es 'La Catrina'"*, *dijo Jamie González.*
"My great-grandmother is 'La Catrina'," said Jamie González.

Titanic *es **nuestra** película favorita.*
Titanic is our favorite movie.

*Mis amigos me informaron que Cuzco es **su** ciudad favorita.*
My friends informed me that Cuzco is their favorite city.

*"**Vuestro** tío os ama mucho", repitió **nuestro** tío Cristóbal.*
"Your uncle loves you all a lot," repeated our Uncle Cristóbal.

*Siempre voy de compras a Sears porque **sus** precios son bajos.*
I always go shopping at Sears because their prices are low.

*"**Tu** voz es divina", gritó un admirador en el concierto de Shakira.*
"Your voice is divine," shouted a fan at the Shakira concert.

*"No veo **sus** recibos", me informó el inspector.*
"I don't see your receipts," the inspector informed me.

*Meryl Streep hace muchas películas; **su** mejor película, en mi opinion, es* Iron Lady.
Meryl Streep makes many movies; her best movie, in my opinion, is *Iron Lady*.

Keep these things in mind as you put these possessive adjectives to use:

1 These adjectives agree with what is <u>possessed</u>, not the <u>possessor</u>!

> my books = ***mis*** *libros*
> their chair = ***su*** *silla*
> our computer = ***nuestra*** *computadora*
> your (fam.) grandparents = ***tus*** *abuelos*

2 Because *"su"* or *"sus"* can mean "his," "her," "your," "their," or "your all's," the context of the sentence is quite important. To avoid confusion, you can choose an alternate construction that uses the preposition *"de"* with a pronoun that follows a preposition.

EXAMPLES: *su primo* = *el primo **de él***   his cousin
     *el primo **de ella***   her cousin
     *el primo **de Ud.***   your cousin
     *el primo **de ellos***   their cousin
     *el primo **de ellas***   their cousin
     *el primo **de Uds.***   your (pl.) cousin

      sus primos = *los primos **de él***   his cousins
     *los primos **de ella***   her cousins
     *los primos **de Ud.***   your cousins
     *los primos **de ellos***   their cousins
     *los primos **de ellas***   their cousins
     *los primos **de Uds.***   your (pl.) cousins

1. Translate the following into Spanish:

   a. my papers   _____

   b. our grandmother _____

   c. their salad (two ways)

   _____   _____

   d. her movie (two ways)

   _____   _____

   e. his glass of water (two ways)

   _____   _____

   f. your all's table (two ways)

   _____   _____

   g. my mosquito   _____

   h. our tomatoes   _____

2. Complete the following sentences by translating the possessive adjective in parentheses into the appropriate form:

   a. Cuando _____ guitarrista no llegó, yo acompañé a Shakira. (his)

   b. Tenemos muy buenos recuerdos de _____ vacaciones en las Islas Galápagos. (our)

   c. De todos los éxitos *(hits)* de los BeeGees, *Saturday Night Fever* fue

   _____ disco más popular. (their)

d. _____ amigos comieron todos los Doritos y por eso tuve que volver a la tienda. (my)

e. Vosotros no tenéis _____ raquetas de tenis hoy; ¿preferís jugar al fútbol? (your)

f. _____ amigas nunca recuerdan _____ aniversario. (her/her)

g. "_____ suerte va a cambiar pronto", me susurró la mujer después de leerme la mano. (your, familiar)

h. El colombiano Juanes tiene mucho talento; _____ álbum *Más futuro que pasado es* un gran éxito. (his)

i. "_____ perro, Pal, es mi mejor amigo", dice Arthur. (my)

j. "Tenemos mucha confianza en _____ alumnos", dijo el maestro cuando habló con el periodista. (our)

3. The following paragraph contains six errors. Underline each error and write the correct word above it:

Mi hermanos organizaron una fiesta de sorpresa. Todos nuestro amigos recibieron invitaciones, pero yo no. Mi invitación no llegó nunca. Todos gritaron mis nombre cuando volví a casa. Carla y Miguel decoraron las tortas; comí la torta bonita de Carla, no la torta feo de Miguel. Dije: "¡Muchas gracias por todo sus trabajo!". Mis amigos y mis hermanos son fantásticos. ¿Cómo son tu amigos?

C) INDIRECT OBJECT PRONOUNS (IDOPs)

Lección Cinco introduced direct object pronouns *(me, te, lo, la, nos, os, los, las)*. These pronouns took the place of nouns that took a "direct hit" from a verb *(¿El dinero? Bonnie y Clyde **lo** robaron)*.

This lesson introduces another type of object pronoun. **Indirect object pronouns (IDOPs)** take the place of nouns that receive an action <u>indirectly</u>.

In the sentence, "I wrote Elvis a letter," the word "letter" clearly is the direct object — the letter is what was written. "Elvis," however, is the <u>indirect object</u>. He is connected to the action of writing because he will receive the letter, but because he is not the letter, he is not the direct object.

In the sentence "I wrote him a letter," "him" is the <u>indirect object pronoun</u> that stands for Elvis.

Let's look at another example. In the sentence "Elvis told me a secret," "a secret" is the direct object. Elvis told what? A secret. The word "me" is the indirect object pronoun because Elvis told the secret **to** me.

Here are the indirect object pronouns (IDOPs) in Spanish:

Indirect Object Pronouns	
me	nos
te	os
le	les

Helpful Tip: Did you notice that *"me, te, nos, os"* are the exact same forms you used for DOPs — direct object pronouns?

EXAMPLES: *Siempre **le** digo "gracias" al camarero cuando **me** trae la comida.*
    I always say "thanks" to the waiter when he brings me the food.

*Cuando los turistas comenzaron a sacar fotos en la iglesia, el guía **les** gritó: "¡Señores, por favor, no se permite!"*
    When the tourists began to take pictures in the church, the guide shouted at them: "Please, it isn't allowed!"

***Le** debo mucho dinero a mi amigo; tengo que conseguir otro empleo.*
    I owe a lot of money to my friend; I have to get another job.

***Os** digo que Miguel Cabrera y Manny Machado hablaron anoche por teléfono.*
    I'm telling you all that Miguel Cabrera and Manny Machado talked last night by phone.

*No **te** pido mucho; simplemente **me** vas a dar tu coche y me voy en seguida.*
I'm not asking you for much; you simply are going to give me your car, and I'll leave at once.

To clarify or to emphasize one of these indirect object pronouns, you may choose to add the following words to a sentence:

a mí	*a nosotros, a nosotras*
a ti	*a vosotros, a vosotras*
a él	*a ellos*
a ella	*a ellas*
a Ud.	*a Uds.*

Sometimes this indirect object pronoun may seem redundant to a speaker of English. For example, in *"Le digo 'hola' a José,"* *"le"* and *"a José"* both refer to the same person! But this practice adds clarity or emphasis: *¡Te voy a llamar a ti primero!* (I'm going to call you first!)

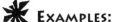 **EXAMPLES:** *Te doy los libros **a ti**, no a Nacha.*
I'm giving the books to you, not to Nacha.

*Chris Rock **nos** informó primero **a nosotros** que iba a hacer el programa de los Óscar este año.*
Chris Rock informed us first that he was going to do the Oscars this year.

In all of the examples above, the indirect object pronouns came directly before the verb. However, just like direct object pronouns, the IDOPs sometimes are attached to verbs. For example, they may be attached to infinitives.

You will see in the examples below that you may choose to put an <u>indirect</u> object pronoun before the first verb, or attach it directly to the infinitive. In later lessons, we will also see DOPs and IDOPs placed after affirmative commands and present participles.

 **EXAMPLES:** *Tengo que decir**te** que no puedo ir al club contigo.*
I have to tell you that I can't go with you to the club.

*Voy a dar**le** a Ud. (**Le** voy a dar a Ud.) la oportunidad de ganar un viaje a Machu Picchu.*
I'm going to give you a chance to win a trip to Machu Picchu.

*Necesitamos reservar**les** (**Les** necesitamos reservar)* una habitación doble.*
We need to reserve you all (them) a double room.

***Note:** Do you remember how to clarify the meaning of *"les"*? Simply add *"a ellos"* or *"a ellas"* or *"a Uds."*: *Les necesitamos reservar una habitación **a ellos/ellas/Uds**.*

1. Write the appropriate indirect object pronoun in the spaces provided:

a. Hace unos años Nicole Kidman ganó un Óscar; _____ dio el trofeo a su hijo.

b. Este año Viola Davis ganó un Óscar; _____ dio un trofeo a su esposo y a su hija.

c. El guitarrista Paco de Lucía no _____ dedicó una canción a mí; estoy muy triste.

d. "Siempre _____ doy muchos besos", _____ dijo la madre a su hijo.

e. Madonna _____ ofrece música nueva a nosotros cada década.

f. Siempre _____ digo muchos secretos a mis amigas.

g. "_____ voy a escribir mañana después de la entrevista", _____ comentó George Clooney a su amigo Brad Pitt.

2. Insert the correct indirect object pronoun (me, te, le, nos, os, les) **or direct object pronoun** (me, te, lo, la, nos, os, los, las) **into the following letter:**

Paco:

     Cuando _____ escribí una carta a Marisela, no _____

contestó. Voy a escribir_____ otra vez. ¿Recuerdas que

_____ dije que ella no _____ ama? ¡Es verdad! Tiene otro

novio. ¿Su nombre? _____ sé. Se llama Paco y vive en la Calle

Ocho. ¿_____ conoces? Vive en tu calle, en el mismo número.

Marisela dice que va a llamar_____ luego.

Hasta luego,

Javier

3. **There is one error in each of the following five sentences. Underline each error and write the correction above it:**

1) *"No debo nada", les dijo el hombre orgulloso al*

   presidente del banco.

2) *Después de recibir tu premio, tienes que llamarme*

   a mi primero.

3) *"Pronto voy a les tocar el Concierto de Aranjuez", les*

   prometió Paco de Lucía a los invitados.

4) *"Siempre lo digo la verdad a la policía", dice el ladrón.*

5) *Un día Britney Spears va a nos decir exactamente qué*

   pasó aquella noche en Las Vegas cuando se casó con

   su amigo Jason.

D) THE VERB "GUSTAR"

Back in the **FIRST STEPS** section of this text, you had the chance to practice a little with the verb *"gustar."* You learned that *"me gusta"* is usually translated as "I like" in Spanish. In fact, the literal translation of *"me gusta"* is not "I like"; it actually means "it is pleasing to me."

"Gustar" is one of a number of Spanish verbs that always use indirect object pronouns. The construction of a sentence with *"gustar"* places an indirect object first, then a form of *"gustar"* and, finally, the subject:

Indirect Object Pronoun *(me, te, le, nos, os, les)*	**+**	**Form of "Gustar"** (usually **gusta, gustan**)	**+**	**Subject**

Because the subject is most often an object or some objects, the form of *"gustar"* will normally be in the 3rd person singular or 3rd person plural.

EXAMPLES: *Me gusta el clima de Guayaquil en primavera.*
I like the climate in Guayaquil in the spring (The climate in Guayaquil is pleasing to me in the spring).

Nos gusta la Casa Rosada de Buenos Aires.
We like the Pink House in Buenos Aires.

¿Te gustan los trajes de baño que llevan los chicos?
Do you like the bathing suits that the boys are wearing?

Os gustan los equipos de fútbol que hacen muchos goles.
You all like soccer teams that score a lot of goals.

Me gustan las películas que tienen en Netflix.
I like the films that they have in Netflix.

A ella le gustó el mes que pasó en Ibarra.
She liked the month that she spent in Ibarra.

¿Les gusta a Uds. la nueva novela de Isabel Allende?
Do you all like the new novel of Isabel Allende?

Helpful Tips: **1)** Did you notice that in the last two sentences above, the speaker added some additional words to emphasize or make clear who received the indirect action of the verb?
2) For example, in the sentence, *"A ella le gustó el mes que pasó en Ibarra,"* the words *"a ella"* make it clear that the month was pleasing to her rather than to him or to you (formal).
3) Similarly, in *"¿Les gusta a Uds. la nueva novela de Isabel Allende?"*, the words *"a Uds."* inform the listeners that the speaker wanted to know if the novel is pleasing <u>to you all</u>, rather than <u>to them</u>.

What happens if an infinitive is the subject of one of these sentences? Will the verb be singular or plural? The answer — singular!

 EXAMPLES: *Me **gusta** leer en la cama.*
I like to read in bed (Reading in bed pleases me).

*Nos **gusta** poner las cartas en el buzón.*
We like to put the letters in the mailbox.

What happens if there are multiple infinitives? Will the form of *"gustar"* still be singular? The answer — yes!

 EXAMPLES: *Te **gusta** leer y escribir poesía en el parque.*
You like to read and write poetry in the park (Reading and writing poetry in the park pleases you).

*A mis amigos les **gusta** bailar y cantar en la playa.*
My friends like to dance and sing on the beach.

PRACTICE EXERCISES ▶

1. In the sentences below, insert the correct form of the verb *"gustar"*:

a. Nos _____ la lluvia en la primavera.

b. Me _____ más los equipos de hockey que los de fútbol americano.

c. Te _____ cantar en la casa cuando no hay nadie.

d. A mi prima le _____ las noches románticas de Lima.

e. A nuestro abuelo le _____ beber vino bueno y comprar coches viejos.

f. Cuando Eva Longoria tiene mucho tiempo libre, le _____ visitar a su familia en México.

g. A nosotros nos _____ las canciones de Alejandro Sanz y las de Luis Miguel — son fantásticas.

h. No me _____ la carne que me sirvieron anoche en el restaurante.

2. **Choose an indirect object pronoun (IDOP)** *(me, te, le, nos, os, les)* **for each of the following sentences:**

   a. A nosotras no _____ gusta el frío en diciembre.

   b. Siempre _____ escribimos muchas cartas a mi abuela.

   c. A mí _____ gustan los precios en esta tienda.

   d. ¡_____ voy a llamar a ti primero!

   e. ¡_____ voy a escribir a ellos luego!

   f. _____ digo a vosotros otra vez: ¡No!

3. **Now translate these sentences into Spanish, always being certain to use a form of** *"gustar"*:

   a. We like tacos with cheese; they are delicious.

   _____

   _____

   b. I like to listen to classical music; Bach and Beethoven are great!

   _____

   _____

   c. My teachers like the truth.

   _____

   _____

   d. She likes to talk and walk; I like dogs and cats.

   _____

   _____

ORAL PRACTICE
PREGUNTAS EN GRUPOS DE DOS

These two sets of questions use grammatical structures and vocabulary from this lesson. Working with a partner, alternate asking and answering each question. When you get to the bottom of each list, start over at the top, switching roles. As a variation, write out the answers in complete sentences.

A) ¿Anduviste hoy a la escuela o tomaste el autobús?

¿Tuviste una entrevista ayer con un representante de la universidad?

¿Viste el cartel para el concierto el sábado?

¿Te gusta besar una rana?

¿Es mejor susurrar o gritar en la biblioteca?

¿Les escribes muchas cartas a tus padres?

¿Dónde pusiste los libros esta mañana?

B) ¿Fuiste de compras con tu mamá recientemente?

A tus amigos, ¿les gusta más la natación o el remo?

A ti, ¿te gustan las zanahorias?

¿Tienes mucho tiempo libre en un día típico?

¿Es mejor contar o escuchar un cuento?

¿Quién te dijo "hola" hoy?

¿A quién le dijiste "hola" hoy?

PRUEBA DE REPASO

1. Answer in complete sentences:

a. ¿A qué hora hiciste la tarea anoche?

_____

b. ¿Viniste a la escuela el domingo?

_____

c. A ti, ¿te gustan las toallas nuevas o las viejas?

_____

d. ¿Trajiste hoy un buen libro a la playa?

_____

e. ¿Estás orgulloso/a de tu familia?

_____

2. Conjugate the following six verbs fully in the preterite tense.

tener (to have)	**decir** (to say)	**dar** (to give)
_____ _____	_____ _____	_____ _____
_____ _____	_____ _____	_____ _____
_____ _____	_____ _____	_____ _____

leer (to read)	**andar** (to walk)	**poder** (to be able to)
_____ _____	_____ _____	_____ _____
_____ _____	_____ _____	_____ _____
_____ _____	_____ _____	_____ _____

3. Conjugate each verb in the appropriate form of the preterite:

a. Mi amiga _____ muy rápido para llegar a tiempo al concierto de Maroon 5. (conducir)

b. Yo no _____ dormir en la cama de mi abuelita porque es muy pequeña. (poder)

c. Ud. no _____ nada anoche. ¿Por qué no trabaja Ud. más? (hacer)

d. Mi abuelo _____ muchas millas en el parque para mejorar su salud. (andar)

e. Maluma y sus amigos _____ en Nueva York ayer para promocionar su nueva canción *"Hawái"*. (estar)

f. Cameron Díaz no _____ a la fiesta la semana pasada porque fue a Hawaii con su amiga Drew Barrymore. (ir)

g. El camarero nos _____ la cuenta a la mesa. (traer)

h. Ellos nunca me _____ cerca del buzón. (ver)

i. Ya te _____ que me gusta mucho el programa de George López. (decir)

j. Mi madre _____ en una revista que Pitbull tiene mucho éxito ahora. (leer)

4. **Write the correct form of the possessive adjectives in the spaces provided:**

a. _____ iglesia (our)   f. _____ precio (your all's)

b. _____ empleos (their)   g. _____ toallas (his)

c. _____ traje de baño (her) h. _____ toallas (my)

d. _____ bebida (their)   i. _____ revistas (your, formal)

e. _____ escuelas (our)   j. _____ camarero (her)

5. **Fill in the blanks with either the correct form of "gustar" or the proper indirect object pronoun** (me, te, le, nos, os, les)**:**

a. A nosotros nos _____ las zanahorias.

b. A ella _____ gusta gritar en la iglesia.

c. A ti no te _____ esquiar cuando hace mucho frío.

d. A él _____ gustó besar a su novia enfrente de sus amigos.

e. Me _____ las calles estrechas.

f. Nos _____ escuchar la música de Tommy Torres.

6. **Translate the following sentences into Spanish:**

a. You like to read and write romantic books.

_____

b. She said: "I like my school, my church and my family."

_____

c. I gave a lot of money to my best friend. ¡CUIDADO! (Don't forget an indirect object pronoun!)

_____

7. Underline and correct the five errors in the following paragraph:

Estoy furiosa. No hay mucha cartas en el buzón hoy. ¿No tuvieran tiempo María y Claudia de escribirme la semana pasada? Mis amigas nunca escriben me. No me gusto mis amigas. Como soy muy orgullosa, no voy a les decir nada. En el futuro, nunca voy a ir al parque con ellas en mi tiempo libre.

ECUADOR &VENEZUELA

ECUADOR

CAPITAL:	Quito
POBLACIÓN:	17.800.000
GOBIERNO:	república
PRESIDENTE:	Lenín Moreno
DINERO ($):	dólar (EEUU), sucre
PRODUCTOS:	bananas, gambas, madera, petróleo
MÚSICA, BAILE:	cachullape, salsa, sanjuanes
SITIOS DE INTERÉS:	Chimborazo, Islas Galápagos
COMIDA TÍPICA:	caldo de patas, ceviche, llapingachos (cheese and potato cakes), locro, patacones

VENEZUELA

CAPITAL:	Caracas
POBLACIÓN:	28.000.000
GOBIERNO:	república federal presidencialista
PRESIDENTE:	Nicolás Maduro / Juan Guaidó
DINERO ($):	bolívar fuerte
PRODUCTOS:	arroz, café, petróleo
MÚSICA, BAILE:	boleros, joropo, salsa
SITIOS DE INTERÉS:	Gran Sabana, Llanos, Mérida, Parque Central (Caracas), Río Orinoco, Salto del Ángel (highest waterfall in world), San Juan
COMIDA TÍPICA:	arepas, cachapas, empanadas, hallaca, merengada, pabellón criollo, sancocho

ECUATORIANOS FAMOSOS:

Eugenio Espejo
(ESCRITOR, MÉDICO)

Oswaldo Guayasamín
(PINTOR)

Jefferson Pérez
(ATLETA)

VENEZOLANOS FAMOSOS:

Baruj Benacerraf (CIENTÍFICO)

Simón Bolívar
(GENERAL, "EL LIBERTADOR")

Miguel Cabrera (BEISBOLISTA)

Hugo Chávez (POLÍTICO)

Gustavo Dudamel
(MÚSICO)

Rómulo Gallegos (ESCRITOR)

Mercedes Pardo (ARTISTA)

Teresa de la Parra (ESCRITORA)

THEME WORDS:
"CLOTHES"

el	abrigo	coat
el	arete	earring
la	blusa	blouse
la	bota	boot
la	bufanda	scarf
los	calcetines/	
	las medias	socks
la	camisa	shirt
la	chaqueta	jacket
el	cinturón	belt
la	corbata	tie
la	falda	skirt
la	gorra	cap, hat
los	guantes	gloves
los	pantalones	pants
el	pendiente	earring
la	ropa	clothes
el	sombrero	hat
el	suéter, jersey	sweater
el	traje de baño	swimsuit
el	vestido	dress
los	zapatos	shoes

OTHER NOUNS

el	asiento, la silla	seat
la	billetera	wallet
la	entrada	admission ticket, entrance
la	milla	mile
la	palabra	word
el	teléfono	telephone
la	vaca	cow

ADJECTIVES

alegre, feliz	cheerful, happy
atlético/a	athletic
caliente	warm, hot
cansado/a	tired
estúpido/a	stupid
misterioso/a	mysterious
preocupado/a	upset

VERBS

acompañar	to accompany
acostarse (ue)	to go to bed
afeitar(se)	to shave (oneself)
casarse	to get married
cepillarse	to brush one's (hair, teeth)
crear	to create, to make
decidir	to decide
despertarse (ie)	to wake up
hacer	to do, to make
lavarse	to wash oneself
levantarse	to get up
llamar	to call
ocurrir, pasar	to occur, to happen
peinarse	to comb one's hair
ponerse	to put on (clothing)
reírse (i)	to laugh
sentar (ie)	to seat (someone)
sentarse (ie)	to sit down
volar (ue)	to fly

MISCELLANEOUS

de nuevo, otra vez	again
despacio	slowly
por eso	therefore
si	if

LECCIÓN SIETE

KEY GRAMMAR CONCEPTS

A) THE IMPERFECT TENSE → *El imperfecto*

B) REFLEXIVE OBJECT PRONOUNS (ROPs) → *Los pronombres reflexivos*

C) ADVERBS → *Los adverbios*

D) TALKING ABOUT THE WEATHER → *¿Qué tiempo hace hoy?*

A) THE IMPERFECT TENSE

💻 (Online access offers recordings of all sample sentences.) 💻

The **imperfect** is another verb tense used to describe action from the past. It differs from the preterite in a number of ways and is used in different situations.

Let's first take a look at the conjugations of the regular verbs. The good news is that there are only three irregular verbs in Spanish: *"ir," "ser,"* and *"ver"*! All of these irregular conjugations will be covered in *Lección Ocho*.

All other verbs in Spanish are <u>completely</u> regular: there are no stem-changing forms or any special spelling changes. For this reason, the imperfect tense is often a favorite among Spanish students.

Here are the regular forms of the imperfect tense:

HABLAR		COMER		VIVIR	
hablaba	hablábamos	comía	comíamos	vivía	vivíamos
hablabas	hablabais	comías	comíais	vivías	vivíais
hablaba	hablaban	comía	comían	vivía	vivían

Helpful Tips: **1)** Did you notice that there are accents only on the *nosotros/nosotras* form of **-AR** verbs *(hablar)* and on every form of the **-ER** and **-IR** verbs *(comer, vivir)*? **2)** Did you also notice that **-ER** and **-IR** endings are identical?

The three verbs on the next page are representative of those that are irregular in the present. You will recall that *cerrar* and *pedir* are "boot" verbs, while *conocer* has a spelling change in the *"yo"* form. You will notice, however, that these verbs are completely normal in the imperfect!

Here are two "boot" verbs and one "spelling-changer" in the imperfect:

CERRAR		CONOCER		PEDIR	
cerraba	cerrábamos	conocía	conocíamos	pedía	pedíamos
cerrabas	cerrabais	conocías	conocíais	pedías	pedíais
cerraba	cerraban	conocía	conocían	pedía	pedían

WHEN IS THE IMPERFECT USED?

1) INCOMPLETE ACTIONS — ACTIONS IN PROGRESS

Unlike the preterite, which describes completed action, the imperfect can describe action that hadn't been completed yet or that was ongoing.

✳ **EXAMPLES:** *Leíamos el libro cuando el teléfono sonó.*
    We were reading the book when the phone rang.

Dorina jugaba a las cartas cuando su amigo, el chico del pendiente, llegó.
    Dorina was playing cards when her friend, the boy with the earring, arrived.

Nadie quería ir al parque; por eso todos se quedaron a la mesa.
    No one wanted to go to the park; therefore, everyone stayed at the table.

David Ortiz dijo que iba a hacer un jonrón en Boston anoche, pero no lo hizo.
    David Ortiz said that he was going to hit a homerun in Boston last night, but he didn't do it.

Helpful Tip: In all of the examples above, did you notice that the verb in the imperfect tense described actions that <u>hadn't</u> been completed (We were in the middle of reading the book; Dorina was in the middle of a card game; No one was interested in going to the park; David Ortiz was planning to hit a homerun)?

2) DESCRIPTION

The imperfect is used for descriptions in the past. This use really makes a lot of sense. When you describe someone as tall or clever, for example, these descriptions are clearly not completed actions. The ongoing nature of a description, with no clear ending point, is a good clue for the imperfect.

✳ **EXAMPLES:** *La mujer misteriosa del sombrero tenía ojos azules.*
    The mysterious woman with the hat had blue eyes.

*¡La sopa de tomate **estaba** muy caliente!*
The tomato soup was very hot!

La nueva película de Mateo Gil, Project Lazarus, ***parecía**
fantástica.*
The new Mateo Gil movie, *Project Lazarus,* seemed fantastic.

*Después de correr diez millas, **estábamos** muy cansados.*
After running ten miles, we were very tired.

3) TELLING TIME

A special use of the imperfect is for telling time in the past. Now is the time to memorize two irregular forms of the imperfect of *"ser"* used below *(era, eran)*. The rest of the irregular forms will be covered in *Lección Ocho.*

 EXAMPLES: ***Eran** las diez de la noche cuando me dormí.*
It was ten at night when I fell asleep.

***Era** la una de la mañana cuando descubrí que no tenía mi billetera, ni mi suéter, ni mi chaqueta.*
It was one A.M. when I discovered that I didn't have my wallet, sweater or jacket.

4) HABITUAL ACTIONS

The imperfect is also used to describe habitual actions in the past. Anything that a person used to do regularly calls for the imperfect.

 EXAMPLES: *Cuando tenía diez años, **comía** Frosted Flakes cada mañana con mis hermanos.*
When I was ten years old, I used to eat Frosted Flakes every morning with my brothers.

*Mi amigo Nick **contaba** los mejores chistes; todos **se reían** mucho.*
My friend Nick used to tell the best jokes; everyone used to laugh a lot.

*Mis amigos y yo **leíamos** The Boxcar Children durante la siesta; nuestra historia favorita se **llamaba** The Yellow House Mystery.*
My friends and I used to read *The Boxcar Children* series during rest time; our favorite was called *The Yellow House Mystery.*

*Antes siempre me **invitabas** a las fiestas; ¿por qué nunca me llamas ahora?*
In the past you always used to invite me to parties; why don't you ever call me now?

PRACTICE EXERCISES

1. Conjugate the following verbs fully into the imperfect:

andar (to walk)   **comprender** (to understand)

_____ _____   _____ _____

_____ _____   _____ _____

_____ _____   _____ _____

escribir (to write)   **comenzar** (to begin)

_____ _____   _____ _____

_____ _____   _____ _____

_____ _____   _____ _____

escoger (to choose)   **repetir** (to repeat)

_____ _____   _____ _____

_____ _____   _____ _____

_____ _____   _____ _____

2. Now change each of the following verbs from the present or preterite tense to the corresponding form of the imperfect. Also, add all possible subject pronouns:

Examples: tienen → <u>**(ellos, ellas, Uds.) tenían**</u> compraste → <u>**(tú) comprabas**</u>

a. comienza → _____   **f.** pedí → _____

b. pierdes → _____   **g.** cupo → _____

c. bebemos → _____   **h.** pintaste → _____

d. admite → _____   **i.** vienen → _____

e. limpian → _____   **j.** estuvimos → _____

3. Complete the following sentences using the appropriate form of the imperfect tense:

a. Yo nunca _____ a mis profesores en las clases de español; por eso no sé hablar bien el español ahora. (escuchar)

b. Rob Thomas _____ la letra de la canción *"Smooth"* mientras Carlos Santana tocaba la guitarra. (cantar)

c. El ladrón del abrigo gris _____ la puerta del banco cuando un coche de la policía llegó a la escena. (abrir)

d. Nuestros amigos siempre hacían excursiones con la familia a Caracas; mis

hermanos y yo siempre _____ acompañarlos. (querer)

e. Penélope Cruz y Antonio Banderas _____ muy contentos cuando anunciaron que Pedro Almodóvar ganó un Óscar. (parecer)

f. Cuando García Márquez tenía cinco años, _____ en Aracataca, un pueblo de Colombia. (vivir)

g. Todos _____ sorprendidos cuando vieron el vestido verde que llevaba Jennifer López en los Grammys. (estar)

h. Nosotros siempre _____ los discos nuevos de Led Zeppelin cuando vivíamos en Ohio. (comprar)

i. De niño, Jim Carrey siempre _____ cuentos cómicos; de adulto hizo una película cómica extraordinaria: *Liar, Liar.* (escribir)

j. _____ las once y media de la noche cuando Juan Pablo Montoya me llamó para hablar de NASCAR. (Ser)

4. The following paragraph contains six errors. The preterite has been used in some instances where the imperfect was a better choice, and there are some spelling problems with a couple of imperfect verb forms.

 Esta tarde jugué al tenis cuando comenzó a llover. Fueron las tres de la tarde. El cielo estuvo muy gris cuando mi amigo me dijo: "Vamos. Llueve mucho". Mi amigo pareció agitado, y yo le dije: "Bueno, vamos". Vuelvíamos a casa cuando el sol apareció. Decidimos jugar más. Mi amigo y yo estabamos muy contentos.

 B) REFLEXIVE OBJECT PRONOUNS (ROPS)

So far we have learned two categories of object pronouns:
   1) Direct Object Pronouns *(me, te, lo, la, nos, os, los, las)*
   2) Indirect Object Pronouns *(me, te, le, nos, os, les).*

A speaker chooses between these pronouns depending on whether the noun being replaced is the direct object or the indirect object of the verb.

This lesson presents a final list of pronouns that are associated with verbs. These pronouns are **reflexive**.

In the sentence: "I see myself in the mirror," the word "myself" is the reflexive object pronoun. This type of pronoun can easily be identified because the subject of the verb is also an object of the verb. Whom do I see in the mirror? I see myself!

In the sentence: "Daniel bought himself a new computer," "himself" is the reflexive object pronoun. The subject, "Daniel," bought something to give to himself.

Reflexive Object Pronouns	
me	*nos*
te	*os*
se	*se*

Helpful Tip: Once again, *"me, te, nos, os"* should look familiar. They also serve as DOPs (direct object pronouns) and IDOPs (indirect object pronouns).

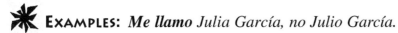 **EXAMPLES:** *Me llamo Julia García, no Julio García.*
My name is (I call myself) Julia García, not Julio García.

Nos lavamos las manos antes de comer.
We wash our hands before eating. (In this sentence, we are clearly washing ourselves . . . *"las manos"* identifies what part of our body we are washing. In a reflexive sentence, a definite article, rather than a possessive adjective, is used in Spanish with body parts and articles of clothing.)

Mi amigo se pone los pantalones y la corbata muy despacio.
My friend puts on his pants and tie very slowly.

Tú te consideras muy guapo, ¿verdad?
You consider yourself very good-looking, don't you?

Os ponéis en una buena posición otra vez.
You all are putting yourselves in a good position again.

Esos actores se llaman Jencarlos Canela y Gaby Espino.
Those actors are named (call themselves) Jencarlos Canela y Gaby Espino.

Mi hermano se acuesta a las diez.
My brother goes (puts himself) to bed at ten o'clock.

Mi papá se sienta en la silla cómoda.
My dad sits down in the comfortable chair.

To clarify or to emphasize one of these reflexive object pronouns, you may choose to add the following words:

a mí	*a nosotros, a nosotras*
a ti	*a vosotros, a vosotras*
a sí	*a sí*

To add even extra emphasis, the words *"mismo, misma, mismos, mismas"* can follow any of the words above. You simply choose the form that agrees with the subject.

 **EXAMPLES:** *Muchas veces me digo a mí misma que tengo mucho talento.*
Many times I tell <u>myself</u> that I have a lot of talent.

Nos miramos a nosotras mismas en el espejo antes de salir para la escuela.
We look at <u>ourselves</u> in the mirror before leaving for school.

No necesitas admirtirme a mí que no eres perfecto; necesitas admitírtelo a ti mismo.
You don't have to admit to me that you aren't perfect; you need to admit it to <u>yourself</u>.

Si ellas quieren recibir una carta, ¡tienen que escribirse a sí mismas!
If they want to receive a letter, they have to write to themselves!

PRACTICE EXERCISES

1. Complete the following sentences using the appropriate reflexive object pronoun *(me, te, se, nos, os, se)***:**

a. _____ siento en mi silla favorita cuando estoy muy cansado.

b. El álbum más romántico de Miguel Bosé _____ llama *Papito*.

c. _____ lavamos la cara y las manos cuando vamos a misa.

d. _____ dices que nunca vas a comer en ese restaurante otra vez.

e. Mi amiga _____ cepilla los dientes con Crest.

f. ¿Por qué _____ comprasteis un regalo para Navidad?

g. Cuando nadie me llama por teléfono, _____ pregunto por qué no tengo más amigos.

2. Now add the following words *(a mí, a ti, a sí, a nosotros/nosotras, a vosotros/vosotras, a sí)* **to emphasize the reflexive pronoun found in each sentence. Add** *"mismo, misma, mismos, mismas"* **to at least a few of the sentences:**

a. Me digo _____ que necesito encontrar otro trabajo.

b. Mi padre siempre se dice _____: "De tal palo, tal astilla *(Like father, like son)*".

c. Ellos se consideran _____ los chicos más atléticos del universo.

d. Mi vecina se miente _____ cuando dice que no tiene muchos zapatos.

e. ¿Por qué os dais _____ los mejores asientos?

f. Mi hermana se conoce muy bien _____; nunca trata de hacer nada si está cansada.

🔑 C) ADVERBS

Adverbs are words that are used to modify or qualify verbs, adjectives, or other adverbs. These words tell how, when, where, or with what intensity something is done.

In the sentence **"I stupidly bought a car last year that was so poorly made,"** there are a number of adverbs:

- ◆ **"stupidly"** is an adverb that qualifies the verb "bought."
- ◆ **"last year"** is an adverbial phrase which modifies the verb "bought," telling the listener when the action was done.
- ◆ **"so"** is an adverb because it lets us know how poorly the car was made; it modifies the adverb "poorly."
- ◆ **"poorly"** is also an adverb which modifies "made"; it tells us how the car was made.

In Spanish, adverbs are commonly placed <u>after</u> verbs and <u>before</u> adjectives or other adverbs.

Here is a list of twenty common adverbs in Spanish:

Common Adverbs			
allí → there		*muy* → very	
antes → before		*nunca* → never	
aquí → here		*poco* → a little	
ayer → yesterday		*pronto* → soon	
bien → fine, well		*siempre* → always	
después → after		*también* → also	
hoy → today		*tan* → so	
mal → poorly, badly		*tanto* → so much	
mañana → tomorrow		*tarde* → late	
mucho → a lot		*temprano* → early	

Helpful Tips: **1)** Be aware that some of these words have more than one grammatical use. For example, *"ayer"* and *"hoy"* are both nouns in this sentence: *"Ayer fue martes, pero hoy es miércoles,"* but they are adverbs in this one: *"Comí en McDonald's ayer, pero como en Taco Bell hoy."*
2) In the following sentence, *"mucho"* and *"poco"* are adjectives: *"Tengo mucho talento y poco dinero,"* but in this one they are adverbs: *"Bailamos mucho, pero estudiamos poco."*
3) As adverbs, *"mucho"* and *"poco"* have <u>one</u> form. As adjectives, they have <u>four</u>: *mucho, mucha, muchos, muchas; poco, poca, pocos, pocas.*

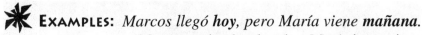 **EXAMPLES:** *Marcos llegó hoy, pero María viene mañana.*
Marcos arrived today, but María is coming tomorrow.

Mi amigo es tan estúpido que cree que las vacas vuelan.
My friend is so stupid that he thinks cows can fly.

Luis Miguel está muy enfermo; no puede cantar bien ahora.
Luis Miguel is very sick; he can't sing well now.

Siempre compro las entradas temprano porque el espectáculo es popular.
I always buy the tickets early because the show is popular.

Syracuse tiene un equipo de baloncesto muy bueno, y Duke, también.
Syracuse has a very good basketball team, and Duke, too.

Carolina Herrera trabaja mucho en la industria de la moda; dicen que pronto va a abrir una nueva tienda en Caracas.
Carolina Herrera works a lot in the fashion industry; they say that soon she is going to open a new store in Caracas.

"Más vale tarde que nunca" es un refrán muy común en español.
"Better late than never" is a very common saying in Spanish.

 # PRACTICE EXERCISES

1. Complete the following sentences using any adverb from this list that makes sense (*allí, antes, aquí, ayer, bien, después, hoy, mal, mañana, mucho, muy, nunca, poco, pronto, siempre, también, tan, tanto, tarde, temprano*)**.**
A number of sentences may have more than one correct answer:

a. Paul McCartney todavía es _____ popular que es difícil conseguir una entrada para sus conciertos.

b. Marcos no llegó ni _____, ni hoy; va a llegar mañana.

c. Estoy _____ cansada y no me siento _____; voy a acostarme después de las clases.

d. Mi hermana es una fanática; siempre se cepilla los dientes por la mañana,

pero yo _____ lo hago.

e. "Uds. necesitan sentarse _____ en las sillas y comenzar a estudiar", les dijo la profesora a los alumnos.

f. _____ yo siempre bebía café con leche, pero ahora prefiero tomar té con limón.

g. Mis primos, Luis, Dalia, Domingo y Loli vienen a la fiesta . . . y, claro,

Roberto viene _____.

h. Raúl de Molina, el periodista en *El Gordo y La Flaca,* come _____ y por eso se llama "El Gordo".

i. No te preocupes; mi padre viene con el coche en dos minutos.

Sí, viene muy _____.

j. No me gusta ir _____ al cine porque no quiero perderme ni un minuto de la película.

2. Now write your own original sentences using the following adverbs. In some sentences, you will be asked to incorporate more than one adverb into the sentence:

a. temprano

_____

b. hoy; mañana

_____

c. mal

_____

d. antes; pronto

_____

e. también

_____

D) TALKING ABOUT THE WEATHER

Talking about the weather is a common topic of conversation in almost every culture. At the beginning of this book, you learned a few expressions to describe the weather. In this section, you will find even more ways to do so. Now that you understand more about the various parts of speech, you will see that the constructions themselves differ in English and Spanish.

Here is a good list of expanded vocabulary for talking about the weather:

¿Qué tiempo hace hoy?	How's the weather today? (Literally: What weather is it doing/making today?)
Hace frío. Hace mucho frío.	It's cold. It's very cold. (Literally: It's making cold. It's making a lot of cold.)
Hace calor. Hace mucho calor.	It's hot. It's very hot. (Literally: It's making heat. It's making a lot of heat.)
Hace sol. Hace mucho sol.	It's sunny. It's very sunny. (Literally: It's making sun. It's making a lot of sun.)
Llueve. Llueve un poco.	It's raining. It's raining a little.
Nieva.	It's snowing.
Está nublado.	It's cloudy.
Está soleado.	It's sunny.
Graniza.	It's hailing.
Hace (mucho) viento.	It's (very) windy. (Literally: It's making [a lot of] wind.)
Hay (mucha) niebla.	It's (very) foggy. (Literally: There is [a lot of] fog.)

PRACTICE EXERCISES

1. Using the weather vocabulary that you just learned, write an appropriate expression that you associate with each picture:

a. _____

b. _____

c. _____

d. _____

2. Pretend that you have just been hired at your local television station as the new meteorologist. Prepare a script for a telecast which describes not only the current weather in your area, but also the national forecast. Be certain that there are a number of different weather patterns in play across the country:

_____

_____

_____

_____

_____

_____

These two sets of questions use grammatical structures and vocabulary from this lesson. Working with a partner, alternate asking and answering each question. When you get to the bottom of each list, start over at the top, switching roles. As a variation, write out the answers in complete sentences.

A) Cuando tenías ocho años:

¿dónde vivías?

¿bebías más jugo de naranja o jugo de tomate?

¿cómo se llamaba tu mejor amigo?

¿recibías muchas cartas de tus abuelos?

¿hablaban tus padres por teléfono durante la comida?

¿te reías mucho con tus amigos?

¿llevabas guantes y bufanda cuando nevaba?

B) ¿Te sientes alegre hoy?

¿Te compraste una entrada para la nueva exposición en el museo?

¿Te preguntas por qué no vuelan las vacas?

¿Normalmente hablas despacio o rápidamente?

¿Puedes decirme un buen chiste ahora?

¿Prefieres llegar tarde o temprano a una película?

¿Estás alegre cuando hace mucho viento?

DIALOGUE

The following dialogue contains grammar and vocabulary that you've seen in this lesson and in the introductory section. After listening to the dialogue, read it aloud, alone or with friends. Afterwards, try to answer the questions that follow either aloud or in written form.

LAS AVENTURAS DE RAFAEL, ELISA Y "EL TIGRE"
ESCENA CUATRO
🖥 (Online access offers recordings of this adventure series.) 🖥

Rafael, "El Tigre" y Elisa duermen tranquilamente en un apartamento en Nueva York. A las ocho en punto, Marisela, la prima de Javier (el amigo de Rafael), los llama.

Marisela: Buenos días. Buenos días. ¡Levántense Uds.!

El Tigre: ¿Qué hora es, Marisela?

Marisela: Son las ocho de la mañana. Es hora de desayunar. En unos minutos tenemos que ir a la comisaría (police station) para ver si tienen información sobre tu mochila.

Rafael: Buenos días. Tengo hambre, Javier y Marisela. ¿Qué hay de comer?

Javier: Cereal, tostadas, jugo, Pop-Tarts y café.

El Tigre: Oye, Marisela, tomé una decisión anoche. No importa la mochila. Puedo comprar más ropa hoy. Y todavía tengo dinero en la billetera.

Javier: Te puedo prestar mi ropa vieja, Tigre. Creo que usamos la misma talla (size) más o menos.

Elisa: Rafael, tus amigos son simpáticos. ¡Tenemos mucha suerte!

Rafael: Gracias. Pero ese hombre que robó la mochila . . . soñé con él (I dreamt about him) anoche. Creo que lo conozco.

Elisa: No pienses en eso. Todo va bien ahora. Hablé con mis padres anoche y estaban muy felices. Les dije que el campamento de tenis es bonito y que tenía muchas ganas de practicar el tenis. Mi padre estaba muy contento.

Suena el teléfono. Javier lo contesta.

Javier: Aló. Aló.

Javier cuelga el teléfono.

Javier: ¡Qué extraño! No habla nadie.

Marisela: Pues, ¿quién sabe? A lo mejor (probably) un número equivocado. Pero, vamos, chicos. Tengo un día fantástico para Uds. Primero vamos al Museo Metropolitano de Arte para ver una exposición de Frida Kahlo y Diego Rivera, y después vamos a almorzar en mi favorito restaurante cubano, "Victor's Café".

Rafael:	Javier me dijo que Uds. vieron a Elvis Crespo en "Victor's Café" la semana pasada. ¿Es verdad?
Javier:	Claro, chico. Es toda la verdad.
Elisa:	Elvis canta muy bien y es muy guapo, también. Me encanta la canción *"Suavemente"*.

Los chicos se preparan para el día. Se duchan, se peinan y se visten.

Javier:	¿Es verdad que Uds. tienen que irse mañana? Nueva York es tan grande y hay tanto que hacer.
Marisela:	Es verdad. Esta tarde filman una película de Spike Lee en Central Park. Si hay tiempo después de almorzar, vamos a ver si podemos ver un poquito.
El Tigre:	Spike Lee es fantástico. Me gustaría mucho.
Javier:	¿Saben Uds. que Nueva York es el sitio más popular en la historia del cine? ¿Se dan cuenta (Do you realize?) de todas las películas que filmaron aquí?
El Tigre:	Pues, *King Kong* es una.
Javier:	También *West Side Story, Kramer vs. Kramer, When Harry Met Sally, Serpico, Fame, Sleepless in Seattle, Breakfast at Tiffany's, Taxi Driver* y *Saturday Night Fever.*
Elisa:	¡Es increíble! Vamos.
El Tigre:	Si hay tiempo esta tarde, ¿podemos comer un helado en "Serendipity"*?* Rafael me dijo que tienen una bebida de chocolate fantástica.
Marisela:	Sí, chico. Te prometo que vamos por allí.

Elisa, "El Tigre", Rafael, Javier y Marisela salen del apartamento. Al salir, el teléfono suena de nuevo. Javier decide no contestarlo.

PREGUNTAS

1) ¿Dónde duermen Rafael, Elisa y El Tigre?

_____

2) ¿A qué hora se levantaron?

_____

3) ¿Qué van a comer para el desayuno?

_____

4) ¿Por qué no van a la comisaría (police station)?

_____

5) ¿Por qué no necesita comprar ropa nueva El Tigre?

_____

6) ¿Qué exposición especial hay en el Museo Metropolitano de Arte?

_____

7) ¿Dónde van a almorzar?

_____

8) ¿Qué cantante famoso comió recientemente en ese restaurante?

_____

9) ¿Cómo se llaman tres películas famosas que fueron filmadas en Nueva York?

_____

10) ¿Qué problema hay con el teléfono en esta escena?

_____

PRUEBA DE REPASO

1. Answer in complete sentences:

a. ¿Qué tiempo hace hoy en Caracas, Venezuela?

_____

b. Cuando tenías dos años, ¿hablabas español?

_____

c. Cuando tenías diez años, ¿comías más carne o más pescado?

_____

d. ¿Te lavas las manos antes de comer?

_____

e. ¿Adónde vas después de clase hoy?

_____

2. Conjugate the following six verbs fully in the imperfect tense:

hablar (to talk)   **comer** (to eat)   **vivir** (to live)

_____ _____   _____ _____   _____ _____

_____ _____   _____ _____   _____ _____

_____ _____   _____ _____   _____ _____

cerrar (to close)   **volver** (to return)   **pedir** (to ask for)

_____ _____   _____ _____   _____ _____

_____ _____   _____ _____   _____ _____

_____ _____   _____ _____   _____ _____

3. Conjugate each verb into the appropriate form of the imperfect:

a. Mis padres me _____ a la tienda cuando me perdí en las calles atestadas de Nueva York. (acompañar)

b. Cuando tenía ocho años, yo _____ frecuentemente la casa de mis abuelos cerca del Salto de Ángel. (visitar)

c. ¿Qué tiempo _____ ayer en las montañas de Chile? (hacer)

d. Normalmente mi papá no _____ nada; mi madre siempre tomaba todas las decisiones. (decidir)

e. Cuando mi tío _____ de Progressive Field, José Ramírez marcó otro jonrón. (salir)

f. ¿Cómo _____ esa famosa cocinera que murió en 2004? –Julia Child. (llamarse)

g. Los padres de Steve Carell siempre _____ cuando él, de niño, les contaba chistes. (reírse)

h. Mi hija, Sarita, siempre _____ ranas en el río cerca de nuestra casa. (encontrar)

i. Nosotros no _____ nada hasta que el profesor nos lo explicó todo. (entender)

j. En mi barrio todos _____ agitados debido al *(due to the)* misterioso robo en la iglesia. (estar)

4. Complete the following sentences with one of the following reflexive object pronouns *(me, te, se, nos, os, se)*:

a. _____ llamo Óscar de la Hoya y soy boxeador y cantante.

b. El álbum de Enrique Iglesias que más me gusta _____ llama *Uno*.

c. Mis hijos nunca _____ cepillaban los dientes cuando eran pequeños.

d. Nunca _____ admites los problemas que tienes. ¿Por qué no eres más honesto contigo mismo?

e. Vosotros _____ laváis las manos antes de comer.

f. _____ dije que soy atlética y que puedo correr veintiséis millas.

g. Ellos no _____ conocen muy bien a sí mismos; por eso no son muy felices.

h. Mis abuelos _____ prepararon una comida exquisita con empanadas, ceviche y frutas tropicales.

5. Write the "opposite" of the following adverbs:

a. bien _____

b. poco _____

c. nunca _____

d. tarde _____

e. mañana _____

f. aquí _____

g. después _____

6. Translate the following sentences into Spanish:

a. It's hailing, and we are very upset.

_____

b. She always used to call her friends after each party.

_____

c. Paco laughs so much during math class!

_____

7. The following postcard contains six errors. Underline each error and write the correction above it:

Hola Chita:

Estoy en San Cristóbal, Venezuela. Llueva mucho hoy, pero estoy alegre. Ayer en el hotel, yo duermía a las siete de la mañana cuando alguien entró en mi habitación. Un señor anunció: "Es miércoles. El hotel está cerrada hoy". Yo estabo muy confundida. Decidí salir de allí. Primero lavé me la cara y me cepillé el pelo. Me puse una falda nueva y una camisa blanca. Tomé las maletas y pagé la cuenta. ¡Nunca voy a volver al "Hotel California"!

Muchos besos,

Consuelo

_____

_____

_____

BOLIVIA & CHILE

BOLIVIA

CAPITALES:	La Paz (¡La capital más alta del mundo!), Sucre
POBLACIÓN:	11.800.000
GOBIERNO:	república
PRESIDENTE:	Luis Arce
DINERO ($):	boliviano
PRODUCTOS:	agricultura, artesanía, minerales
MÚSICA, BAILE:	auqui-auqui, cueca, tinku
SITIOS DE INTERÉS:	El lago Titicaca, Parque Nacional Madidi, Salar de Uyuni
COMIDA TÍPICA:	empanadas, humitas, marraqueta (pan), salsa picante

CHILE

CAPITAL:	Santiago
POBLACIÓN:	19.200.000
GOBIERNO:	república
PRESIDENTE:	Sebastián Piñera
DINERO ($):	peso chileno
PRODUCTOS:	agricultura, cobre, vino
MÚSICA, BAILE:	costillar, cueca, refalosa
SITIOS DE INTERÉS:	Los Andes, desierto de Atacama, Isla de Pascua, Tierra del Fuego, Valle de la Luna
COMIDA TÍPICA:	cazuela de ave, empanadas, parrillada de mariscos, pastel de chocho, sopaipillas, vino

BOLIVIANOS FAMOSOS:

Marina Núñez del Prado
(ESCULTORA)

Víctor Paz
(POLÍTICO)

Edmundo Paz Soldán
(ESCRITOR)

Javier Taborga
(ATLETA)

CHILENOS FAMOSOS:

Isabel Allende
(NOVELISTA)

Salvador Allende
(POLÍTICO)

Gabriela Mistral
(POETA)

Pablo Neruda
(POETA)

Bernardo O'Higgins
(HÉROE NACIONAL)

181

Practice this vocabulary with our mobile app! Visit tobreak.com/app for more details.

VOCABULARIO LECCIÓN OCHO

THEME WORDS: "AT HOME"

la	alfombra	carpet, rug
el	armario, el clóset	closet
la	bañera, tina	tub
las	cortinas	curtains
el	(cuarto de) baño	bathroom
la	cuchara	spoon
el	cuchillo	knife
la	ducha, la regadera	shower
las	escaleras	stairs
la	escoba	broom
el	fregadero	sink (in kitchen)
el	grifo	faucet
el	lavamanos (Sp.), el lavabo	sink (in bathroom)
el	plato	plate, dish
el	sofá	sofa
el	tenedor	fork

OTHER NOUNS

el	accidente	accident
el/la	asistente/a (el auxiliar) de vuelo	flight attendant
el	boleto	ticket
el	enemigo	enemy
el	lago	lake

el	pastel	cake
la	torta	cake
el	tostador/ la tostadora	toaster

ADJECTIVES

cariñoso/a	affectionate
generoso/a	generous
mayor	older
menor	younger
sabroso/a	tasty, delicious
solo/a	alone

VERBS

cortar	to cut
desear	to wish, want, desire
mostrar (ue)	to show
prestar	to lend
repetir (i)	to repeat
sonar (ue)	to ring, to sound

MISCELLANEOUS

todavía	still
todavía no	not yet

LECCIÓN OCHO

KEY GRAMMAR
CONCEPTS

A) **IRREGULAR VERBS IN THE IMPERFECT TENSE** → *Los verbos irregulares en el imperfecto*

B) **DOUBLE OBJECT PRONOUNS** → *Cuando hay dos pronombres complementos*

C) **ADVERBS THAT END WITH "-MENTE"** → *Los adverbios que terminan con "-mente"*

 A) IRREGULAR VERBS IN THE IMPERFECT TENSE

As you learned in the last lesson, there are only three irregular verbs in the imperfect tense: *"ir," "ser,"* and *"ver."* Every other verb is completely regular — no stem changes, no strange spelling, no tricks.

Here are the three verbs that are irregular in the imperfect:

IR		SER		VER	
iba	íbamos	era	éramos	veía	veíamos
ibas	ibais	eras	erais	veías	veíais
iba	iban	era	eran	veía	veían

 ¡CUIDADO! At first glance, some students wonder why *"ver"* is irregular. If it were regular, however, the conjugations would be: *vía, vías, vía,* etc., and not *veía, veías,* and *veía,* etc.

Let's look at these common verbs in action:

✳ **EXAMPLES:** *Eran las diez de la noche cuando me dormí.*
It was ten P.M. when I fell asleep.

Mientras íbamos a la casa de la abuela, tuvimos un accidente.
When we were going to Grandma's house, we had an accident.

Yo siempre veía a mi tío cuando vivía en La Paz.
I always used to see my uncle when I lived in La Paz.

Mi profesora de inglés era una mujer alta.
My English teacher was a tall woman.

Taylor Swift y David Bisbal iban a cantar en Central Park el año pasado.
Taylor Swift and David Bisbal were going to sing in Central Park last year.

*Cuando **éramos** niños, **veíamos** el programa* I Love Lucy *porque Desi Arnaz fue uno de los primeros actores cubanos en la televisión.*

When we were kids, we used to watch the show *I Love Lucy* because Desi Arnaz was one of the first Cuban actors on television.

***Era** la una y media de la mañana cuando mi hermano mayor volvió a casa; mis padres estaban furiosos.*

It was one-thirty in the morning when my older brother returned home; my parents were furious.

 PRACTICE EXERCISES

1. Now change each of the following verbs from either the present or preterite tense to the corresponding form of the imperfect:

Example: vas → <u>**ibas**</u>

a. soy → _____

b. viste → _____

c. sois → _____

d. vieron → _____

e. van → _____

f. vamos → _____

g. ven → _____

h. somos → _____

i. veo → _____

j. fue → _____

2. Complete the following sentences using the appropriate form of the imperfect tense:

a. _____ las diez de la noche cuando comenzó mi programa favorito de WWE. (Ser)

b. Mi hermana nunca _____ conmigo al restaurante; prefería la comida sabrosa de mi mamá. (ir)

c. Anoche nosotros _____ *Dancing with The Stars* en la sala cuando sonó el teléfono. (ver)

d. Uds. siempre _____ a sus amigos cuando iban al lago durante el verano. (ver)

e. Cuando mi padre _____ al trabajo, vio a Lance Armstrong enfrente del hotel. (ir)

f. Mi mejor amigo nunca _____ divertido; siempre tomaba todo en serio. (ser)

3. **In the following "family tale," fill in the blanks with the appropriate imperfect form of *"ir," "ser,"* or *"ver"*:**

Cuando mi abuelo _____ niño, siempre _____ a la casa de mi

abuela. Como vivían en la misma calle, él la _____ todas las tardes. Se

sentaban en un sofá grande. Mi abuela _____ mayor que él, pero eso no

_____ importante para mi abuelo. Un día anunció que _____ a casarse

con ella. Y _____ la verdad. Ahora hace cincuenta años que están casados.

🗝 B) Double object pronouns

Do you remember all of the object pronouns we have studied thus far?

Here is a review of object pronouns:

Reflexive Object Pronouns (ROPs)		Indirect Object Pronouns (IDOPs)		Direct Object Pronouns (DOPs)	
me	*nos*	*me*	*nos*	*me*	*nos*
te	*os*	*te*	*os*	*te*	*os*
se	*se*	*le*	*les*	*lo, la*	*los, las*

Oftentimes, a speaker will choose to use two object pronouns in the same sentence. The nouns for which these pronouns stand will already have been made clear to the listener or reader.

For example, the English sentence "I gave a present to my sister" could be rewritten: "I gave it to her," which uses both a direct object pronoun (DOP) — "it" — and an indirect object pronoun (IDOP) — "her."

Similarly, the sentence "My aunt sang some lullabies to herself" could be rewritten: "My aunt sang them to herself," which uses both a DOP — "them" — and a reflexive object pronoun (ROP) — "herself."

ARE THERE SPECIAL RULES ABOUT USING MULTIPLE OBJECT PRONOUNS?

Yes, indeed! Here are some things to keep in mind when using multiple object pronouns.

1) ORDER OF THESE PRONOUNS: "RID"

The order for these pronouns is always reflexive object pronoun first, then indirect object pronoun, and finally direct object pronoun. By memorizing the word "**RID**," (**R**eflexive, **I**ndirect, and **D**irect), you should be able to keep the order straight. Let's look at a few sample sentences:

EXAMPLES: *¿El plato? Mi hermana **me lo** dio.*
The plate? My sister gave it to me.
(**Note:** In this sentence, *"me"* is the IDOP and *"lo"* is the DOP.)

*¿Las manos? **Nos las** lavamos antes de comer.*
Our hands? We wash them before eating.
(**Note:** In this sentence, *"nos"* is the ROP, and *"las"* is the DOP.)

*¿Las palabras? **Me las** repito cada día.*
The words? I am repeating them to myself every day.

*Angélica me compró el nuevo álbum de BTS. **Te lo** pongo mañana.*
Angélica bought me the new BTS album. I'll play it for you tomorrow.

> **Helpful Tip:** Did you notice that these object pronouns are placed directly before the conjugated verb?

2) THE USE OF "SE" TO REPLACE "LE" OR "LES"

There is a special case in Spanish in which the 3rd person <u>indirect</u> object pronoun *le* or *les* is replaced by the word *se*. This change occurs when *le* or *les* is followed by any 3rd person <u>direct object</u> pronoun: *lo, la, los,* or *las*.

What was the thinking behind this rule? Probably to avoid putting two short words next to each other that begin with "l," e.g., *"le lo" or "les la."* It is easier for the ear to distinguish these words when the first word is changed to *se*:

> *Se*
> *¿La pizza? L̶e̶ la doy a mi amigo.*

EXAMPLES: *¿El secreto del enemigo? **Se lo** dije al coronel.*
The enemy's secret? I told it to the colonel.
(**Note:** In this sentence, *"le"* meaning "to him" was replaced by the word *"se."*)

¿La revista nueva? **Se la** *llevo a mi madre.*
> The new magazine? I'm taking it to my mother.
>
> (**Note:** In this sentence, *"le"* meaning "to her" was replaced by the word *"se."*)

¿Los regalos que están en la mesa? **Se los** *doy a mis mejores amigos.*
> The presents on the table? I'm giving them to my best friends.
>
> (**Note:** In this sentence, *"les"* meaning "to them" was replaced by the word *"se."*)

¿Las instrucciones para operar el tostador? **Se las** *dejé a mi hermano.*
> The instructions for operating the toaster? I left them for my brother.
>
> (**Note:** In this sentence, *"le"* meaning "to him" was replaced by the word *"se."*)

¿Las palabras de la canción Louie, Louie*?* **Se las** *repetí a mi madre, pero no las entendió.*
> The words to *Louie, Louie?* I repeated them to my mom, but she didn't understand them.
>
> (**Note:** In this sentence, *"le"* meaning "to her" was replaced by the word *"se."*)

El futbolista chileno Gary Medel me prestó una camisa amarilla, pero nunca **se la** *devolví.*
> The Chilean soccer player Gary Medel lent me a yellow shirt, but I never returned it to him.
>
> (**Note:** In this sentence, *"le"* meaning "to him" was replaced by the word *"se."*)

3) VERB FOLLOWED BY AN INFINITIVE

When one verb is followed by an infinitive, you may choose to put these multiple object pronouns before the first verb, or you may attach them to the infinitive. You may not separate them, however, by putting one object pronoun before the first verb and attaching the second to the infinitive!

✳ **EXAMPLES:** *¿La invitación? Voy a dár***tela** *a ti (***Te la** *voy a dar a ti).*
> The invitation? I'm going to give it to you.

¿Los vasos de cristal? **Se los** *tengo que comprar a mi amiga (Tengo que comprár***selos** *a mi amiga).*
> The crystal glasses? I need to buy them for my friend.

Manolo me escribe cartas a mí, pero no **se las** *quiere escribir a su mamá (. . . no quiere escribír***selas** *a su mamá).*
> Manolo writes letters to me, but he doesn't want to write them to his mother.

Helpful Tip: You may have noticed that when you add two object pronouns to an infinitive, it is necessary to place a written accent mark on the third syllable from the end of the new word created (e.g., *dártela . . . comprárselos . . . escribírselas*).

---

1. Rewrite the following sentences, by substituting an object pronoun for the underlined words. Remember to replace "le/les" with "se":

a. Roberto me compra <u>la alfombra</u> mañana.

_____

b. Luis Miguel le dedica <u>muchas canciones</u> a su familia.

_____

c. Nuestros abuelos nos regalaron <u>la nueva revista de Oprah Winfrey</u>.

_____

d. Te voy a sacar <u>muchas fotos</u> mañana durante el viaje a la Isla de Pascua.

_____

e. Necesitamos mostrarles <u>los pasaportes</u> a los guardias.

_____

f. Iba a confesarte <u>un secreto importante</u>.

_____

g. Los incas nos enseñaron <u>lecciones importantes de agricultura</u>.

_____

h. Mis primos les dieron <u>botellas de vino chileno</u> a sus amigos para la fiesta.

_____

i. Mi hermano mayor es fantástico. Nos va a limpiar <u>la ducha y la bañera</u>.

_____

2. **In the following sentences, write the appropriate double object pronouns in the space provided. Add an accent mark when necessary:**

   a. ¿La nueva película de Diego Luna? Voy a mostrar_____ a mi amiga.

   b. ¿Los pasaportes? _____ necesito mostrar al asistente de vuelo.

   c. ¿Las baladas de Beyoncé? Ella _____ va a cantar a nosotros.

   d. ¿El teléfono? Mi madre _____ va a contestar (a mí).

   e. ¿Una torta de cumpleaños? Mi abuela desea hacer_____ a mi hermana.

3. **The following paragraph contains six object pronoun errors. Underline each error and write the correction above it:**

   El día de mi cumpleaños, mi abuela quería me hacer una torta. Me preparó la por la mañana. Era de chocolate. Cuando mis amigos llegaron, mi abuela la quería darles a ellos también. Ella siempre era muy generosa. Pero la torta era para mí. Yo no quería se la dar a mis amigos porque sabía que iban a comer mucho. Pero, ¡qué sorpresa! Mi abuela me hizo dos tortas. Por eso, la primera les la di a mis amigos y la otra la me comí yo solito.

C) ADVERBS THAT END WITH "-MENTE"

Last lesson you learned how adverbs modify verbs, adjectives, and other adverbs. The adverbs presented helped to tell how, when, where, or how intensely something was done. This lesson will present other adverbs, all of which end with "*-mente*." This ending is equivalent to the "-ly" ending in English (e.g., quickly, patiently, stubbornly, etc.).

Here is a simple formula for transforming most adjectives into adverbs:

◆ Take the feminine form of an adjective and add "*-mente*":

Masculine Adjective		Feminine Adjective		Adverb	English Equivalent
rápido	→	*rápida*	→	*rápidamente*	quickly
loco	→	*loca*	→	*locamente*	crazily
intenso	→	*intensa*	→	*intensamente*	intensely

◆ As adjectives that end in a vowel other than "*o*" or "*a*" are already both feminine and masculine, there is no need to change them at all!

alegre	→	**alegremente** (happily)
fuerte	→	**fuertemente** (strongly)

◆ Add "*-mente*" to adjectives that end in a consonant.

cortés	→	**cortésmente** (courteously)
leal	→	**lealmente** (loyally)

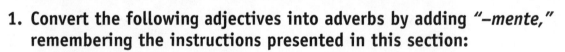

PRACTICE EXERCISES

1. Convert the following adjectives into adverbs by adding "*–mente*," remembering the instructions presented in this section:

Example: lento → <u>**lentamente**</u>

a. rápido → _____

b. feliz → _____

c. cordial → _____

d. triste → _____

e. alegre → _____

f. ruidoso → _____

g. paciente → _____   **i.** general → _____

h. contento → _____   **j.** extraño → _____

2. **Translate the following sentences into Spanish, using the adverbial construction found in this section:**

   a. The boys ran quickly to the bathroom when the class ended.

   _____

   _____

   b. José Feliciano sang the song intensely.

   _____

   _____

   c. Consuelo said sadly that her friend was sick.

   _____

   _____

3. **Identify and correct the four errors in this list of things to do:**

 Para hacer mañana:

1) Cortar el césped cuidadosomente

2) Hablar con mi mamá cariñosamente

3) Llegar a la clase puntualamente

4) Lavar los tenedores, cucharas y cuchillos rápidomente en el fregadero

5) Entregar la tarea alegramente

ORAL PRACTICE
PREGUNTAS EN GRUPOS DE DOS

These two sets of questions use grammatical structures and vocabulary from this lesson. Working with a partner, alternate asking and answering each question. When you get to the bottom of each list, start over at the top, switching roles. As a variation, write out the answers in complete sentences.

A) ¿Eras un/una niño/niña muy alto/alta?

¿Ibas de viaje frecuentemente con tus padres?

¿Te gustaba nadar en el agua fría?

¿Veías mucho la televisión cuando eras niño/niña?

¿Cuántos años tenían tus padres cuando se casaron?

A ti, ¿te gusta cortar el césped?

¿Escribes las composiciones alegremente?

B) Un chiste . . . ¿vas a decírmelo ahora?

Unas Coca-Colas . . . ¿vas a comprármelas luego?

Los regalos . . . ¿quieres mostrármelos ahora?

Las fotos . . . ¿deseas prestármelas esta noche?

¿Todavía tienes muchos enemigos?

¿Haces la tarea intensamente?

¿Hablas con los adultos cordialmente?

PRUEBA DE REPASO

1. Answer in complete sentences:

a. ¿Adónde ibas de vacaciones cuando eras más joven?

_____

b. ¿Siempre deseabas estudiar español?

_____

c. ¿Prefieres las tortas de chocolate o las de vainilla?

_____

d. ¿Limpias las escaleras alegremente o tristemente?

_____

e. El secreto . . . ¿vas a decírmelo ahora?

_____

2. Conjugate the following three verbs fully in the imperfect tense:

      ir (to go)   **ser** (to be)   **ver** (to see)

_____ _____   _____ _____   _____ _____

_____ _____   _____ _____   _____ _____

_____ _____   _____ _____   _____ _____

3. Conjugate each verb into the appropriate form of the imperfect:

a. _____ las siete y media de la tarde cuando Lucero me llamó por teléfono. (Ser)

b. Yo _____ a comprar el nuevo disco de Los Tigres del Norte, pero descubrí que no tenía dinero. (ir)

c. Yo siempre _____ a mi abuela cuando vivíamos en Santa Cruz. (ver)

d. Nosotros nunca _____ la televisión cuando estábamos de vacaciones cerca del lago Titicaca. (ver)

e. Cuando mis padres _____ a Chile en avión, los asistentes de vuelo siempre los atendían bien. (ir)

f. José _____ mi vecino cuando yo era niño. (ser)

g. Mi esposa y yo _____ a la playa cuando comenzó a llover fuertemente. (ir)

h. Ricardo Montalbán _____ mi actor favorito cuando era niña. (ser)

4. **Rewrite the following sentences, replacing the underlined words with an appropriate object pronoun:**

a. Mi tío me dio <u>un regalo</u> para mi cumpleaños.

_____

b. Te voy a sacar <u>una foto</u> en unos minutos.

_____

c. Siempre le decía <u>los secretos</u> a mi mejor amiga.

_____

d. Les voy a repetir <u>las palabras</u> a los profesores.

_____

e. Mis primos nunca me mostraban <u>el armario secreto</u>.

_____

f. Uds. quieren prestarme <u>un teléfono</u>, ¿verdad?

_____

5. Convert the following adjectives into adverbs:

a. cariñoso →_____   **e.** general →_____

b. generoso →_____   **f.** obvio →_____

c. leal →_____   **g.** sincero →_____

d. fuerte →_____   **h.** elegante →_____

6. Translate the following sentences into Spanish. Pay close attention to the verbs: one is in the present, two are in the preterite, and two more are in the imperfect.

a. Before, I used to work intensely; now I sleep day and night.

_____

b. The lawn? I cut it for you yesterday.

_____

c. It was eight o'clock when the accident happened in the dining room.

_____

7. Find and correct the five errors in this diary entry:

 11 de febrero

Hacían mucho frío hoy. Era las seis de la mañana cuando comenzó a

nevar. Le escribí una carta a mi novia. Era una carta muy negativa y

decidí no enviárlela. Todavía quiero Raquela, pero no me trata tan

cariñosomente como antes. Creo que la nieve es el problema. Voy a

dormir un poco más.

NICARAGUA

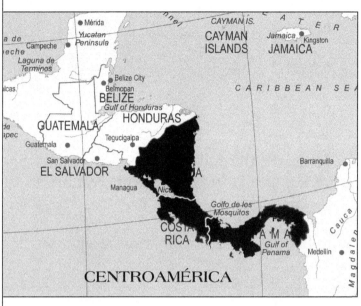

HONDURAS

Puerto
Cabezas

CORDILLERA ISABELIA

NICARAGUA

SELVA TROPICAL

Chinadera

León

★ Managua

Granada

LAGO DE NICARAGUA

Bluefields

Océano
Pacífico

San
Carlos

El
Caribe

COSTA RICA

Mérida

Campeche

Yucatan
Peninsula

CAYMAN IS.

CAYMAN
ISLANDS

Jamaica

JAMAICA

Kingston

Laguna de
Terminos

Belize City

Belmopan

BELIZE

Gulf of Honduras

HONDURAS

CARIBBEAN SEA

GUATEMALA

Guatemala

Tegucigalpa

San Salvador

EL SALVADOR

Managua

Nica

Barranquilla

COSTA
RICA

Golfo de los
Mosquitos

PANAMA

Gulf of
Penama

Cauca

Medellin

Magdalena

CENTROAMÉRICA

COSTA RICA

NICARAGUA

El Caribe

COSTA RICA

SELVA DE NUBES

SELVA TROPICAL

Puntarenas

★ San José

Puerto
Limón

Océano
Pacífico

Golfito

PANAMÁ

PANAMÁ

COSTA
RICA

El Caribe

GOLFO DE
LOS MOSQUITOS

Colón

Ciudad de
Panamá ★

Balboa

Volcán
Barú

David

PANAMÁ

GOLFO DE
PANAMÁ

Santiago

La
Palma

Península
de Azuero

ISLA DE
COIBA

ISLA DE
CÉBACO

COLOMBIA

Océano Pacífico

NICARAGUA, COSTA RICA & PANAMÁ

NICARAGUA

CAPITAL:	Managua
POBLACIÓN:	6.700.000
GOBIERNO:	república
PRESIDENTE:	José Daniel Ortega Saavedra
DINERO ($):	córdoba
PRODUCTOS:	algodón, café, fruta, petróleo, plátano
MÚSICA, BAILE:	bamba, rumba
SITIOS DE INTERÉS:	La Flor, las huellas de Acahualinc, El lago de Nicaragua
COMIDA TÍPICA:	baho, gallo pinto, nacatamales

NICARAGÜENSES FAMOSOS:

Violeta Barrios de Chamorro
(POLÍTICA)

Ernesto Cardenal
(POLÍTICO)

Rubén Darío
(POETA)

COSTA RICA

CAPITAL:	San José
POBLACIÓN:	5.100.000
GOBIERNO:	república democrática
PRESIDENTE:	Carlos Alvarado Quesada
DINERO ($):	colón costarricense
PRODUCTOS:	azúcar, bananas, café, melón, muebles, piña
MÚSICA, BAILE:	merengue, punto guanacasteco, salsa
SITIOS DE INTERÉS:	Monte Verde, Parques Nacionales Tortuguero y Corcovado, Volcán Arenal, Volcán Irazú
COMIDA TÍPICA:	casado, gallo pinto, gallos (filled tortillas), olla de carne, pan de yuca, sopa negra

COSTARRICENSES FAMOSOS:

Óscar Arias Sánchez
(POLÍTICO, GANADOR DE PREMIO NOBEL)

Franklin Chang
(ASTRONAUTA)

Editus
(CONJUNTO MUSICAL)

Claudia Poll
(ATLETA)

Silvia Poll
(ATLETA)

PANAMÁ

CAPITAL:	La Ciudad de Panamá
POBLACIÓN:	4.400.000
GOBIERNO:	democracia constitucional
PRESIDENTE:	Laurentino Cortizo
DINERO ($):	balboa, dólar americano
PRODUCTOS:	cacao, petróleo, piña, plátano
MÚSICA, BAILE:	afro-caribeña
SITIOS DE INTERÉS:	Archipiélago de San Blas, El canal de Panamá, Península Azuero, Volcán Barú
COMIDA TÍPICA:	arroz con coco, ceviche, chicha dulce, corvina, ropa vieja, sancocho de gallina, saos

PANAME—OS FAMOSOS:

Rubén Blades
(MÚSICO)

Roberto Durán
(BOXEADOR)

Mireya Moscoso
(POLÍTICA)

Mariano Rivera
(BEISBOLISTA)

Practice this vocabulary with our mobile app! Visit tobreak.com/app for more details.

VOCABULARIO
LECCIÓN NUEVE

THEME WORDS: "AT SCHOOL"

la	bandera	flag
el	calendario	calendar
la	campana	bell
el	escritorio	desk
el	examen	test
el	mapa	map
la	mochila	backpack
la	oficina	office
la	pizarra	blackboard
el/la	profesor/a	teacher
la	prueba	proof, quiz, test
el	pupitre	student desk
la	tiza	chalk
la	universidad	university

OTHER NOUNS

el	acondicionador de aire	air conditioner
el	beso	kiss
el	campeonato	championship
el	código postal	zip code
la	libra	pound
la	lotería	lottery
la	llegada	arrival
el	meteorólogo	meteorologist

la	tempestad	storm
la	tormenta	storm
el/la	vecino/a	neighbor

ADJECTIVES

barato/a	cheap
corto/a	short
demasiado/a	too much (pl., too many)
emocionado/a	excited
largo/a	long
próximo/a	next

VERBS

colgar (ue)	to hang (up)
enojarse	to become angry
graduarse	to graduate
mudarse	to move (relocate)
negar (ie)	to deny
probar (ue)	to taste, to try

MISCELLANEOUS

montar en bicicleta	to ride a bicycle
por fin	finally
por supuesto	of course
saber de memoria	to know by heart
tranquilamente	calmly

LECCIÓN NUEVE

KEY GRAMMAR CONCEPTS

A) CHOOSING BETWEEN THE PRETERITE AND IMPERFECT → *¿El pretérito o el imperfecto?*

B) CHOOSING BETWEEN "SABER" AND "CONOCER" → *"Saber" vs. "conocer"*

C) SPECIAL EXPRESSIONS WITH "HACER" → *Expresiones con "hacer"*

D) THE CONSTRUCTION WITH "ACABAR DE" — TALKING ABOUT WHAT YOU'VE JUST DONE → *"Acabar de"*

 A) CHOOSING BETWEEN THE PRETERITE AND IMPERFECT

The ability to **choose wisely between the preterite and imperfect** is a sign of a good Spanish speaker. Oftentimes, sentences can make perfect sense using either the preterite or imperfect; however, the meaning of each sentence may be quite different.

Let's first review the key concepts of each of these past tenses:

Preterite	Imperfect
◆ Single, complete event	◆ Incomplete, ongoing event
◆ The beginning or ending point of an action	◆ Description
	◆ Telling time in the past
◆ When you tell how long an action lasted	◆ Habitual actions

Let's take a look at a number of sentences that contain both a preterite and imperfect verb. Try to figure out why the speaker has chosen each tense.

 EXAMPLES: *Eran las once de la noche cuando mi hermano volvió a casa.*
It was eleven at night when my brother returned home.

Comíamos en el restaurante cuando Wilmer Valderrama entró.
We were eating in the restaurant when Wilmer Valderrama entered.

En el pasado, Ricky Martin siempre cantaba "Livin' la Vida Loca" *durante los conciertos, pero anoche no la cantó.*
In the past, Ricky Martin always used to sing *"Livin' la Vida Loca"* during his concerts, but last night he didn't sing it.

Aunque el atleta era muy fuerte, ayer sólo levantó doscientas libras.
Although the athlete was very strong, he only lifted two hundred pounds yesterday.

*Mientras **veía** el programa* República Deportiva *anoche, **descubrí** que Julián Gil **era** muy guapo.*

> While I was watching the program *República Deportiva* last night, I discovered that Julián Gil was very good-looking.

***Estuve** en San José sólo tres días porque **hacía** muchísimo calor allí.*

> I was in San José for only three days because it was so hot there.

*Mi perrito **estaba** tan cansado que por fin se **durmió** en el sofá.*

> My puppy was so tired that he finally fell asleep on the sofa.

*Mi hermana menor normalmente no **comía** hamburguesas, pero un día **tenía** muchísima hambre y las **probó**.*

> My little sister normally didn't eat hamburgers, but one day she was very hungry and she tried them.

*Los campistas **esperaban** en las montañas cuando **comenzó** a nevar.*

> The campers were waiting in the mountains when it began to snow.

In the above sentences, the contrast between the preterite and imperfect is striking. Did you notice the following?

◆ The descriptive use of the imperfect *(Mi perrito **estaba** cansado . . .; . . . el atleta **era** muy fuerte . . .)*

◆ The habitual use of the imperfect *(. . . normalmente no **comía** hamburguesas . . .; . . . siempre **cantaba** "Livin' la Vida Loca" . . .)*

◆ The use of the imperfect to tell time *(**Eran** las once de la noche . . .)*

◆ An incomplete event is "interrupted" by a preterite action *(**Comíamos** en el restaurante cuando Wilmer Valderrama **entró**; Mientras **veía** el programa* Cristina *anoche, **descubrí** que Fernando Colunga . . .)*

◆ When the speaker tells how long an event lasted, the preterite was used *(**Estuve** en San José sólo tres días . . .)*

◆ If there was no clear ending point, the imperfect was chosen *(Los campistas **esperaban** en las montañas . . .)*

As you work through the practice exercises on the next page, try to ask yourself what the speaker is intending.

¿ ◆ ❓ Is there a clear ending point of a completed action? If so, use the preterite. If not, you will likely choose the imperfect.

---

1. In the following paragraphs, choose between the preterite and imperfect. Try to pick the tense that you think best captures the feel of the narrative:

a. Cuando yo _____ (ser) joven, vivía en Chicago. Nuestra familia

_____ (tener) una casa bonita cerca de un parque. Un día

_____ (hacer) mucho calor. Mi mamá _____ (decir) que los

meteorólogos _____ en la televisión (anunciar) que

_____ (ir) a llover mucho esa noche. _____ (Ser) las siete

de la noche cuando _____ (comenzar) la tormenta. Mis hermanos

y yo _____ (tener) mucho miedo. _____

(Llover) fuertemente por doce horas. Por la mañana, por fin, _____

(salir) el sol. Mis hermanos y yo _____ (decir): "¡Bravo!".

b. Yo _____ (leer) una revista tranquilamente en casa anoche cuando

_____ (sonar) el teléfono. Lo _____ (contestar) y un

hombre _____ (decir): "¡Felicidades! Ud. _____ (ganar) la

lotería". No _____ (saber) qué hacer. _____ (Estar) muy

contenta y emocionada. _____ (Colgar) el receptor (*receiver*) y

_____ (comenzar) a buscar el boleto. _____

(Buscar) y _____ (buscar), pero no lo _____ (poder)

encontrar. ¿Dónde _____ (estar)? Unos momentos más tarde, mi perro,

Eugenio, _____ (entrar) en el cuarto. _____ (Tener) el

boleto en la boca. Lo _____ (tomar) y le _____ (dar)

un beso muy grande.

Spanish has two ways to say "to know": *"saber"* and *"conocer."*

1 *"Saber"* **is used when a person is speaking about a fact or giving information, something that usually could be articulated easily.**

For example, if you were to ask: "Do you know where I live?", you would use the verb *"saber,"* because the answer is a fact: *¿Sabes dónde vivo? –Sí, lo sé . . . Calle Mango 129.*

If a person says that he or she knows how to do something, (e.g., dance the cha-cha), that speaker will also use *"saber." (María sabe bailar el chachachá* — Mary knows how to dance the cha-cha. The steps of the cha-cha can be explained or diagrammed.

Note: You <u>don't</u> need the word *"como"* meaning "how."

2 *"Conocer"* **conveys the idea of being acquainted with a person or place.**

For example, if you want to say that Lola knows Lili, you say *"Lola conoce a Lili."* Remember, *"saber"* is used with facts; clearly a person is not a fact. A person cannot be easily articulated, explained or diagrammed!

If you wanted to ask someone if he or she knows the city of Lima well, you choose *"conocer." ¿Conoces Managua? –Sí, la conozco.* A city, of course, is not something that can be articulated.

If, however, you wanted to know the <u>name</u> of a city, you would ask: *¿Sabes la capital de Nicaragua? –Sí, lo sé; es Managua.*

The following sentences highlight the differences between *"saber"* and *"conocer."*

EXAMPLES: *¿**Sabe** Ud. si llueve ahora? –No, no lo **sé**.*
Do you know if it's raining now? –No, I don't know.

***Conozco** a muchas personas de Nicaragua.*
I know many people from Nicaragua.

*¿**Conoces** bien la Ciudad de Panamá?*
Do you know Panama City well?

***Sabemos** que no hay muchos restaurantes buenos por aquí.*
We know that there aren't many good restaurants around here.

*¿**Sabes** la hora? –Por supuesto, son las seis y media.*
Do you know what time it is? –Of course, it's six-thirty.

*Hoy en día es muy importante **conocer** bien a los vecinos.*
Nowadays it's very important to know one's neighbors well.

*Como no **sabes** bailar bien, prefiero no ir al baile contigo.*
Since you don't know how to dance well, I prefer not to go to the dance with you.

Sé de memoria todas las palabras del poema "Lola".
I know by heart all the words of the poem "*Lola.*"

¿Conoces a mi primo Charlie? Es alto, moreno y muy atlético.
Do you know my cousin, Charlie? He is tall, dark and very athletic.

¡CUIDADO! Pay attention to the special uses of *"saber"* **and** *"conocer"* **in the preterite and imperfect tenses.** When you decide that you want to use a past tense of *"saber"* and *"conocer,"* you should know that the translations in English are a little different.

	Preterite	Imperfect
saber	*supe* → I found out (a fact)	*sabía* → I knew, I used to know (a fact)
conocer	*conocí* → I met (a person)	*conocía* → I knew, I used to know (a person, a place)

Let's look at a few examples of these sentences:

EXAMPLES: *Anoche **conocí** a un hombre muy guapo . . . se llama Cristian.*
I met a very good-looking man . . . his name is Cristian.

*Cuando era joven, **conocía** a muchas personas que jugaban al baloncesto.*
When I was young, I knew (used to know) a lot of people who played basketball.

*Mi bisabuela **conoció** a una mujer que sobrevivió el hundimiento del Titanic.*
My great-grandmother met a woman who survived the sinking of the Titanic.

***Conocíamos** muchos restaurantes baratos en Heredia, Costa Rica.*
We used to know a lot of inexpensive restaurants in Heredia, Costa Rica.

*Anoche **supe** que mi novia tiene otro novio.*
Last night I found out that my girlfriend has another boyfriend.

*Todo el mundo **sabía** que la profesora era muy exigente.*
Everyone knew that the teacher was very hard.

*Cuando mis padres **supieron** que yo no tenía el coche, se enojaron muchísimo.*
When my parents found out that I didn't have the car, they got very mad.

*No **sabía** que Libertad Lamarque era una actriz tan famosa.*
I didn't know that Libertad Lamarque was such a famous actress.

PRACTICE EXERCISES

1. Write the correct form of the present tense of *"saber"* or *"conocer"* in the following sentences:

    a. Yo no _____ bien a la profesora de inglés en esta escuela.

    b. Nadie _____ si hay un buen restaurante cerca de la playa.

    c. ¿_____ (tú) dónde viven los nuevos vecinos?

    d. Nosotras _____ que es peligroso montar en bicicleta sin casco.

    e. Mi prima _____ bien la ciudad de Granada; hace mucho tiempo que vive allí.

    f. Eva Arguiñano y Ferrán Adrià _____ preparar muchos platos riquísimos.

    g. Yo _____ una tienda donde hay mochilas, banderas y campanas.

    h. Ellos _____ que no puedo ir a la fiesta esta tarde por el examen de mañana.

    i. ¿_____ Uds. la música nueva de Camila? –Sí, la _____, pero no nos gusta.

    j. Mis padres _____ que no me gusta volver a casa antes de la medianoche.

2. In this paragraph, you will once again decide between *"saber"* and *"conocer."* This paragraph, however, was written in the past, so you will also have to decide between the preterite and imperfect.

Mi primo Eduardo _____ a Albert Pujols un día en

Anaheim. Eduardo _____ que Albert iba a salir por la puerta

de atrás. También _____ personalmente a un policía que

trabajaba en Anaheim. Cuando yo _____ que Eduardo tenía el

autógrafo de Albert, estaba muy celoso. ¿Por qué no fui con él al partido?

C) SPECIAL EXPRESSIONS WITH "HACER"

You have seen the word *"hacer"* throughout this text. As you remember, it is commonly used to mean "to do" or "to make." You also know that *"hacer"* is used when talking about the weather. This section presents a number of expressions or constructions that use the word *"hacer."*

Here are a number of expressions or constructions that use the word *"hacer"*:

hacerse amigo de →	to become friends with
hacer caso a →	to pay attention to
hacer cola →	to stand in line
hacer frente a →	to face up to
hacer frío, calor, etc. →	to be cold, hot, etc. (outside)
hacer la maleta →	to pack one's suitcase
hacer las paces →	to make up (to make peace)
hacer una pregunta →	to ask a question

Let's look at these expressions used in sentences:

EXAMPLES: *Primero Eva Longoria y Tony Parker **se hicieron** muy buenos amigos y después se casaron en París. Por desgracia, ya no están casados.*
First Eva Longoria and Tony Parker became very good friends, and afterwards they got married in Paris. Unfortunately, they are no longer married.

*Nunca les **hago caso** a mis padres cuando me gritan.*
I never pay attention to my parents when they shout at me.

*Como no me gusta **hacer cola**, nunca voy a los estrenos de las películas nuevas.*

> Because I don't like to stand in line, I never go to the premieres of new movies.

*Tienes que **hacer frente** al hecho de que no tienes muchos amigos.*

> You have to face up to the fact that you don't have many friends.

*¿Te puedo **hacer una pregunta**? ¿Por qué **hace muchísimo frío** en Patagonia?*

> May I ask you a question? Why is it very cold in Patagonia?

*Marco **hace la maleta** porque va de viaje a Costa Rica.*

> Marco is packing his bag because he is going on a trip to Costa Rica.

*Cuando peleo con mis hermanas, siempre me gusta **hacer las paces** rápidamente.*

> When I fight with my sisters, I always like to make up quickly.

There is also a special construction using *"hacer"* that describes something that began in the past and continues into the present.

"Hace" + **X** + *que* + **Verb** = **I have been doing something for X.**

(period of time)   (in present tense)   (period of time)

✳ **EXAMPLES:** *Hace mucho tiempo que Gloria Estefan **vive** en Miami.*

> Gloria Estefan has been living in Miami for a long time.

*Hace dos años que **trabajo** en el restaurante.*

> I have been working in the restaurant for two years.

*¿Cuánto tiempo hace que **tienes** tu propio televisor? –**Hace seis años que lo tengo**.*

> How long have you had your own television set? –I've had it for six years.

*Hace dos horas que **leo** este libro nuevo de Julia Álvarez.*

> I have been reading this new book of Julia Álvarez for two hours.

PRACTICE EXERCISES

1. **Complete the following sentences by using the correct form of one of the following expressions using *"hacer"*** *(hacerse amigos, hacer caso a, hacer cola, hacer frente, hacer frío, calor, etc., hacer la maleta, hacer las paces, hacer una pregunta).* **Use each expression just once:**

   a. ¿Te puedo _____? ¿Dónde está San José?

   b. ¡Qué pena! Había demasiada gente que quería ver la producción de Broadway de Emilio y Gloria Estefan, *On Your Feet*. Como nunca me gusta _____, fui a ver otro musical.

   c. Cuando mi amiga _____, ¡siempre coge demasiada ropa!

   d. El profesor anunció: "En esta clase es esencial _____ todo lo que digo".

   e. Cuando era más joven, nunca me gustaba _____ con mi hermana; prefería estar enojada con ella todo el tiempo.

   f. Mi hijo y el niño del nuevo vecino _____ muy rápidamente; ahora juegan juntos a menudo.

   g. Necesito comprar un acondicionador de aire porque _____ en esta casa.

   h. Muchas personas no pueden _____ a sus problemas; necesitan negar la realidad.

2. **Now complete these sentences by conjugating the following infinitives in the present tense. Then translate the sentences into English:**

   a. Hace dos horas que yo _____ en este avión. (estar)

   _____

b. Hace muchas semanas que ellos _____ el programa *NCIS* en la tele. (ver)

_____

c. Hace un año que nosotros _____ en Nueva York. (vivir)

_____

d. Hace muchos años que los Cleveland Indians no _____ un campeonato de béisbol. (ganar)

_____

e. Hace muchos meses que mi tío no _____ trabajo. (tener)

_____

3. Finally, translate the following sentences into Spanish, using the new construction with *"hacer"*:

Example: I've been studying for ten minutes.
         Hace diez minutos que estudio. _____

a. I've been speaking Spanish for one year.

_____

b. Alejandro Fernández has been singing for many years.

_____

c. I have been studying the map for twenty minutes.

_____

d. We have been living in San José for fifteen months.

_____

e. I haven't seen you for a long time.

_____

D) THE CONSTRUCTION WITH "ACABAR DE"

Spanish has a very useful construction for describing events that just took place. For example, if you want to say "I just arrived," you say *"Acabo de llegar."* This construction makes use of the present tense of *"acabar,"* which means "to end," along with the preposition *"de"* and an infinitive.

Here is the formula for saying that something just happened:

> The present tense of *"acabar"* **+** *"de"* **+** Infinitive

Let's take a look at some more sentences with this handy construction:

EXAMPLES: *Javier Bardem y Penélope Cruz* **acaban de salir.**
Javier Bardem and Penélope Cruz just left.

Acabo de ver The Social Network, *la película sobre Facebook.*
I've just seen the Facebook movie, *The Social Network.*

Tú **acabas de mentir.**
You just lied.

Acabamos de oír *que va a llover mañana.*
We just heard that it is going to rain tomorrow.

Mi amiga **acaba de comprar** *entradas para el próximo concierto de Tiësto.*
My friend just bought tickets for the next Tiësto concert.

Acabo de contestar *el teléfono. Era mi abogada.*
I just answered the phone. It was my lawyer.

PRACTICE EXERCISES

1. Write the appropriate form of *"acabar"* **in the following sentences:**

a. Tú _____ de escribir tu código postal.

b. Nosotras _____ de ver una película muy aburrida.

c. Alguien _____ de entrar por la puerta de atrás.

d. Mis padres _____ de escribir una carta muy bonita.

e. Muchos de mis amigos _____ de graduarse de la universidad.

2. Now translate the following sentences into Spanish:

a. I just bought a new desk.

_____

b. They just woke up.

_____

c. My friend just asked me a question.

_____

d. He just tasted the rice with coconut.

_____

e. We just discovered that our crazy neighbor wants to sell her house.

_____

ORAL PRACTICE
PREGUNTAS EN GRUPOS DE DOS

These two sets of questions use grammatical structures and vocabulary from this lesson. Working with a partner, alternate asking and answering each question. When you get to the bottom of each list, start over at the top, switching roles. As a variation, write out the answers in complete sentences.

A) ¿En cuántos años vas a graduarte de la universidad?

Cuando eras niño/niña, ¿te enojabas frecuentemente?

¿Montabas mucho en bicicleta durante los veranos?

¿Cuál es tu código postal?

¿Tienes una mochila para tus libros?

¿Escribes con tiza en la pizarra?

¿Bailabas frecuentemente con tus amigos cuando eras más joven?

B) ¿Conoces bien la ciudad de Lima?

¿Sabes dónde podemos comprar boletos de lotería?

¿Conoces personalmente a los padres de nuestro/a profesor/a de español?

¿Sabes de memoria todas las capitales de los países de Centroamérica?

¿Acabas de comer antes de llegar a clase?

¿Con quién acabas de hablar?

¿Cuánto tiempo hace que vives en tu casa?

DIALOGUE

The following dialogue contains grammar and vocabulary that you've seen in this lesson and in the introductory section. After listening to the dialogue, read it aloud, alone or with friends. Afterwards, try to answer the questions that follow either aloud or in written form.

LAS AVENTURAS DE RAFAEL, ELISA Y "EL TIGRE"

ESCENA CINCO

Son las nueve de la noche. Rafael, "El Tigre", Elisa, Javier y Marisela caminan por la Tercera Avenida en Nueva York. Deciden tomar un café en una cafetería llamada "E.J.'s".

Rafael:	¡Qué día más increíble!
Elisa:	Rafael tiene razón. Los cuadros que vimos de Kahlo en el museo eran impresionantes.
Javier:	A mí me gustaron más los murales de Rivera.
El Tigre:	Para decirles la verdad, el chocolate caliente en "Serendipity" fue lo que a mí más me gustó.
Rafael:	Siempre piensas en la comida. Pues, la película de Spike Lee en Central Park fue fantástica, también. No sabía cuánto trabajo es necesario para filmar sólo unos minutos de acción.
Elisa:	¿Reconocieron Uds. a algunos actores conocidos?
Javier:	Yo, sí. Creo que vi a Javier Bardem; oí que tiene un papel (role) importante en la película. Me gusta mucho Javier porque su nombre es tan distinguido.

Una camarera llega a la mesa.

Camarera:	Buenas noches. ¿Les gustaría tomar algo?
Marisela:	Un café con leche, por favor.
Elisa:	Para mí, una Coca-Cola.
Javier:	Un café solo.
Rafael:	Y yo, una Coca-Cola, también.
El Tigre:	Para mí, una Coca-Cola y un pedazo de torta de chocolate, con cinco tenedores, por favor.

Los chicos se ríen. En este momento un hombre con bigote y una mujer vestida de blanco llegan y se sientan en una mesa al fondo de la cafetería. Los chicos no los ven, pero el hombre y la mujer los miran cuidadosamente.

Javier:	¡Qué pena que Uds. tengan que (What a shame that you all have . . .) irse mañana!

Marisela:	Es verdad. Todavía hay tanto que hacer.
Rafael:	Uds. son tan generosos. Pero tenemos la idea loca de ir también a Chicago. Creo que podemos llegar allí en veinticuatro horas por tren. Vamos a pasar un día allá y volver a Washington para este fin de semana.

La camarera vuelve a la mesa con las bebidas y la torta de chocolate.

Elisa:	Es una idea loca. Uds. nunca me dijeron que pensaban hacer eso.
El Tigre:	Pues, ¿no te encantan las sorpresas?
Elisa:	Pues, sí, pero pensaba que íbamos a pasar tres o cuatro días aquí.
Rafael:	Pero, tenemos que ver el mundo. ¡Somos jóvenes!

Javier y Marisela se susurran algo al oído.

Javier:	Y tengo una sorpresa para Uds. ¡Marisela y yo vamos con Uds. a Chicago!
Elisa:	Fantástico. Pero, ¿y tus padres? ¿No vuelven esta noche?
Javier:	Decidieron quedarse unos días más en Dallas. Marisela les dijo que íbamos a pasar unos días en su apartamento en Greenwich Village.
Rafael:	Es una idea fenomenal. Todos vamos juntos a Chicago. Pero vamos al apartamento ahora. Tenemos que acostarnos temprano. El tren sale a las seis de la mañana.
El Tigre:	Un momentico. Tengo que comer más torta.

Todos se ríen. Elisa, "El Tigre", Rafael, Javier y Marisela se levantan, pagan la cuenta y salen de la cafetería. El hombre del bigote y la mujer vestida de blanco los siguen a la calle.

1) ¿Dónde están los jóvenes cuando la escena comienza?

   _____

2) ¿Qué parte del día les gustó más a Elisa y a Rafael?

   _____

3) ¿Cuál fue la mejor parte del día según El Tigre?

   _____

4) ¿A qué actor famoso vio Javier?

   _____

5) ¿Qué bebidas pidieron los jóvenes en la cafetería?

   _____

6) ¿Quiénes entran ahora al restaurante?

   _____

7) ¿Qué ciudad famosa piensan visitar los chicos?

   _____

8) ¿Quiénes van también?

   _____

9) ¿A qué hora sale el tren por la mañana?

   _____

10) ¿Quiénes siguen a los jóvenes a la calle?

   _____

1. Answer in complete sentences:

    a. ¿Ibas frecuentemente a la playa cuando eras joven?

    _____

    b. ¿Conoces a mis mejores amigos?

    _____

    c. ¿En dónde tienes que hacer cola muchas veces?

    _____

    d. ¿Siempre les haces caso a todos tus profesores?

    _____

    e. ¿Qué lección de este libro acabas de estudiar?

    _____

2. Conjugate each verb fully first in the preterite AND then in the imperfect tense:

    cerrar (to close)   **vender** (to sell)   **ir** (to go)

_____ _____ _____ _____ _____ _____

_____ _____ _____ _____ _____ _____

_____ _____ _____ _____ _____ _____

_____ _____ _____ _____ _____ _____

_____ _____ _____ _____ _____ _____

_____ _____ _____ _____ _____ _____

3. **In the following paragraph, conjugate each verb into the proper form of either the preterite or imperfect tense:**

Cuando mis abuelos _____ (ser) jóvenes, _____

(vivir) en Managua, Nicaragua. En 1943, ellos _____ (casarse)

y _____ (mudarse) a Nueva York. La vida en Nueva York no

_____ (ser) fácil, pero mi abuelo _____

(conseguir) un buen trabajo en una fábrica de Long Island. Mi abuela

_____ (aprender) a hablar inglés primero, pero mi abuelo

_____ (tardar) muchos años en dominar la lengua. Cuando mi

padre _____ (nacer) en 1951, mis abuelos _____

(estar) muy orgullosos. Mi padre _____ (graduarse) de la

Universidad de Nueva York en 1972 y ahora es profesor de español.

4. **Fill in the following sentences with the correct form of the verb *"saber"* or *"conocer"*:**

   a. Estoy muy emocionado porque acabo de _____ a Juan Soler.

   b. Mi abuela _____ el secreto íntimo de la vecina.

   c. Nosotros no _____ a qué hora nos va a decir el pronóstico del tiempo el meteorólogo.

   d. Mi tía _____ muy bien el pueblo de León.

   e. ¿_____ Ud. cuánto cuesta una libra de tomates?

   f. Yo _____ personalmente a Emilio Estévez y a su padre Martin Sheen.

5. Match the following *"hacer"* expressions with their English equivalent:

a) *hacer cola*   **1)** to face up to

b) *hacer una pregunta*   **2)** to make up

c) *hacer la maleta*   **3)** to pack

d) *hacerse amigos*   **4)** to ask a question

e) *hacer las paces*   **5)** to stand in line

f) *hacer frente a*   **6)** to become friends

6. Translate the following sentences into Spanish:

a. My friend just met the Mexican actor Gael García Bernal.

_____

_____

b. I just bought an air conditioner because it's hot in our house.

_____

_____

c. Our uncle has been living in Panama City for two years. (Use an *"hacer"* expression.)

_____

_____

d. He packed his luggage, stood in line, and finally left on the airplane.

_____

_____

7. The following newspaper account contains five errors. Underline each error and write the correction above it:

Julio Iglesias acabba de grabar otro disco nuevo

El famoso cantante español presentó hoy en una reunión

en Madrid su nuevo álbum, titulado "Romantic Classics".

Canta música muy romántica, ideal para hacer las pazes

con un viejo amigo o hacerse amigo de alguien nuevo.

Todos conocen que Julio tiene talento, pero pocos lo

saben personalmente. Sólo sus hijos, Enrique y Julio, Jr.,

lo conocen bien. En la reunión de ayer, Julio dijio que

este álbum es el mejor de su carrera. ¡Adelante, Julio!

Te queremos.

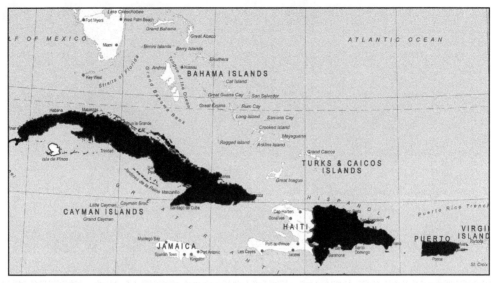

Breaking the Spanish Barrier Level 1 (Beginner)

CUBA, REPÚBLICA DOMINICANA & PUERTO RICO

CUBA

CAPITAL:	La Habana
POBLACIÓN:	11.200.000
GOBIERNO:	república socialista
PRESIDENTE:	Miguel Díaz-Canel
DINERO ($):	peso cubano
PRODUCTOS:	azúcar, minerales, tabaco
MÚSICA, BAILE:	habanera, jazz, mambo, rumba, son
SITIOS DE INTERÉS:	Castillo del Morro
COMIDA TÍPICA:	congris, fruta, moros y cristianos, plátanos

REPÚBLICA DOMINICANA

CAPITAL:	Santo Domingo
POBLACIÓN:	10.900.000
GOBIERNO:	república democrática
PRESIDENTE:	Luis Abinader
DINERO ($):	peso dominicano
PRODUCTOS:	azúcar, cacao, carne, fruta, minerales, tabaco
MÚSICA, BAILE:	bachata, marimba, merengue
SITIOS DE INTERÉS:	Lago Enriquillo, Pico Duarte
COMIDA TÍPICA:	chivo asado, comida criolla, mondongo, sancocho

PUERTO RICO

CAPITAL:	San Juan
POBLACIÓN:	2.800.000
GOBIERNO:	estado libre asociado (commonwealth)
GOBERNADOR:	Pedro Pierluisi
DINERO ($):	dólar americano
PRODUCTOS:	agricultura, azúcar, café, piña, ron, tabaco
MÚSICA, BAILE:	bomba, salsa
SITIOS DE INTERÉS:	Isla Mona, Ponce, El Yunque
COMIDA TÍPICA:	arroz con habichuelas, asopao, empanadillas, mofongo, pollo frito con tostones

CUBANOS FAMOSOS:

José Capablanca
(AJEDRECISTA)

Fidel Castro
(DICTADOR)

Celia Cruz
(CANTANTE)

Gloria Estefan
(CANTANTE)

José Martí
(POETA)

DOMINICANOS FAMOSOS:

Julia Álvarez
(ESCRITORA)

Francisco Casanova
(CANTANTE)

Alex Rodríguez
(BEISBOLISTA)

Óscar de la Renta
(DISEÑADOR)

PUERTORRIQUEÑOS FAMOSOS:

Roberto Clemente
(BEISBOLISTA)

José Feliciano
(MÚSICO)

José Ferrer
(ACTOR)

Ricky Martin
(CANTANTE)

Concha Meléndez
(ESCRITORA)

Rita Moreno
(ACTRIZ)

Chichi Rodríguez
(GOLFISTA)

Practice this vocabulary with our mobile app! Visit tobreak.com/app for more details.

VOCABULARIO
LECCIÓN DIEZ

THEME WORDS: "OUTDOORS"

el *árbol*	tree
el *arbusto*	bush
el *césped*	lawn
el *cielo*	sky
la *estrella*	star
la *flor*	flower
la *hierba*	grass
el *jardín*	garden
la *luna*	moon
la *pala*	shovel
la *piscina*	swimming pool
la *puesta de(l) sol*	sunset
la *rosa*	rose
la *salida del sol*	sunrise
la *tierra*	soil, earth
el *tulipán*	tulip

OTHER NOUNS

la *fila*	row
la *luna de miel*	honeymoon
el *resultado*	result
el *vídeo (Sp.)*/el *video*	video

ADJECTIVES

humilde	humble
pelirrojo/a	red-headed

VERBS

bañarse	to take a bath
caer	to fall
casarse con	to get married to
charlar	to chat
compartir	to share
conducir/ manejar	to drive
ducharse	to shower
equivocarse	to make a mistake
felicitar	to congratulate
freír (i)	to fry
nadar	to swim

MISCELLANEOUS

este	east
norte	north
oeste	west
sur	south
ya	already
ya no	no longer, anymore

LECCIÓN DIEZ

KEY GRAMMAR CONCEPTS

A) THE PROGRESSIVE TENSE → *El progresivo*

B) REFLEXIVE AND RECIPROCAL CONSTRUCTIONS → *Las construcciones reflexivas y las construcciones recíprocas*

C) EQUAL AND UNEQUAL COMPARISONS → *Las comparaciones iguales y desiguales*

 ## A) THE PROGRESSIVE TENSE

The **progressive** is a verb tense that gives extra emphasis to an act that is actually <u>in progress</u> — an event that is occurring at the exact moment that a speaker is describing. It can describe an event in the present or an event from the past.

EXAMPLES: *El teléfono está sonando ahora, pero yo estoy cortando el césped.*
The phone is ringing right now, but I am cutting the lawn.

Mi novio estaba durmiendo cuando llegué a su casa.
My boyfriend was sleeping when I arrived at his house.

HOW IS THE PROGRESSIVE TENSE FORMED?

This tense is normally constructed by combining a form of the verb *"estar"* (usually the present or the imperfect) with a present participle. The present participle is equivalent to the *"–ing"* form of a verb in English.

The present participle in Spanish is formed as follows:

> **-AR verbs: Remove the *"ar"* from the infinitive and add *"ando."***

EXAMPLES:

bailar	→ *bailando*	(dancing)
hablar	→ *hablando*	(speaking)
trabajar	→ *trabajando*	(working)

✳ **EXAMPLES:**

comer	→	comiendo	(eating)
romper	→	rompiendo	(breaking)
vender	→	vendiendo	(selling)

✳ **EXAMPLES:**

abrir	→	abriendo	(opening)
escribir	→	escribiendo	(writing)
vivir	→	viviendo	(living)

IRREGULAR FORMS

-IR "boot" verbs have a special vowel change, the same vowel change that occurs in the 3rd person of the preterite:

dormir	→	d**u**rmiendo
pedir	→	p**i**diendo
repetir	→	rep**i**tiendo
sentir	→	s**i**ntiendo

Note: *"decir"* → d**i**ciendo

You will need to memorize these other common irregular forms:

caer	→	cayendo
ir	→	yendo
leer	→	leyendo
traer	→	trayendo

Here is the formula for the progressive tense:

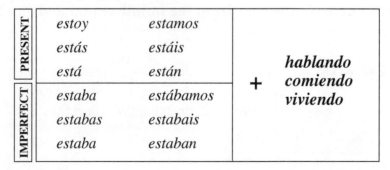

PRESENT	estoy	estamos	
	estás	estáis	
	está	están	**+** *hablando*
IMPERFECT	estaba	estábamos	*comiendo*
	estabas	estabais	*viviendo*
	estaba	estaban	

Here are some more examples of sentences using the progressive tense:

✳ **EXAMPLES:** *¡Qué mala suerte!* **Está lloviendo** *y no podemos ver la Luna.*
       What bad luck! It's raining and we can't see the Moon.

 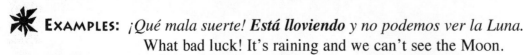

*Arturo Sandoval **estaba tocando** la trompeta anoche en Boston durante las celebraciones del 4 de julio cuando comenzaron los fuegos artificiales.*
Arturo Sandoval was playing the trumpet last night in Boston during the Fourth of July celebrations when the fireworks began.

*Un momento . . . **estoy pensando** . . . no sé qué voy a hacer.*
One moment . . . I am thinking . . . I don't know what I'm going to do.

*María **estaba charlando** con su mamá cuando el cartero llegó.*
María was chatting with her mom when the mailman arrived.

***Estamos esperando** la llegada del próximo autobús.*
We're waiting for the arrival of the next bus.

Helpful Tip: The progressive is a combination of verb forms. The present participle does not have a feminine or plural form . . . i.e., it will always be *"hablando,"* for example, and never *hablanda or *hablandos!

If you ever have an object pronoun associated with the progressive tense, you have the option of putting this pronoun before the form of *"estar,"* or attaching it to the end of the present participle. If you attach the pronoun, be certain to add an accent mark.

EXAMPLES: *¿La música de Luis Fonsi? **La** estoy escuchando (Estoy **escuchándola**).*
The music of Luis Fonsi? I'm listening to it.

*¿Los tulipanes? **Los** estamos cortando (Estamos **cortándolos**).*
The tulips? We're cutting them.

PRACTICE EXERCISES

1. Change these verbs into the corresponding form of the progressive:

Examples: comes → __estás comiendo__   vivían → __estaban viviendo__

a. bebe   → _____

b. estudian → _____

c. vivo   → _____

d. leíamos → _____

e. duermes → _____

f. caminan → _____

g. vendía   → _____

h. sirvo   → _____

i. escribían → _____

j. aprendes → _____

2. Complete the following sentences by writing the correct form of the progressive tense. Be careful when deciding whether to use the present progressive *(estoy hablando)* **or the imperfect progressive** *(estaba hablando)***:**

a. Mi amiga _____ ahora y no puede ir al Museo del Prado conmigo. (estudiar)

b. Anoche la policía _____ cuando el ladrón entró en el jardín. (esperar)

c. Mucha gente _____ durante la película; por eso no podía oír nada. (hablar)

d. Sé que tú _____ una carta ahorita, pero ¿no puedes hablar un minuto conmigo? (escribir)

e. ¡Caramba! _____ mucho y no podemos ver los árboles. (Nevar)

f. ¿El desayuno? Loretta Sánchez lo _____ cuando su hermana Silvia la llamó por teléfono. (comer)

g. Nosotras _____ las noticias cuando el hombre misterioso llamó a la puerta. (leer)

h. Ella no desea ir contigo a la piscina porque _____ en este momento. (dormir)

i. Muchas personas _____ anoche en Puerto Rico los resultados de la pelea de Edgar Berlanga. (celebrar)

j. En este momento creo que nuestros amigos _____ del avión. (salir)

k. ¿En qué dirección _____ (nosotros) ahora: este, oeste, norte o sur? –Pues, no lo sé. (viajar)

B) REFLEXIVE AND RECIPROCAL CONSTRUCTIONS

1) REFLEXIVE CONSTRUCTIONS

In *Lección Siete*, we had the chance to look at sentences that use a reflexive construction.

 EXAMPLES: *Cada noche **me lavo** las manos antes de comer.*
   Each night I wash my hands before eating.

   *Mi hermano siempre **se mira** en el espejo cuando está en el baño.*
   My brother always looks at himself in the mirror when he is in the bathroom.

In these sentences, the verb and the object pronoun refer to the same person. Reflexive sentences make use of one of these pronouns:

me	nos
te	os
se	se

 EXAMPLES: ***Me hablo a mí misma** cuando estoy nerviosa.*
   I talk to myself when I am nervous.

   *Siempre **te dices a ti mismo** que lo sabes todo.*
   You always tell yourself that you know everything.

   *¿No recuerdan Uds. que **nos compramos** boletos para el concierto de Shakira?*
   Don't you all remember that we bought ourselves tickets for the Shakira concert?

Helpful Tip: Do you remember that for extra emphasis or clarity, you can add the following words after the verb: *a mí (mismo/a), a ti (mismo/a), a sí (mismo/a), a nosotros (mismos), a nosotras (mismas), a vosotros (mismos), a vosotras (mismas), a sí (mismos/as)*?

---

2) RECIPROCAL CONSTRUCTIONS

What happens, however, when you want to say that you do something for each other rather than for yourselves? How would I say "They write each other" rather than "They write themselves"?

Spanish speakers make use of the following three pronouns for reciprocal action:

nos
os
se

You will notice that these object pronouns are the same ones used with plural verbs (we, you all, they). In order to have a reciprocal action, you need more than one person!

WHAT EXACTLY IS A RECIPROCAL ACTION?

Reciprocal action conveys a sense of "back and forth": I do something to you that you do to me, he does something to her that she does to him, one group of people does something to another group that the other group does to the first group, etc.

EXAMPLES: *Raúl Castro y yo* **nos hablamos** *por teléfono anoche.*
   Raúl Castro and I spoke to each other last night by phone.

   Marco y Ana siempre **se besan** *antes de despedirse.*
   Marco and Ana always kiss each other before saying goodbye.

   Vosotros **os insultáis** *frecuentemente. ¡No me gusta!*
   You all insult each other frequently. I don't like that!

Although the translations above indicate that the sentences are reciprocal in nature, they theoretically could be interpreted as being reflexive (Raúl and I talk to ourselves . . . Marco and Ana kiss themselves . . . You all insult yourselves). Although the context of the sentence would probably give the listener the clue, how do we make a reciprocal sentence unambiguous?

For emphasis, or to distinguish a reciprocal sentence from a reflexive one, a Spanish speaker will simply add one of the following: *(el) uno a (al) otro, (la) una a (la) otra, (los) unos a (los) otros, (las) unas a (las) otras.*

EXAMPLES: *Mis amigos siempre* **se hablan** *(el) uno a (al) otro cuando tienen problemas.*
   My friends always talk to each other when they have problems.

   Serena Williams y Maria Sharapova **se felicitaron** *(la) una a (la) otra después de su emocionante partido.*
   Serena Williams and Maria Sharapova congratulated each other after their exciting match.

   Nosotros **nos prometimos** *(los) unos a (los) otros que nunca íbamos a pelear otra vez.*
   All of us promised each other that we weren't going to fight again.

   Vosotras **os escribisteis** *(la) una a (la) otra dos veces el verano pasado.*
   You all wrote each other twice last summer.

¡CUIDADO! It is not possible to "mix" genders: *"una a otro" is incorrect. In a group of men and women, you must use the *"o"* ending: *"uno a otro"* or *"unos a otros."*

PRACTICE EXERCISES

1. **Insert one of the following words to complete the following REFLEXIVE sentences** (*me, te, se, nos, os, se, mí, ti, sí, nosotros/as, vosotros/as, mismo, misma, mismos, mismas*)**:**

   a. _____ llamo Sergio García, no Andy García.

   b. Antes de comer _____ lavamos las manos y la cara.

   c. Soy artista y siempre me digo a _____ que debo pintar estrellas, el cielo y puestas de sol bonitas.

   d. Cuando entras en la clase, normalmente _____ sientas en la primera fila, ¿verdad?

   e. David Bisbal y Chenoa se miraron a _____ en el televisor que está al lado del podio.

   f. Uds. nunca _____ afeitan por la mañana. ¿Por qué?

2. **Now insert one of the following to complete the following RECIPROCAL sentences** (*nos, os, se, uno a otro, una a otra, unos a otros, unas a otras*)**:**

   a. Ramón Castro y Raúl Castro _____ saludaron esta mañana en una calle de la Habana.

   b. Mi novia y yo _____ besamos por última vez cuando me fui de viaje la semana pasada.

   c. Pedro Almodóvar y Penélope Cruz se hablaban mucho _____ cuando hacían la película *Los abrazos rotos*.

   d. Las chicas en ese equipo nunca _____ ayudan unas a otras; por eso pierden frecuentemente.

   e. Mis tías se dicen _____ que no hay mal que por bien no venga. ("Every cloud has a silver lining.")

3. Translate the following three sentences into Spanish. Use emphasis in "c":

    a. We call ourselves cooks, but we don't know how to do anything in the kitchen.

    _____

    b. They promised to see each other in the summer.

    _____

    c. I sat myself down in the chair, and you and I told each other the secrets.

    _____

C) EQUAL AND UNEQUAL COMPARISONS

Often a person wants to compare one thing to another. There are two basic types of comparative sentences: those that express equality, and those that express inequality.

1) EQUAL COMPARISONS

It is common to compare nouns, adjectives, adverbs, and verbs. When you want to say that you have as many as, or that someone is as tall as, or that someone runs as quickly as, or dances as much as someone else, you will need a construction of equality. In Spanish, these sentences of equal comparison are constructed as follows:

a) Nouns

When comparing nouns, use the adjectives _"tanto," "tanta," "tantos,"_ or _"tantas"_ (meaning "as much" or "as many") <u>before</u> a noun and use the word _"como"_ (meaning "as") <u>after</u> the noun.

> _tanto/tanta/tantos/tantas_ **+ Noun +** _como_
> (as many, as much)   (as)

    EXAMPLES: _Compré **tantas flores como** tú._
                   I bought as many flowers as you.

                  María tiene **tanta paciencia como** su madre.
                   María has as much patience as her mother.

                  Julio Iglesias, Jr. no **tiene tanto talento como** su papá.
                   Julio Iglesias, Jr. doesn't have as much talent as his dad.

b) Adjectives/adverbs

When comparing adjectives or adverbs, use the adverb *"tan"* (meaning "as") <u>before</u> the adjective or adverb and the word *"como"* (meaning "as") <u>after</u> the adjective or adverb.

> *tan* + **Adjective/Adverb** + *como*
> (as)   (as)

EXAMPLES: *Serena juega **tan bien como** su hermana Venus.*
Serena plays as well as her sister Venus.

*Jamie lee **tan rápidamente como** sus amigos.*
Jamie reads as quickly as his friends.

La película Iron Man 3 *no es **tan buena como*** Man of Steel.
The movie *Iron Man 3* is not as good as *Man of Steel*.

c) Verbs

When comparing verbs, the expression *"tanto como"* (meaning "as much as") follows the verb. Notice that in both languages, the second verb in the comparison is understood but not usually expressed.

> **Verb** + *tanto como*
> (as much as)

EXAMPLES: *Paula no baila **tanto como** Jennifer (baila).*
Paula doesn't dance as much as Jennifer.

*Leemos **tanto como** nuestros padres.*
We read as much as our parents.

*No estudié **tanto como** mi amiga.*
I didn't study as much as my friend.

2) UNEQUAL COMPARISONS

The following chart offers the construction for all sentences that express an unequal comparison:

Subject	+	Verb	+	*más*/*menos*	+	Noun	+	*que*	+	Noun
				(more/less)		**Adjective**		(than)		**Pronoun**
						Adverb				

a) Nouns

When comparing nouns, the words *"más"* and *"menos"* (meaning "more" and "less") precede a noun, and the word *"que"* (meaning "than") follows it.

 EXAMPLES: *Yo tengo **más amigas que** mi hermana.*
I have more friends than my sister.

*Los gatos comen **menos carne que** los perros.*
Cats eat less meat than dogs.

*Condujimos el coche **más millas que** tú.*
We drove the car more miles than you.

b) Adjectives/adverbs

When comparing adjectives or adverbs, the words *"más"* and *"menos"* (meaning "more" and "less") precede an adjective or adverb, and the word *"que"* (meaning "than") follows it.

 EXAMPLES: *Yo corro **más despacio que** mi hermano*
I run more slowly than my brother.

*Lola es **más alta que** Mario.*
Lola is taller than Mario.

*A veces me siento **menos inteligente que** mis amigos.*
At times I feel less intelligent than my friends.

*Los soldados lucharon **más intensamente que** sus enemigos.*
The soldiers fought more intensely than their enemies.

c) Verbs

When comparing verbs, the expression *"más que"* (meaning "more than") or the expression *"menos que"* (meaning "less than") is used.

 EXAMPLES: *Yo me equivoco **más que** Ud.*
I make more errors than you.

*Yo **grito menos que** ellos.*
I shout less than they do.

¡CUIDADO! Some comparatives have special forms:

◆ The comparative form of *bueno* is *mejor,* not *más bueno.

◆ The comparative form of *malo* is *peor,* not *más malo.

PRACTICE EXERCISES

1. **Choose the word or words that you feel best complete the following sentences that offer comparisons. You should choose one of the following** *(tanto, tanta, tantos, tantas, tanto como, tan, como, más, menos, más que, menos que, que)***:**

   a. Tengo _____ discos compactos como tú.

   b. Estudié _____ Ana, pero saqué una nota más baja

   _____ ella.

   c. Hay _____ días en diciembre _____ en enero.

   d. Hay _____ días en febrero _____ en marzo.

   e. Cristina Saralegui es _____ famosa como Oprah Winfrey.

   f. No podemos trabajar _____ Uds.

   g. Alex Morgan es más atlética _____ yo.

   h. Breezy Johnson esquía _____ rápido como los otros miembros del equipo nacional de esquí.

   i. Yo tengo diez libros y mi amigo tiene ocho. Yo tengo _____

   libros _____ mi amigo.

   j. Todos dicen que Brad Pitt es _____ guapo que Antonio

   Banderas, pero yo creo que Antonio es más guapo _____ Brad.

2. Now translate these sentences into Spanish:

a. We work as much as our parents.

_____

b. There are more chairs than tables here.

_____

c. Do you have as much talent as Breanna Stewart?

_____

3. The following paragraph contains five errors. Underline each error and write the correction above it:

Mi amigo Will se casó ayer con Diana. Todos lloraron durante la misa; Will lloró tan como Diana. Will tiene treinta y ocho años y Diana tiene treinta y uno. Will es profesor y Diana es médica. Los dos trabajan mucho. Will trabaja tanta como Diana. Will y Diana tienen muchísimos amigos . . . Will tiene tan amigos como Diana. Después de la luna de miel, van a vivir cerca de Boston. Boston no es tanto vieja como muchas otras ciudades en Europa, pero es mucho más buena.

ORAL PRACTICE
PREGUNTAS EN GRUPOS DE DOS

These two sets of questions use grammatical structures and vocabulary from this lesson. Working with a partner, alternate asking and answering each question. When you get to the bottom of each list, start over at the top, switching roles. As a variation, write out the answers in complete sentences.

A) ¿Estás hablando en inglés o en español?

¿Estás llorando ahora?

¿Quién estaba charlando cuando entraste en la clase hoy?

¿Adónde vas para tu luna de miel?

¿Te gustan las personas humildes?

¿Cómo se llama una actriz pelirroja famosa?

¿Te equivocas frecuentemente?

B) ¿Te cantas a ti mismo/a cuando te bañas?

¿Se hablan tus padres uno a otro mucho?

¿Se felicitan los republicanos y los demócratas frecuentemente?

¿Compras tantos regalos como tus amigos?

¿Lees tan rápidamente como tus amigos?

¿Ves más películas que tus padres?

¿Hablas español más despacio que tus amigos?

1. Answer in complete sentences:

a. ¿Estás escribiendo con lápiz o con pluma ahora?

_____

b. ¿Estabas viendo la televisión a las nueve?

_____

c. ¿Se escriben tus amigos unos a otros en el verano?

_____

d. ¿Te hablas a ti mismo/misma cuando te bañas?

_____

e. ¿Viste más películas que tus padres este año?

_____

2. Change these verbs into the corresponding form of the progressive:

a. vuelves → _____   **d.** tenía   → _____

b. dormís → _____   **e.** comemos→ _____

c. preparan→ _____   **f.** piden   → _____

3. **Complete the following sentences by writing the correct form of the progressive tense:**

a. Mi madre _____ con una amiga cuando llegué a casa. (charlar)

b. Ahora yo _____ porque mi luna de miel fue un desastre. (llorar)

c. Ramón no está en casa ahorita porque _____ un examen en la escuela. (hacer)

d. Nosotros _____ las instrucciones porque nadie nos escuchó la primera vez. (repetir)

e. Tú no _____ tu parte en el incidente; voy a llamar a la policía. (admitir)

f. Acabo de volver de la tienda. Hoy ellos _____ televisores por un precio increíble: ¡200 dólares! (vender)

4. **Insert one of the words or expressions that you learned this lesson to give emphasis to the following reflexive and reciprocal sentences:**

a. Mi amiga y yo nos hablamos _____ por teléfono todas las noches.

b. José se miró _____ en el espejo grande del baño.

c. Mis vecinos nunca se invitan _____ a ningún evento.

d. Nosotros tenemos que admitirnos a _____ que nuestro equipo va a perder todos los partidos este año.

e. Cuando Raúl está en Santo Domingo y Olivia está en Tokio, se escriben

_____ frecuentemente.

f. Por no haber muchos asistentes de vuelo en el avión, mis padres tuvieron

que sentarse _____.

5. Choose the word or words that you feel best complete the following sentences that express comparison *(tanto, tanta, tantos, tantas, tanto como, tan, como, más, menos, que, más que, menos que):*

a. Yo tengo tres discos y tú tienes dos. Yo tengo _____ discos _____ tú.

b. Nosotros nunca podemos correr _____ tú.

c. Hay _____ días en diciembre _____ en enero.

d. Mi madre es _____ alta que yo.

e. Ellos juegan _____ intensamente como nosotros.

f. Martina Navratilova no tenía _____ paciencia como Chris Evert Lloyd.

g. Hay _____ personas en California que en Rhode Island.

h. No te creo. Tú no comiste tantas pizzas _____ yo.

i. Trevor Bauer gana _____ dinero que otros jugadores de béisbol.

6. Translate the following sentences into Spanish:

a. I am showering now; I can't talk with you.

_____

b. The girls are taller than the boys.

_____

c. The actors congratulated themselves after the movie.

_____

d. I already bought the television set . . . it cost more than the telephone.

_____

7. The following police report contains six errors. Underline each error and write the correction above it:

Anoche yo estaba conducido el coche cuando vi a un hombre pelirrojo con un televisor en las manos. El televisor era más grande como un elefante. El hombre era tan bajo que un tostador. La situación era un poco cómico. Le dije: "Señor, ¿adónde va Ud. caminanda con ese televisor?". El hombre no quería charlar. Comenzó a llorar. Después me dijo: "Lo siento". Yo dije: "¿Quiere Ud. acompañarme?". Luego el hombre me insultió y ahora está en la cárcel.

PARAGUAY & URUGUAY

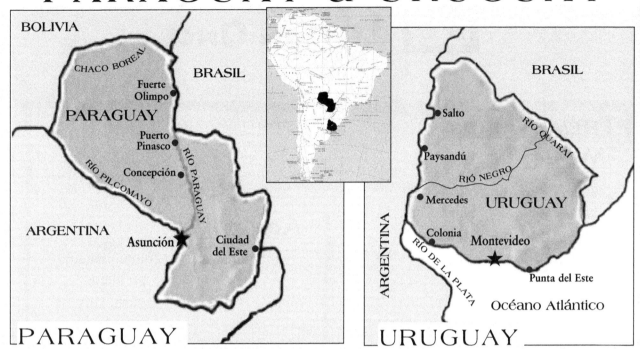

PARAGUAY

URUGUAY

PARAGUAY

CAPITAL:	Asunción
POBLACIÓN:	7.200.000
GOBIERNO:	república constitucional
PRESIDENTE:	Mario Abdo Benítez
DINERO ($):	guaraní
PRODUCTOS:	agricultura, algodón, ganadería, madera, maíz
MÚSICA, BAILE:	danza de la botella, polka
SITIOS DE INTERÉS:	Chaco, Ciudad del Este, El río Paraguay, Las Ruinas Jesuitas
COMIDA TÍPICA:	bori-bori, chipas, palmitos, so'o ku'i, sopa paraguaya, tereré

PARAGUAYOS FAMOSOS:

Agustín Barrios
(MÚSICO)

Augusto Roa Bastos
(ESCRITOR)

José Luis Chilavert
(FUTBOLISTA)

Luis Alberto
del Paraná
(CANTANTE)

URUGUAY

CAPITAL:	Montevideo
POBLACIÓN:	3.500.000
GOBIERNO:	república constitucional
PRESIDENTE:	Luis Lacalle Pou
DINERO ($):	peso uruguayo
PRODUCTOS:	carne, cemento, cuero, vino
MÚSICA, BAILE:	música gauchesca, tango, vals
SITIOS DE INTERÉS:	Colonia del Sacramento, Punta del Este
COMIDA TÍPICA:	asado, cazuela, chivitos, mate, parrillada, puchero

URUGUAYOS FAMOSOS:

Juan Manuel Blanes
(PINTOR)

José Gervasio Artigas
(HÉROE NACIONAL)

Pedro Figari (PINTOR)

Juan Carlos Onetti
(ESCRITOR)

Horacio Quiroga
(ESCRITOR)

Enrique Rodó
(ESCRITOR)

 *Practice this vocabulary with our mobile app! Visit tobreak.com/app for more details.*

 # VOCABULARIO LECCIÓN ONCE

THEME WORDS: "MUSIC"

el	*acordeón*	accordion
la	*banda*	band
el	*clarinete*	clarinet
el	*concierto*	concert
la	*flauta*	flute
la	*guitarra*	guitar
la	*orquesta*	orchestra
el	*piano*	piano
el	*saxofón*	saxophone
los	*tambores*	drums
el	*trombón*	trombone
la	*trompeta*	trumpet
el	*violín*	violin

OTHER NOUNS

el	*actor*	actor
la	*actriz*	actress
el	*billete*	ticket
la	*boda*	wedding
el	*episodio*	episode
el	*luchador*	wrestler

el	*mensaje*	message
la	*mentira*	lie
la	*respuesta*	reply

ADJECTIVES

contaminado/a	contaminated, polluted
tonto/a	foolish, silly, stupid
último/a	last (of a group)

VERBS

fumar	to smoke
invitar	to invite
mojar	to moisten, to wet
pasar (tiempo)	to spend (time)
perder (tiempo)	to waste (time)
preocuparse	to worry
regresar	to return

ADVERBS

cerca	near(by)
lejos	far (away)

LECCIÓN ONCE

KEY GRAMMAR CONCEPTS

A) FORMAL COMMAND FORMS USING UD. AND UDS. → *Mandatos con Ud. y Uds.*

B) DEMONSTRATIVE ADJECTIVES → *Los adjetivos demostrativos*

C) SOME USEFUL IDIOMATIC EXPRESSIONS AND PROVERBS → *Algunas expresiones idiomáticas y refranes útiles*

A) FORMAL COMMAND FORMS USING UD. AND UDS.

Commands express a desire that someone else either do or not do something. In Spanish, the endings of the verb forms themselves show that a command is intended. When reading, you will often find exclamation points acting as brackets, framing the beginning and the end of the command! Most interesting to English speakers is the fact that the first exclamation point is upside down.

Here are some sentences that use commands:

EXAMPLES: *¡Cierre Ud. la puerta!*
        Close the door!

      ¡Abra Ud. el libro!
        Open the book!

      ¡Escriban Uds. la composición ahora mismo!
        Write the composition right now!

      ¡No cierre Ud. la puerta!
        Don't close the door!

      ¡No abra Ud. el libro!
        Don't open the book!

      ¡No escriban Uds. la composición ahora mismo!
        Don't write the composition right now!

In this section, we will study the formula for creating these formal commands. Right off the bat, do you notice that the verb endings are exactly the same whether a *Ud./Uds.* command is affirmative or negative (*¡Abra!* → *¡No abra!*, *¡Cierre!* → *¡No cierre!*, *¡Escriban!* → *¡No escriban!*)?

1) REGULAR VERBS

Here are the forms for formal commands of regular verbs:

	Ud. (+)	Ud. (–)	Uds. (+)	Uds. (–)
HABLAR	¡Hable Ud.!	¡No hable Ud.!	¡Hablen Uds.!	¡No hablen Uds.!
COMER	¡Coma Ud.!	¡No coma Ud.!	¡Coman Uds.!	¡No coman Uds.!
VIVIR	¡Viva Ud.!	¡No viva Ud.!	¡Vivan Uds.!	¡No vivan Uds.!

Note: Affirmative and negative *Ud./Uds.* commands are exactly the same.

As you noticed in this chart, **-AR** verbs end with *"e"* or *"en,"* while **-ER** and **-IR** verbs end with *"a"* or *"an."* These endings are often described as the "opposite" of what you use in the regular present tense. Hearing these endings alerts a listener that the speaker has just barked out an order!

2) STEM-CHANGING "BOOT" VERBS

What happens with stem-changing "boot" verbs? To form the *Ud.* and *Uds.* command forms, follow the same idea as above, but remember the stem change!

	Ud. (+)	Ud. (–)	Uds. (+)	Uds. (–)
CERRAR	¡Cierre Ud.!	¡No cierre Ud.!	¡Cierren Uds.!	¡No cierren Uds.!
VOLVER	¡Vuelva Ud.!	¡No vuelva Ud.!	¡Vuelvan Uds.!	¡No vuelvan Uds.!
PEDIR	¡Pida Ud.!	¡No pida Ud.!	¡Pidan Uds.!	¡No pidan Uds.!

3) IRREGULAR VERBS

How do we form commands using verbs that are irregular in the *"yo"* form — words like *hacer, tener,* or *salir*? The process is simple — begin with the irregular *"yo"* form of the present tense. Then add the new endings that you have seen throughout this section.

		"yo" form of present	*"Ud."* command form	*"Uds."* command form
EXAMPLE:	**TENER**	tengo	tenga	tengan

	Ud. (+)	Ud. (−)	Uds. (+)	Uds. (−)
CONDUCIR	¡Conduzca Ud.!	¡No conduzca Ud.!	¡Conduzcan Uds.!	¡No conduzcan Uds.!
DECIR	¡Diga Ud.!	¡No diga Ud.!	¡Digan Uds.!	¡No digan Uds.!
HACER	¡Haga Ud.!	¡No haga Ud.!	¡Hagan Uds.!	¡No hagan Uds.!
PONER	¡Ponga Ud.!	¡No ponga Ud.!	¡Pongan Uds.!	¡No pongan Uds.!
SALIR	¡Salga Ud.!	¡No salga Ud.!	¡Salgan Uds.!	¡No salgan Uds.!

4) SUPER-IRREGULAR VERBS

Finally, there are some verbs whose command forms you simply need to memorize. They do not follow the rules that have been presented thus far. Practice them carefully; because they are such common words, you will use them all the time.

	Ud. (+)	Ud. (−)	Uds. (+)	Uds. (−)
IR	¡Vaya Ud.!	¡No vaya Ud.!	¡Vayan Uds.!	¡No vayan Uds.!
SABER	¡Sepa Ud.!	¡No sepa Ud.!	¡Sepan Uds.!	¡No sepan Uds.!
SER	¡Sea Ud.!	¡No sea Ud.!	¡Sean Uds.!	¡No sean Uds.!

FINALLY, WHAT HAPPENS TO OBJECT PRONOUNS IN COMMANDS?

The rules are simple:

◆ Attach all object pronouns to the end of AFFIRMATIVE (+) commands.

◆ Place all object pronouns before NEGATIVE (−) commands.

✳ **EXAMPLES:** *¿Los perritos calientes? ¡Cómalos Ud.! . . . ¡No los coma Ud.!*
The hot dogs? Eat them! . . . Don't eat them!

¿Los vecinos? ¡Invítenlos Uds! . . . ¡No los inviten Uds!
The neighbors? Invite them! . . . Don't invite them!

¡CUIDADO! When you attach an object pronoun to a command of two syllables or more, you must add an accent mark: *¡Invítenlos! ¡Hágame! ¡Cómalos!*

PRACTICE EXERCISES

1. **Review the instructions for forming "Ud./Uds." commands carefully. Now fill in this table, following the example provided. The "+" and "−" indicate affirmative and negative respectively:**

	Ud. (+)	Uds. (−)
Example: bailar	¡Baile!	¡No bailen!
a. trabajar		
b. aprender		
c. vivir		
d. entender		
e. mostrar		
f. repetir		
g. salir		
h. sentarse		
i. tener		
j. ir		
k. ser		

2. **Complete the following sentences by conjugating the verb in parentheses into the appropriate *"Ud."* or *"Uds."* command form. In the last three sentences, you will need to insert an object pronoun:**

a. ¡_____ Uds. las respuestas en la pizarra! (Escribir)

b. ¡_____ Ud. el televisor ahora mismo! ¡Está comenzando el último episodio de *American Idol*! (Encender)

c. ¡No me _____ Ud. otra mentira . . . necesito la verdad! (decir)

d. ¡_____ Uds. todos los vegetales! (Comer)

e. ¡_____ Ud. la tarea primero, y después _____ con los amigos! (Hacer/salir)

f. ¡No _____ Uds. esas preguntas tontas! (repetir)

g. ¿Las chicas? ¡_____ Uds. a la fiesta! (Invitarlas)

   ¡CUIDADO! *(Remember, attach the object pronoun to the end of an **affirmative** command!)*

h. ¿La canción de Coldplay *Viva la Vida*? ¡No _____ Ud. aquí! (cantarla)

   ¡CUIDADO! *(Remember, put the object pronoun before the negative command!)*

i. ¿El nuevo disco de Alejandro Sanz? ¡_____ Uds. en la tienda! (Comprarlo)

B) DEMONSTRATIVE ADJECTIVES

Demonstrative adjectives help to identify and distinguish one noun from other nouns of the same type. These adjectives generally precede the noun that they modify. The corresponding words in English are "this," "these," "that," and "those."

Here are the demonstrative adjectives:

Demonstrative Adjectives		
este	*esta*	this
estos	*estas*	these
ese	*esa*	that
esos	*esas*	those
aquel	*aquella*	that (way over there)
aquellos	*aquellas*	those (way over there)

Aquel, aquella, aquellos, and *aquellas* help to identify something that is a great distance away, the farthest distance away of a number of objects, or something quite removed in time from the speaker's framework.

 **EXAMPLES:**

este libro	this book
esta mesa	this table
estos libros	these books
estas mesas	these tables
ese actor	that actor
esa actriz	that actress
esos actores	those actors
esas actrices	those actresses
aquel árbol	that tree (over yonder)
aquella montaña	that mountain (over yonder)
aquellos árboles	those trees (over yonder)
aquellas montañas	those mountains (over yonder)

Helpful Tip: Some students have trouble remembering if *"este"* means "this" or "that," or if *"estos"* means "these" or "those." The following rhyme may help to keep these forms straight in your mind:

"This" and "these" have "t's." *(es**t**e/es**t**a* and *es**t**os/es**t**as)*

PRACTICE EXERCISES

1. **Translate the demonstrative adjective in parentheses into Spanish, being certain that it agrees with the noun it describes:**

a. _____ flautas (these)

b. _____ reloj (that, over yonder)

c. _____ hamburguesa (that)

d. _____ guitarras (those)

e. _____ día (this)

f. _____ padre (this)

g. _____ restaurantes (those, over yonder)

h. _____ trompeta (that)

i. _____ hospitales (those)

j. _____ computadoras (these)

2. **The following narrative contains seven errors. Underline each error and write the correction above it:**

Esta chicas no saben nada. Cuando yo era niña, nunca hablaba con eso tipo de chicas. Sé que aquelos días eran diferentes, pero a veces pienso que los jóvenes de hoy están locos. Por ejemplo, mi nieta, quien va a ese escuela cerca de la casa, siempre habla con el chico del trombón . . . ¿lo conoces? Es eso chico con bigote que siempre fuma aquellas cigarrillos. Un día ella va a casarse con él. No importa. Voy a ese boda y no voy a decirle nada a nadie.

C) SOME USEFUL IDIOMATIC EXPRESSIONS AND PROVERBS

This section will present a number of **useful idiomatic expressions and proverbs.** Some of these expressions cannot be translated literally into English. Feeling at ease when using expressions such as the ones in the following chart is a sign of a good Spanish speaker.

Idiomatic Expressions and Proverbs	
a fines de →	around the end of
dar las gracias →	to thank
dar por entendido →	to consider it understood
dejar un recado →	to leave a message
de repente →	suddenly
de hoy en adelante →	from now on
echar al correo →	to mail
enamorarse (de) →	to fall in love (with)
estar de acuerdo (con) →	to agree (with)
extrañar el nido →	to be homesick
ida y vuelta →	roundtrip
La práctica hace al maestro. →	Practice makes perfect.
llamar a la puerta →	to knock on the door
llover a cántaros →	to rain a lot
Más vale tarde que nunca. →	Better late than never.
No hay mal que por bien no venga. →	Every cloud has a silver lining.
ponerse enfermo/a →	to become ill
sano y salvo →	safe and sound
tener cuidado →	to be careful
tener en cuenta →	to keep in mind
volverse loco/a →	to go crazy

Let's take a look at each of these expressions used in a sentence:

 **EXAMPLES:** *Voy a ver* No Time to Die, *la película de James Bond,*
 a fines de *este mes.*
  I'm going to see *No Time to Die,* the James Bond movie,
  at the end of this month.

 Mi amigo no ***me dio las gracias*** *después de la fiesta.*
  My friend didn't thank me after the party.

 Doy por entendido *que todos van a llegar a las seis.*
  I consider it understood that everyone will arrive at six.

 Penélope Cruz no me ***dejó un recado*** *en el hotel.*
  Penélope Cruz didn't leave me a message in the hotel.

De repente *sonó la alarma y tuvimos que salir.*
  Suddenly the alarm sounded, and we had to leave.

De hoy en adelante *sólo voy a decir la verdad.*
  From now on, I'm only going to tell the truth.

*Mañana voy a **echar al correo** una carta para mi novia.*
  Tomorrow I'm going to mail a letter to my girlfriend.

*La infanta Cristina de Borbón **se enamoró de** Iñaki Urdangarín hace muchos años.*
  Princess Cristina de Borbón fell in love with Iñaki Urdangarín many years ago.

Estoy de acuerdo *contigo: Eddy Álvarez es uno de los mejores patinadores americanos.*
  I agree with you: Eddy Álvarez is one of the best American skaters.

*Como **extrañaba** tanto **el nido,** volví a mi pueblo, Cuéllar.*
  Because I was so homesick, I returned to my hometown of Cuéllar.

*Es mucho más barato comprar un billete de **ida y vuelta.***
  It's much cheaper to buy a roundtrip ticket.

*Mi profesora de piano siempre me decía: **"La práctica hace al maestro"**; por eso decidí no estudiar con ella.*
  My piano teacher always used to tell me: *"Practice makes perfect."* For that reason, I decided not to study with her.

Estaba llamando a la puerta *cuando alguien gritó: "¿Qué pasa?"*
  I was knocking on the door when someone shouted: "What's going on?"

Llovía a cántaros *cuando salí de casa y me mojé mucho.*
  It was raining heavily when I left home, and I got soaked.

*Mi amigo se casó a la edad de cincuenta y cinco años. — **Más vale tarde que nunca.***
  My friend got married at the age of fifty-five. — Better late than never.

*Me rompí el brazo anoche, pero en el hospital conocí a un médico muy guapo . . . **No hay mal que por bien no venga.***
  I broke my arm last night, but in the hospital I met a very handsome doctor . . . Every cloud has a silver lining.

*El día de su concierto en Nueva York, Marc Anthony **se puso enfermo** y no pudo cantar.*
  The day of his concert in New York, Marc Anthony got sick and couldn't sing.

Al final de la película 101 Dálmatas, *todos los perritos volvieron a casa **sanos y salvos.***
  At the end of the movie *101 Dalmatians,* all of the puppies returned home safe and sound.

"¡Tengan cuidado!", *gritó mi madre cuando mi hermano y yo salimos en la Harley.*

"Be careful!", shouted my mother when my brother and I left on the Harley.

Si tocamos la canción "Quisiera" *de Alejandro Fernández, tenemos que* **tener en cuenta** *que mi hermana va a llorar.*

If we play the song *"Quisiera"* by Alejandro Fernández, we have to keep in mind that my sister is going to cry.

Cuando Ricky Martin canta "Livin' la vida loca", *todos todavía* **se vuelven locos.**

When Ricky Martin sings *"Livin' la vida loca,"* everyone still goes crazy.

PRACTICE EXERCISES

1. Choose one of the expressions in this section to complete the following sentences:

a. Creo que la comida que sirvieron estaba contaminada; por eso yo

_____ y tuve que ir al hospital.

b. Como estamos tan ocupados, no podemos ir de vacaciones ahora . . . pero

_____ agosto vamos a tener mucho más tiempo libre.

c. El cartero tenía un paquete urgente; por eso él _____ por cinco minutos. Por fin, dejó el paquete con el vecino.

d. Me robaron el dinero y el equipaje, pero aprendí muchas lecciones importantes en el viaje. Como siempre dice mi mamá:

_____.

e. Lucille Ball y Desi Arnaz _____ cuando eran jóvenes y decidieron casarse en seguida.

f. Cuando mis hijos nadan en la piscina del vecino, yo siempre les digo:

¡_____!

g. Necesito hacer algunos cambios importantes en mi vida:

_____ no voy a fumar más y voy a tocar el clarinete.

h. El novio llegó media hora tarde a la iglesia. Todos estaban furiosos, pero

como decía mi abuela: _____.

i. Sí, tienes razón, yo _____ contigo; Tito
Puente fue uno de los mejores músicos del mundo — ¡su banda era
fantástica!

j. No me gustan las grandes ciudades; deseo regresar a mi pueblo lo más

pronto posible. Es verdad que yo _____.

**2. Now write some original sentences of your own using the following five
expressions:** *dejar un recado, de repente, ida y vuelta, la práctica hace al
maestro, volverse loco/a.* **Translate them afterwards:**

a. _____

_____

_____

_____

_____

b. _____

_____

_____

_____

_____

c. _____

_____

_____

_____

_____

d. _____

_____

_____

_____

_____

e. _____

_____

_____

_____

_____

ORAL PRACTICE
PREGUNTAS EN GRUPOS DE DOS

These two sections use the grammatical structures and vocabulary from this lesson.

(Alternate giving these commands with your partner . . . even though you are likely speaking with a friend, you will be practicing formal *"Ud."* commands . . . the person who receives the command must do it!)

A) ¡Hable Ud. un poco de inglés ahora!

   ¡Muéstreme su libro de español!

   ¡Pídame un autógrafo!

   ¡Levántese!

   ¡Cante una canción tonta!

   ¡Péinese!

   ¡Dígame un secreto!

B) ¿Te gustan estas preguntas?

   ¿Recuerdas aquellos días cuando eras bebé?

   ¿Viste una película de Jennifer López recientemente?

   ¿De hoy en adelante vas a fumar más?

   A fines de este año escolar, ¿me vas a invitar a una fiesta?

   ¿Te vuelves loco/a cuando canta Marc Anthony?

   ¿Siempre estás de acuerdo con tus padres?

DIALOGUE

The following dialogue contains grammar and vocabulary that you've seen in this lesson and in the introductory section. After listening to the dialogue, read it aloud, alone or with friends. Afterwards, try to answer the questions that follow either aloud or in written form.

LAS AVENTURAS DE RAFAEL, ELISA Y "EL TIGRE"

ESCENA SEIS

Son las seis menos diez de la mañana. Elisa, "El Tigre", Rafael, Marisela y Javier esperan en el andén (platform) *al lado de un tren muy largo de Amtrak. En unos minutos van a abordar el tren para su viaje a Chicago.*

El Tigre: ¡Caramba! Es tan temprano.

Elisa: Tienes razón, Tigre. ¿No había otro tren, Rafael?

Rafael: No. Ese tren es ideal . . . va a llegar en veinticinco horas a Chicago. Llegamos a las seis de la mañana.

Javier: ¿A las seis? ¡Qué barbaridad! ¿En qué estábamos pensando?

Marisela: ¡No se preocupen! Podemos dormir en el tren esta tarde y toda la noche. Sé que hay tantas cosas que hacer en Chicago que no vamos a tener sueño.

Rafael: Es verdad. *La Torre Sears* es el edificio más alto de este país y *El Museo de Ciencia e Industria* es uno de los mejores del mundo.

Elisa: Además, me dicen que el lago Michigan es muy bonito y Chicago tiene playas preciosas.

El Tigre: Tengo hambre. ¿Sirven desayuno en el tren?

Javier: Caramba, Tigre. Es verdad lo que dicen tus amigos. Sólo piensas en la comida.

Todos se ríen. Entonces se escucha un anuncio.

Voz: Saliendo en la plataforma dos el tren para Chicago. Por favor, aborden inmediatamente.

En este momento el hombre del bigote y la mujer vestida de blanco llegan al andén.

Elisa: Tigre, Rafael. ¿Ven Uds. a esas dos personas? Creo que los vi recientemente en otro lugar.

Marisela: Esto (This) ocurre frecuentemente en Nueva York, Elisa. Después de unos días, uno cree que conoce a todo el mundo. ¡Abordemos! (Let's board!)

El Tigre:	Pero creo que Elisa tiene razón. El hombre ese con el bigote . . . creo que es el mismo que me robó la mochila.
Marisela:	¿El hombre aquel con la mujer? Pues los vi anoche en la cafetería, también.

El hombre del bigote y la mujer vestida de blanco comienzan a acercarse a los jóvenes.

Javier:	Ellos vienen. ¿Qué hacemos? ¿Llamamos a la policía?
Elisa:	Tengo mi teléfono celular.
Rafael:	No, no. No hay tiempo. Subamos al tren.

Los cinco jóvenes suben al tren un segundo antes de que se cierren las puertas. Se oye un silbido (whistle) *y el tren se pone en marcha.*

Elisa:	¿Saben Uds. si el hombre y la mujer abordaron también?
El Tigre:	Creo que no.
Elisa:	Tengo miedo.
Marisela:	¡No te preocupes! No pasa nada. Somos cinco y ellos sólo son dos.
Javier:	Además, vamos a Chicago y ellos se quedan en Nueva York.

En otra parte del tren el hombre del bigote y la mujer vestida de blanco se sientan.

El hombre:	¡Qué suerte! Por poco nos deja el tren.
La mujer:	Pero saltamos (we jumped) muy bien . . . y ahora no van a poder escaparse de nosotros.
El hombre:	Sí, querida. En unas horas, vamos a hacerles una visita. Por ahora, vamos a descansar un poquito.

1) ¿Qué hora es cuando comienza esta escena?

_____

2) ¿Adónde van los jóvenes?

_____

3) ¿De cuántas horas es el viaje a Chicago?

_____

4) ¿Cómo se llama el edificio más alto de Estados Unidos?

_____

5) ¿Qué museo de Chicago es muy famoso?

_____

6) ¿A quiénes ven ahora en el andén?

_____

7) ¿Van a llamar a la policía? ¿Por qué sí o por qué no?

_____

8) ¿De qué tiene miedo Elisa?

_____

9) ¿Quiénes hablan juntos al final de la escena y dónde están?

_____

10) ¿Qué van a hacer en unas horas?

_____

PRUEBA DE REPASO

1. Answer in complete sentences:

    a. ¿Es bueno fumar en la biblioteca?

_____

_____

    b. ¿Te gusta esta escuela o prefieres otra escuela?

_____

_____

    c. ¡No escriba Ud. nada aquí!

_____

_____

    d. ¿Dejaste un mensaje ayer en el escritorio de tu profesor favorito?

_____

_____

    e. ¿Se pone enferma una persona después de beber agua contaminada?

_____

_____

2. Write formal *"Ud."* commands as indicated:

	Ud. (+)	Ud. (−)
a. hablar	_____	_____
b. vivir	_____	_____
c. volverse	_____	_____
d. decir	_____	_____
e. conocer	_____	_____

	Uds. (+)	Uds. (−)
f. hacer	_____	_____
g. ser	_____	_____
h. ir	_____	_____
i. pedir	_____	_____
j. sentarse	_____	_____

3. Change these five negative commands to affirmative commands, remembering to add an accent mark when needed:

a. ¡No me diga el secreto!

_____

b. ¡No se sienten en esas sillas!

_____

c. ¡No nos muestre los vegetales!

_____

d. ¡No me inviten a la fiesta!

_____

e. ¡No se laven las manos en el río!

_____

4. Translate the demonstrative adjectives in parentheses into Spanish:

a. _____ piano (that)

b. _____ actrices (these)

c. _____ billete (that, over yonder)

d. _____ boda (this)

e. _____ saxofones (those)

f. _____ vegetales (these)

g. _____ orquesta (that)

h. _____ montañas (those, over yonder)

5. Choose one of the following expressions or proverbs for each space in the following sentences *(ida y vuelta, la práctica hace al maestro, llamar a la puerta, llover a cántaros, más vale tarde que nunca, no hay mal que por bien no venga, ponerse enfermo/a, sano y salvo, tener cuidado, tener en cuenta)***:**

a. El accidente fue horrible, pero yo estoy bien, ¿no ves? Aquí estoy

_____.

b. Cuando comencé a estudiar el violín, no sabía nada. Esta noche voy a tocar

en Carnegie Hall. Como decía mi abuelo : _____.

c. Me mojé cuando salí de casa porque _____.

d. "¡_____ con el enemigo!", les dijo el general a los soldados.

e. Prefiero comprar billetes de _____ porque normalmente son más baratos.

f. Mi amigo llegó dos horas tarde al concierto . . . ¡_____

_____!

g. Cuando bebí agua contaminada, _____.

6. Translate the following sentences into Spanish:

a. Don't smoke at the wedding!

_____

b. The actress fell in love with the actor.

_____

c. Do you prefer this flute or that accordion?

_____

7. The following narrative contains five errors. Underline each error and write the correction above it:

Mi hermano prefiere este árbol de Navidad, pero yo prefiero aquella árbol. El hombre de la tienda nos dijo: "¡No se preocupan Uds.! Pueden comprar eses dos árboles". Se los mostré a mi madre. Mi madre estaba de acuerda con mi hermano. De hoy en adelanta, no voy más con él a la tienda.

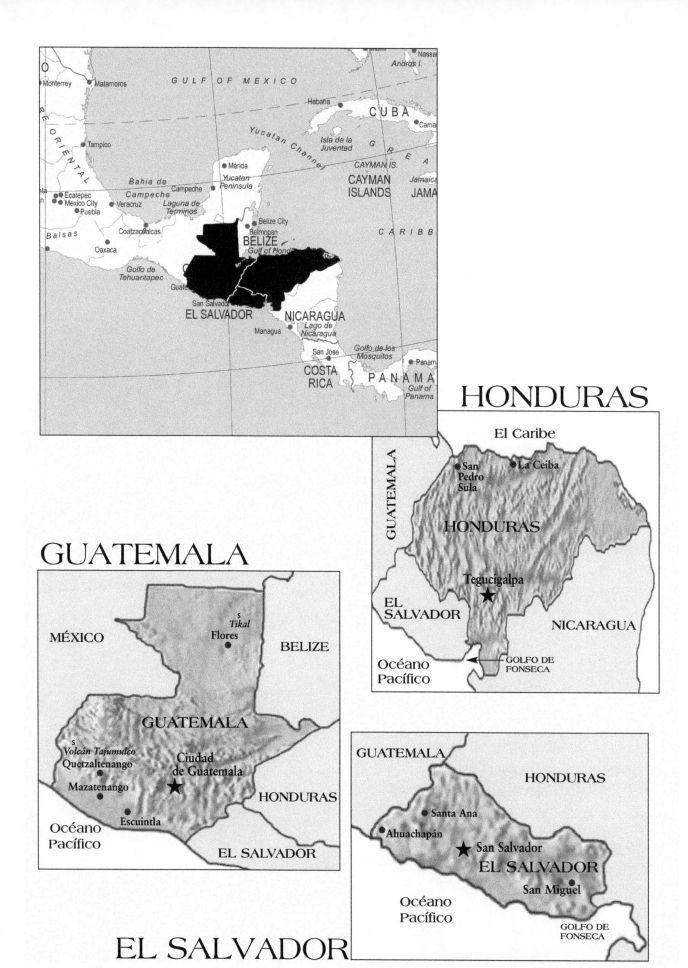

GULF OF MEXICO

Monterrey • • Matamoros

Tampico •

Habana •

CUBA

Isla de la Juventud

Yucatan Channel

CAYMAN IS.

CAYMAN ISLANDS

JAMAICA

JAMA

Mérida •

Yucatan Peninsula

Bahia de Campeche

Campeche •

Ecatepec •
Mexico City •
Puebla •

Veracruz •

Laguna de Terminos

Belize City •

Belmopan •

BELIZE

Gulf of Hond

CARIBB

Balsas

Coatzacoalcos •

Oaxaca •

Golfo de Tehuantepec

Guate

San Salvador •

EL SALVADOR

NICARAGUA

Managua •

Lago de Nicaragua

Golfo de los Mosquitos

San Jose •

COSTA RICA

PANAMA

Panam

Gulf of Panama

HONDURAS

El Caribe

GUATEMALA

San Pedro Sula •

• La Ceiba

HONDURAS

Tegucigalpa ★

EL SALVADOR

NICARAGUA

Océano Pacífico

← GOLFO DE FONSECA

GUATEMALA

MÉXICO

Tikal
Flores •

BELIZE

GUATEMALA

Volcán Tajumulco
Quetzaltenango •

Ciudad de Guatemala ★

HONDURAS

Mazatenango •

Escuintla •

Océano Pacífico

EL SALVADOR

GUATEMALA

HONDURAS

Santa Ana •

Ahuachapán •

San Salvador ★

EL SALVADOR

San Miguel •

Océano Pacífico

GOLFO DE FONSECA

EL SALVADOR

GUATEMALA, HONDURAS & EL SALVADOR

GUATEMALA

CAPITAL:	La Ciudad de Guatemala
POBLACIÓN:	18.100.000
GOBIERNO:	república democrática constitucional
PRESIDENTE:	Alejandro Giammattei
DINERO ($):	quetzal
PRODUCTOS:	azúcar, bananas, café, carne
MÚSICA, BAILE:	marimba, son
SITIOS DE INTERÉS:	Chichicastenango, Islas de la Bahía, Lago Atitlán, El Petén, Tikal, Volcán Pacaya
COMIDA TÍPICA:	chiles rellenos, guacamole, pepián, pescaditos, tamales, tapado, tortillas

HONDURAS

CAPITAL:	Tegucigalpa
POBLACIÓN:	10.100.000
GOBIERNO:	república constitucional democrática
PRESIDENTE:	Juan Orlando Hernández
DINERO ($):	lempira
PRODUCTOS:	azúcar, bananas, cacao, carne, fruta, minerales, tabaco
MÚSICA, BAILE:	punta, sique
SITIOS DE INTERÉS:	Copán (ruinas de los mayas), Santa Bárbara
COMIDA TÍPICA:	aguacate, carne asada, casabe, plátanos, sopa de camarones, tortillas

EL SALVADOR

CAPITAL:	San Salvador
POBLACIÓN:	6.500.000
GOBIERNO:	república
PRESIDENTE:	Nayib Bukele
DINERO ($):	colón, dólar americano
PRODUCTOS:	agricultura, artesanía, azúcar, café
MÚSICA, BAILE:	danza de los historiantes, marimba
SITIOS DE INTERÉS:	Joya de Cerén, Izalco, La Palma, San Andrés, Santa Ana
COMIDA TÍPICA:	pan con pavo, pupusas, tamales

GUATEMALTECOS FAMOSOS:

Ricardo Arjona
(CANTANTE)

Miguel Asturias
(ESCRITOR)

Rigoberta Menchú
(ACTIVISTA)

Carlos Mérida
(ARTISTA)

Augusto Monteroso
(ESCRITOR)

HONDUREÑOS FAMOSOS:

Guillermo Anderson
(MÚSICO)

Julio Escoto
(ESCRITOR)

Lempira
(HÉROE NACIONAL)

Francisco Morazán
(POLÍTICO)

Gabriela Núñez
(POLÍTICA)

José Antonio Velázquez
(PINTOR)

SALVADOREÑOS FAMOSOS:

Raúl Díaz Arce
(FUTBOLISTA)

Jorge González
(FUTBOLISTA)

Claudia Lars
(ESCRITORA)

Alberto Masferrer
(ESCRITOR)

Óscar Romero
(ACTIVISTA, ARZOBISPO)

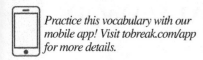

VOCABULARIO
LECCIÓN DOCE

THEME WORDS: "HIGH TECH"

la	aspiradora	vacuum cleaner
la	computadora	computer
el	congelador	freezer
el	contestador automático	answering machine
el	correo electrónico	e-mail
el	(horno de) microondas	microwave (oven)
la	lavadora	washer
el	lavaplatos	dishwasher
la	nevera	refrigerator
el	ordenador (Sp.)	computer
el/la	radio	radio
el	refrigerador	refrigerator
la	secadora	dryer
el	teléfono celular/ el móvil (Sp.)	cellphone
la	televisión	television
el	televisor	television set

OTHER NOUNS

el/la	abogado/a	lawyer
la*	caries/las caries	cavity/cavities

la	carretera	highway
la	docena	dozen
el	fin de semana	weekend
la	galleta	cookie
el	garaje	garage
el	inglés	English
el	perrito caliente	hot dog
el	principio	beginning
la	raqueta	racquet

ADJECTIVES

precioso/a	beautiful, adorable

VERBS

gastar	to spend
terminar	to finish

MISCELLANEOUS

ir de viaje	to travel, to go on a trip
otra vez	again

* This might look like an error, but it's not!
"Caries" is both singular and plural!

LECCIÓN DOCE

KEY GRAMMAR CONCEPTS

A) THE IMMEDIATE FUTURE → *El futuro inmediato*

B) USES OF "POR" AND "PARA" → *Los usos de "por" y "para"*

C) MORE NUMBERS → *Más números*

 A) THE IMMEDIATE FUTURE

In future years of Spanish study, you will learn the verbal endings of the "true" future tense. In the meantime, however, you may want to know how to talk about events that occur subsequent to the present. The **immediate future** is used to refer to events that, in the speaker's mind, will occur relatively soon. You simply use the present tense of *"ir"* with the preposition *"a"* and an infinitive.

Here's the construction of the immediate future:

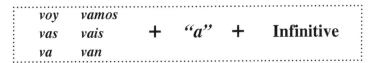

voy	vamos			
vas	vais	**+**	**"a"**	**+** **Infinitive**
va	van			

✳ **EXAMPLES:** *Esta noche* **voy a ver** *a Maynor Figueroa, la estrella hondureña de fútbol.*
Tonight I'm going to see Maynor Figueroa, the Honduran soccer star.

Vamos a regresar de las vacaciones este fin de semana.
We'll be back from vacation this weekend.

A su hijo **le va a encantar** *la nueva película de James Bond.*
Your son is going to love the new James Bond film.

Wisín & Yandel **van a dar** *un concierto en Tegucigalpa este año.*
Wisín & Yandel are going to give a concert in Tegucigalpa this year.

Mi novio **me va a invitar** *al próximo partido de los Bulls.*
My boyfriend is going to invite me to the next Bulls game.

*Mis padres **van a darme** un regalo muy especial para mi cumpleaños: un viaje a* Disney's California Adventure.

My parents are going to give me a very special present for my birthday: a trip to *Disney's California Adventure.*

*Mi dentista **va a estar** muy contento porque tengo muchas caries.*

My dentist is going to be very happy because I have many cavities.

*Mañana **vas a desayunar** a las seis en punto.*

Tomorrow you are going to have breakfast at six sharp.

Helpful Tip: Did you notice that when you use object pronouns with the immediate future, you have the option of placing them before the form of "ir" (**le** *va a encantar,* **me** *va a invitar*) or attaching them to the infinitive *(van a dar**me**)?*

 # PRACTICE EXERCISES

1. Write the forms of the immediate future of the following two infinitives:

        cantar (to sing)   **levantarse** (to get up)

2. Complete the following sentences with the appropriate form of the immediate future:

a. Tenemos mucha suerte porque mañana _____ sol y podemos ir a la playa. (hacer)

b. Creo que Juanes _____ otro Grammy este año. (ganar)

c. Mi hermana y yo _____ el nuevo episodio de *Big Little Lies*. (ver)

d. Esta noche ellos _____ en ese nuevo restaurante hondureño. (comer)

e. Mañana nosotros _____ muy temprano porque vamos a visitar algunas ruinas mayas. (levantarse)

f. Tú _____ enfermo si comes tantos perros calientes. (ponerse)

g. Nadie _____ ahora porque empieza *Modern Family* con Sofia Vergara. (salir)

h. Yo _____ que es buena idea trabajar primero y jugar después. (tener en cuenta)

i. Mi amigo _____ su iPod para escuchar las canciones más recientes. (usar)

 ## B) USES OF "POR" AND "PARA"

In *Lección Cuatro,* you were introduced briefly to the prepositions *"por"* and *"para."* These words are used frequently in Spanish! In English, they can mean "for," "by," "in order to," "along," and "through." Non-native speakers often take a little while to learn which of these prepositions to choose. This section will present four common uses of each of these words.

1) USES OF "POR"

a) *"Por"* **can mean "in exchange for."** It is used when one person gives something to another person in exchange for something else.

> ✳ **EXAMPLES:** *Te doy diez dólares **por** tu raqueta de tenis vieja.*
> I'll give you ten dollars for your old tennis racquet.
>
> *Muchas gracias **por** la invitación.*
> Many thanks for the invitation.
>
> (Here the speaker gives thanks in exchange for the invitation!
> *"Gracias por"* = *"Thank you for"* — remember the rhyme!)

b) *"Por"* **can measure a duration of time.** When you say for how long you did something, you could use *"por."*

✳ EXAMPLES: *Esta mañana sólo estudié **por** diez minutos.*
I only studied for ten minutes this morning.

*Esta noche vamos a dormir **por** ocho horas.*
We are going to sleep for eight hours tonight.

Note: *"Por"* can be omitted in these sentences. In fact, in Spain, *"por"* would not be used here.

c) *"Por"* **expresses rate.**

✳ EXAMPLES: *Normalmente mi amigo conduce a sesenta millas **por** hora en la autopista.*
Normally my friend drives sixty miles an hour on the highway.

*El noventa **por** ciento de mis amigos hablan español.*
Ninety percent of my friends speak Spanish.

d) *"Por"* **describes movement through space.**

✳ EXAMPLES: *Siempre caminamos **por** la playa después de las siete.*
We always walk along the beach after seven.

*¡Salgan Uds. **por** esa puerta verde!*
Leave through that green door!

2) USES OF "PARA"

a) *"Para"* **is used to indicate a destination.**

✳ EXAMPLES: *Caminamos **para** la plaza central.*
We are walking to (towards) the central plaza.

*Este tren sale **para** las afueras.*
This train is heading to the suburbs.

b) *"Para"* **can mean "intended for."** It identifies the recipient of a gift or favor. It also can mean the place where you plan to put something.

✳ EXAMPLES: *"Este anillo es **para** ti", le dijo el actor Aarón Díaz a su nueva novia.*
"This ring is for you," said the actor Aarón Díaz to his new girlfriend.

*La nueva alfombra azul y roja es **para** el comedor.*
The new blue and red rug is for the dining room.

c) *"Para"* indicates a deadline, a time by which something will be completed.

 EXAMPLES: *La tarea **para** mañana es leer su correo electrónico.*
The homework for tomorrow is to read your e-mail.

__Para__ las cinco esta noche voy a terminar este proyecto.
I'm going to finish this project by five tonight.

d) *"Para"* can be used before an infinitive to mean "in order to."

 EXAMPLES: *__Para__ comprender la película, es necesario leer el libro primero.*
In order to understand the movie, it is necessary to read the book first.

*"Dios me trajo a este mundo **para** ser músico", dijo una vez Tito Puente.*
"God brought me to this world in order to be a musician," Tito Puente once said.

Helpful Tip: If we want to say "in order to" in English (though we may choose not to), we must use *"para"* in Spanish.

PRACTICE EXERCISES

1. Complete the following sentences by using the word *"por"* or *"para"*:

a. _____ ganar el partido, tenemos que practicar de sol a sol.

b. Vamos a pasar _____ la casa de la abuela.

c. Estuvimos en Santa Ana _____ tres semanas el verano pasado.

d. Estos regalos son _____ ti, amor mío.

e. Este maíz cuesta cinco dólares _____ docena.

f. ¿Me das tu radio _____ la lavadora?

g. Tengo que terminar toda la tarea _____ esta noche.

h. ¿Puedes venir a mi casa _____ preparar el guacamole conmigo?

i. Estas flores preciosas son _____ mi abuela.

j. "Voy a cantar _____ tres horas", anunció Shakira al principio del concierto.

k. Este avión sale _____ Tegucigalpa en media hora.

2. The following paragraph contains four errors of *"por"* and *"para."* Underline each error and write the correction above it:

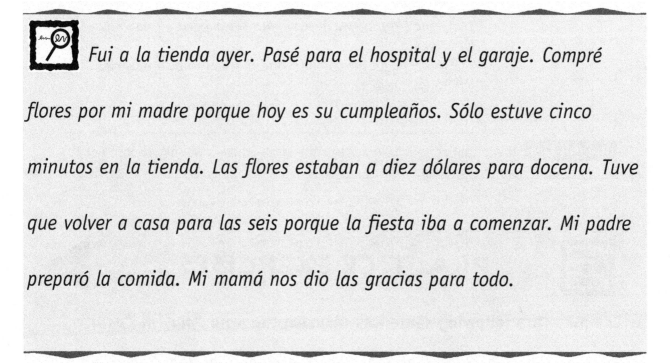

Fui a la tienda ayer. Pasé para el hospital y el garaje. Compré flores por mi madre porque hoy es su cumpleaños. Sólo estuve cinco minutos en la tienda. Las flores estaban a diez dólares para docena. Tuve que volver a casa para las seis porque la fiesta iba a comenzar. Mi padre preparó la comida. Mi mamá nos dio las gracias para todo.

C) MORE NUMBERS

This final section will help you to expand your knowledge of numbers.

1) CARDINAL NUMBERS

In the preliminary pages, you learned to count to thirty-one. Do you remember all of the numbers? All of these numbers are called cardinal numbers.

1	*uno*	11	*once*
2	*dos*	12	*doce*
3	*tres*	13	*trece*
4	*cuatro*	14	*catorce*
5	*cinco*	15	*quince*
6	*seis*	16	*dieciséis (diez y seis)*
7	*siete*	17	*diecisiete (diez y siete)*
8	*ocho*	18	*dieciocho (diez y ocho)*
9	*nueve*	19	*diecinueve (diez y nueve)*
10	*diez*	20	*veinte*

The cardinal numbers 21–29 are written nowadays as one word. Note the accents on *veintidós*, *veintitrés* and *veintiséis*.

21	*veintiuno*	26	*veintiséis*
22	*veintidós*	27	*veintisiete*
23	*veintitrés*	28	*veintiocho*
24	*veinticuatro*	29	*veintinueve*
25	*veinticinco*		

The compound numbers from 31–99 must be written as three words.

30	*treinta*	34	*treinta y cuatro, etc.*	70	*setenta*
31	*treinta y uno*	40	*cuarenta*	80	*ochenta*
32	*treinta y dos*	50	*cincuenta*	90	*noventa*
33	*treinta y tres*	60	*sesenta*	100	*cien(to)*

Helpful Tips: **1)** The word *"ciento"* is shortened to *"cien"* before any noun *(cien televisores, cien mesas)* or before a larger number *(cien mil)*.
2) The word *"y"* is only used in Spanish between groups of tens and ones *(cuarenta y seis)*.

101	*ciento uno*	600	*seiscientos*
200	*doscientos*	700	*setecientos*
300	*trescientos*	800	*ochocientos*
400	*cuatrocientos*	900	*novecientos*
500	*quinientos*	1000	*mil*

Helpful Tips: **1)** When describing a feminine noun, the numerals 200–900 change to agree with that noun *(doscientos libros, doscientas sillas)*.

2) Also, note that the word *"uno"* changes, too. (641 women = ***seiscientas*** *cuarenta y* ***una*** *mujeres*; 641 men = ***seiscientos*** *cuarenta y* ***un*** *hombres*).

2) ORDINAL NUMBERS

Ordinal numbers describe numbers in order (sequence). The most common ordinal numbers in Spanish are the first ten. After that, a Spanish speaker will most often choose to use a cardinal number even though more ordinal numbers exist.

1ST	*primero*	5TH	*quinto*	8TH	*octavo*
2ND	*segundo*	6TH	*sexto*	9TH	*noveno*
3RD	*tercero*	7TH	*séptimo*	10TH	*décimo*
4TH	*cuarto*				

Helpful Tips: **1)** The words *primero* and *tercero* lose their *"o"* **before** a masculine, singular noun *(el primer libro, el tercer episodio)*. All other ordinal numbers retain the *"o"* before a masculine, singular noun *(el quinto hombre, el décimo año)*.

2) All ordinal numbers change the final *"o"* to an *"a"* when describing a singular, feminine noun *(la primera chica, la novena lección, etc.)*.

3) In Spanish, "1ST" is written *"1º"* or *"1ª"*; "2ND" is *"2º"* or *"2ª,"* etc.

PRACTICE EXERCISES

1. **Translate the following words into Spanish:**

   a. twenty-eight computers _____

   b. fifth _____

   c. two hundred thirty-one chairs _____

   d. the sixth book; the sixth week _____

   e. thirteen telephones _____

   f. first _____

   g. eight hundred sixty-nine _____

   h. second _____

   i. nine hundred twenty-five _____

   j. ninth _____

2. **Insert the correct ordinal or cardinal number in the spaces below:**

   a. El _____ presidente de los Estados Unidos fue Thomas Jefferson. (3RD)

   b. Hay _____ días en julio. (31)

   c. ¡Comí _____ galletas ayer! (31)

   d. La _____ lección de este libro es excelente. (5TH)

   e. Encontré _____ dólares en la calle Main. (200)

   f. Vi el _____ perrito que nació en casa de la vecina. (1ST)

   g. ¡Esa palabra tiene _____ letras! (16)

   h. El _____ mes del año es mi favorito. (2ND)

   i. Hay _____ alumnos en mi colegio. (341)

   j. Hay _____ aspiradoras en la casa. (10)

These two sets of questions use grammatical structures and vocabulary from this lesson. Working with a partner, alternate asking and answering each question. When you get to the bottom of each list, start over at the top, switching roles. As a variation, write out the answers in complete sentences.

A) ¿Vas a gastar mucho dinero este fin de semana?

¿Vas a llevar la secadora y la nevera a tu casa nueva?

¿Van a viajar tus padres esta primavera?

¿Vas a poner tu coche en el garaje esta noche?

¿Vas a hablar mucho conmigo hoy?

¿Cuánto dinero me das por mi microondas?

¿Qué tienes que hacer para jugar bien al baloncesto?

B) ¿Te gustan más las hamburguesas o los perritos calientes?

¿Aproximadamente cuántas caries tienes?

¿Por cuánto tiempo hablas español en un día típico?

¿Cuál es el tercer mes del año?

¿Cuál es la quinta letra en la palabra "refrigerador"?

¿Cuál es tu número favorito?

¿Vamos a terminar estas preguntas pronto?

PRUEBA DE REPASO

1. **Answer in complete sentences:**

   a. ¿Vas a acostarte antes de las diez esta noche?

   _____

   b. ¿Cuándo va a llover otra vez?

   _____

   c. ¿Por cuántos años vas a estudiar español?

   _____

   d. ¿Cuál es el primer día de la semana?

   _____

   e. ¿Es posible comer trescientas galletas en un día?

   _____

2. **Write the full conjugations of the following two infinitives in the immediate future:**

   vender (to sell)   **vestirse** (to dress)

   _____ _____   _____ _____

   _____ _____   _____ _____

   _____ _____   _____ _____

3. Complete the following five sentences with the appropriate form of the immediate future:

a. Este fin de semana yo _____ con mi novio. (salir)

b. Esta tarde nosotras _____ mucho dinero en la tienda nueva. (gastar)

c. ¿A qué hora _____ tú esta noche? (acostarse)

d. Mi amigo no _____ su tarea pronto. (terminar)

e. Uds. _____ la verdad ahora mismo. (confesar)

4. Write either *"por"* or *"para"* in the following sentences:

a. Voy a darte quince dólares _____ tu libro de español.

b. _____ llegar a la Ciudad de Guatemala, tienes que seguir todo

derecho _____ 20 kilómetros.

c. Normalmente paseamos _____ el parque cuando estamos en Nueva York.

d. Ese tren va _____ los suburbios; yo necesito ir al centro.

e. La estrella de cine sólo habló con los fotógrafos _____ cinco minutos.

f. "Este perrito caliente es _____ Ud.", me dijo el hombre en Yankee Stadium.

g. Cuando viajo a ochenta millas _____ hora en mi moto, siempre me pongo un poco nervioso.

h. "Necesito la ropa _____ este viernes a las cinco", dijo la mujer en la lavandería.

i. Muchas gracias _____ dejarme tu coche este fin de semana.

j. "Estoy aquí _____ mostrarte fotos nuevas de mis preciosos nietos", anunció la abuela muy orgullosa.

5. Translate the following into Spanish:

a. thirty-five lawyers   _____

b. the first star   _____

c. two hundred and one racquets   _____

d. the fifth cavity   _____

e. 2017   _____

6. Now translate these words to fit into the following sentences:

a. El _____ momento bueno fue cuando Cristina entrevistó a Selena Gómez. (1ST)

b. Bebimos _____ botellas de agua mineral este fin de semana. (21)

c. En mi opinión la _____ lección es la mejor. (5TH)

d. Dicen que Imelda Marcos tenía _____ pares de zapatos. (2341)

e. El _____ fin de semana de agosto pienso ir de viaje con mis cuñados. (2ND)

f. Para tu cumpleaños, te compré _____ rosas. (14)

g. Hay _____ mujeres en esa universidad. (431)

h. Para la boda, van a hacer muchísimo guacamole. Necesitan

_____ aguacates, _____

cebollas, el jugo de _____ limones y

_____ tomates. (120, 21, 42, 35)

7. The following note from your teacher contains seven errors. Underline each error and write the correction above it:

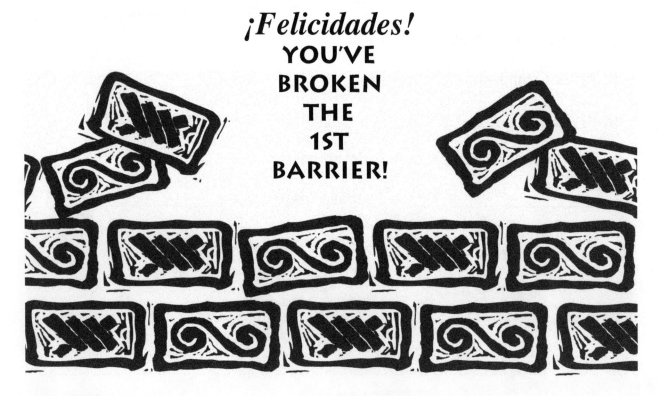

No vas a escribes más ejercicios en este libro. ¡Increíble! Es el fin del libro. Vas a estas muy alegre ahora. Estudiaste para un año y aprendiste mucho español. ¿Fue tu primero año de español o tu segund año? Por hablar bien, tienes que practicar mucho. ¡La práctica hace al maestro! ¿Vas a hablar español este verano con amigos o sólo vas hablar inglés? Ahora, no importa. Tienes que celebrar. ¡Felicidades!

¡Felicidades!
YOU'VE
BROKEN
THE
1ST
BARRIER!

CONJUGACIONES
DE HABLAR,
COMER, VIVIR

REGULAR VERBS

infinitivo	participio	presente	pretérito	imperfecto	Mandatos (commands) Ud./Uds., (+/–)
hablar (to talk, speak)	hablando	hablo hablas habla hablamos habláis hablan	hablé hablaste habló hablamos hablasteis hablaron	hablaba hablabas hablaba hablábamos hablabais hablaban	hable hablen
comer (to eat)	comiendo	como comes come comemos coméis comen	comí comiste comió comimos comisteis comieron	comía comías comía comíamos comíais comían	coma coman
vivir (to live)	viviendo	vivo vives vive vivimos vivís viven	viví viviste vivió vivimos vivisteis vivieron	vivía vivías vivía vivíamos vivíais vivían	viva vivan

IRREGULAR VERBS

infinitivo	participio	presente	pretérito	imperfecto	Mandatos (commands) Ud./Uds., (+/–)
andar (to walk)	andando	ando andas anda andamos andáis andan	anduve anduviste anduvo anduvimos anduvisteis anduvieron	andaba andabas andaba andábamos andabais andaban	ande anden
caber (to fit)	cabiendo	quepo cabes cabe cabemos cabéis caben	cupe cupiste cupo cupimos cupisteis cupieron	cabía cabías cabía cabíamos cabíais cabían	quepa quepan
caer (to fall)	cayendo	caigo caes cae caemos caéis caen	caí caíste cayó caímos caísteis cayeron	caía caías caía caíamos caíais caían	caiga caigan
comenzar (to begin)	comenzando	comienzo comienzas comienza comenzamos comenzáis comienzan	comencé comenzaste comenzó comenzamos comenzasteis comenzaron	comenzaba comenzabas comenzaba comenzábamos comenzabais comenzaban	comience comiencen
conducir (to drive)	conduciendo	conduzco conduces conduce conducimos conducís conducen	conduje condujiste condujo condujimos condujisteis condujeron	conducía conducías conducía conducíamos conducíais conducían	conduzca conduzcan

infinitivo	participio	presente	pretérito	imperfecto	Mandatos (commands) Ud./Uds., (+/−)
conocer (to know)	conociendo	conozco conoces conoce conocemos conocéis conocen	conocí conociste conoció conocimos conocisteis conocieron	conocía conocías conocía conocíamos conocíais conocían	conozca conozcan
construir (to build)	construyendo	construyo construyes construye construimos construís construyen	construí construiste construyó construimos construisteis construyeron	construía construías construía construíamos construíais construían	construya construyan
dar (to give)	dando	doy das da damos dais dan	di diste dio dimos disteis dieron	daba dabas daba dábamos dabais daban	dé den
decir (to say)	diciendo	digo dices dice decimos decís dicen	dije dijiste dijo dijimos dijisteis dijeron	decía decías decía decíamos decíais decían	diga digan
dormir (to sleep)	durmiendo	duermo duermes duerme dormimos dormís duermen	dormí dormiste durmió dormimos dormisteis durmieron	dormía dormías dormía dormíamos dormíais dormían	duerma duerman
estar (to be)	estando	estoy estás está estamos estáis están	estuve estuviste estuvo estuvimos estuvisteis estuvieron	estaba estabas estaba estábamos estabais estaban	esté estén
hacer (to do, make)	haciendo	hago haces hace hacemos hacéis hacen	hice hiciste hizo hicimos hicisteis hicieron	hacía hacías hacía hacíamos hacíais hacían	haga hagan
ir (to go)	yendo	voy vas va vamos vais van	fui fuiste fue fuimos fuisteis fueron	iba ibas iba íbamos ibais iban	vaya vayan
jugar (to play)	jugando	juego juegas juega jugamos jugáis juegan	jugué jugaste jugó jugamos jugasteis jugaron	jugaba jugabas jugaba jugábamos jugabais jugaban	juegue jueguen

infinitivo	participio	presente	pretérito	imperfecto	Mandatos (commands) Ud./Uds., (+/−)
negar (to deny)	negando	niego niegas niega negamos negáis niegan	negué negaste negó negamos negasteis negaron	negaba negabas negaba negábamos negabais negaban	niegue nieguen
oír (to hear)	oyendo	oigo oyes oye oímos oís oyen	oí oíste oyó oímos oísteis oyeron	oía oías oía oíamos oíais oían	oiga oigan
oler (to smell)	oliendo	huelo hueles huele olemos oléis huelen	olí oliste olió olimos olisteis olieron	olía olías olía olíamos olíais olían	huela huelan
pedir (to ask for)	pidiendo	pido pides pide pedimos pedís piden	pedí pediste pidió pedimos pedisteis pidieron	pedía pedías pedía pedíamos pedíais pedían	pida pidan
poder (to be able)	pudiendo	puedo puedes puede podemos podéis pueden	pude pudiste pudo pudimos pudisteis pudieron	podía podías podía podíamos podíais podían	pueda puedan
poner (to put)	poniendo	pongo pones pone ponemos ponéis ponen	puse pusiste puso pusimos pusisteis pusieron	ponía ponías ponía poníamos poníais ponían	ponga pongan
querer (to want, to like)	queriendo	quiero quieres quiere queremos queréis quieren	quise quisiste quiso quisimos quisisteis quisieron	quería querías quería queríamos queríais querían	quiera quieran
reír (to laugh)	riendo	río ríes ríe reímos reís ríen	reí reíste rió reímos reísteis rieron	reía reías reía reíamos reíais reían	ría rían

infinitivo	participio	presente	pretérito	imperfecto	Mandatos (commands) Ud./Uds., (+/–)
saber (to know)	sabiendo	sé sabes sabe sabemos sabéis saben	supe supiste supo supimos supisteis supieron	sabía sabías sabía sabíamos sabíais sabían	sepa sepan
seguir (to follow)	siguiendo	sigo sigues sigue seguimos seguís siguen	seguí seguiste siguió seguimos seguisteis siguieron	seguía seguías seguía seguíamos seguíais seguían	siga sigan
ser (to be)	siendo	soy eres es somos sois son	fui fuiste fue fuimos fuisteis fueron	era eras era éramos erais eran	sea sean
tener (to have)	teniendo	tengo tienes tiene tenemos tenéis tienen	tuve tuviste tuvo tuvimos tuvisteis tuvieron	tenía tenías tenía teníamos teníais tenían	tenga tengan
traer (to bring)	trayendo	traigo traes trae traemos traéis traen	traje trajiste trajo trajimos trajisteis trajeron	traía traías traía traíamos traíais traían	traiga traigan
venir (to come)	viniendo	vengo vienes viene venimos venís vienen	vine viniste vino vinimos vinisteis vinieron	venía venías venía veníamos veníais venían	venga vengan
ver (to see)	viendo	veo ves ve vemos veis ven	vi viste vio vimos visteis vieron	veía veías veía veíamos veíais veían	vea vean

DICCIONARIO
ESPAÑOL-INGLÉS

A

a . . . . at, to
a eso de . . . . at approximately
a la derecha . . . . to the right
a la izquierda . . . . to the left
a lo largo . . . . along
a menudo . . . . often
a pesar de . . . . in spite of
a veces . . . . at times, sometimes
abajo . . . . below
abandonar . . . . to abandon
abeja (la) . . . . bee
abierto/a . . . . open
abogado/a (el/la) . . . . lawyer
abordar . . . . to board
abrazar . . . . to embrace, to hug
abrazo (el) . . . . embrace
abrelatas (el) . . . . can opener
abrigo (el) . . . . coat, overcoat
abril . . . . April
abrir . . . . to open
abuela (la) . . . . grandmother
abuelo (el) . . . . grandfather
aburrido/a . . . . bored, boring
aburrirse . . . . to become (get) bored
acabar de . . to have just (done something)
accidente (el) . . . . accident
acción (la) . . . . action
aceite (el) . . . . oil
acera (la) . . . . sidewalk
acero (el) . . . . steel
acompañar . . . . to accompany
acondicionador de aire (el)
. . . . air conditioner
aconsejar . . . . to advise
acordeón (el) . . . . accordion
acostarse (ue) . . . . to go to bed
acostumbrarse a . . . . to get used to
actitud (la) . . . . attitude
actor (el) . . . . actor
actriz (la) . . . . actress
actual . . . . current, present day
acusar . . . . to accuse
adelante . . . . forward, ahead
adicional . . . . additional
admitir . . . . to admit
adquirir (ie) . . . . to acquire
adversario/a (el/la) . . . . opponent
aeropuerto (el) . . . . airport
afeitar(se) . . . . to shave (oneself)
aficionado/a (el/la) . . . . fan
afilado/a . . . . sharp (e.g., knife)
afuera . . . . outside
afueras (las) . . . . suburbs
agencia de viajes (la) . . . . travel agency
agosto . . . . August
agotado/a . . . . exhausted

agradecer . . . . . to thank, be grateful for
agradecido/a . . . . grateful
agrio/a (amargo/a) . . . . bitter, sour
agua (el) (f.) . . . . water
agudo/a . . . . sharp, astute
águila (el) (f.) . . . . eagle
ahora . . . . now
ahora mismo . . . . right now
ahorrar . . . . to save
ajedrez (el) . . . . chess
ajo (el) . . . . garlic
ala (el) (f.) . . . . wing
alabar . . . . to praise
alarma (la) . . . . alarm
alba (el) (f.) . . . . dawn
albóndiga (la) . . . . meatball
alcalde (el) . . . . mayor
alcanzar . . . . to reach
alcoba (la) . . . . bedroom
alegrarse de . . . . . . to be happy about
alegre . . . . happy
alegría (la) . . . . joy, happiness
alemán (el) . . . . German
alfabeto (el) . . . . alphabet
alfombra (la) . . . . carpet, rug
algo . . . . something
algodón (el) . . . . cotton
alguien . . . . someone
alguno/a . . . . some
allí . . . . there
almacén (el) . . . . . . department store
almohada (la) . . . . pillow
almorzar (ue) . . . . to have lunch
alquilado/a . . . . rented
alquilar . . . . to rent
alrededor . . . . around
alto/a . . . . tall
alumno/a (el/la) . . . . student
alzar . . . . to raise (up)
amable . . . . friendly, kindly, nice
amante (el/la) . . . . lover
amar . . . . to love
amarillo/a . . . . yellow
ambos/as . . . . both
amenazar . . . . to threaten
amigo/a (el/la) . . . . friend
amor (el) . . . . love
amoroso/a . . . . loving
análisis (el) . . . . analysis
anaranjado/a . . . . orange
ancho/a . . . . wide
anchoa (la) . . . . anchovy
andar . . . . to walk
andén (el) . . . . platform
anillo (el) . . . . ring
anillo de compromiso (el)
. . . . engagement ring
anoche . . . . last night

anochecer . . . . to become night
anormal . . . . abnormal
ansioso/a . . . . anxious, eager
anteayer . . . . . . the day before yesterday
anteojos (los) . . . . glasses
antes (de) . . . . before
anuncio (el) . . . . advertisement,
announcement
añadir . . . . to add
año (el) . . . . year
apagar . . . . to turn off
aparecer . . . . to appear
apasionadamente . . . . passionately
apetecer . . . . to appeal to
aplaudir . . . . to applaud
aplazar . . . . to postpone
aplicado/a . . . . applied, dedicated,
industrious
apostar (ue) . . . . to bet
apoyar . . . . to support, to aid
aprender . . . . to learn
aprender de memoria
. . . . to learn by heart
apretar (ie) . . . . . . to tighten, to squeeze
apunte (el) . . . . note
apurado/a . . . . rushed, in a hurry
aquel, aquella . . . . that (over yonder)
aquí . . . . here
árabe (el) . . . . Arabic
arándano (el) . . . . . cranberry, blueberry
araña (la) . . . . spider
árbitro (el) . . . . referee
árbol (el) . . . . tree
arbusto (el) . . . . bush
ardiente . . . . burning, passionate
arena (la) . . . . sand
arete (el) . . . . earring
aretes (los) . . . . earrings
armario (el) . . . . closet
armonía (la) . . . . harmony
arquitecto/a (el/la) . . . . architect
arreglar . . . . to arrange, to fix
arrepentirse (ie) (de) . . . . to regret
arriba . . . . up
arrojar . . . . to throw
arroyo (el) . . . . stream
arroz (el) . . . . rice
arte (el) (f.) . . . . art
asado/a . . . . roasted
asar . . . . to roast
ascensor (el) . . . . elevator
así . . . . in this way
asiento (el) . . . . seat
asistente de vuelo (el/la) . . flight attendant
asistir . . . . to attend
aspiradora (la) . . . . vacuum cleaner
astuto/a . . . . astute
asunto (el) . . . . matter, subject

asustar . . . . to frighten, to scare
atacar . . . . to attack
atado/a . . . . tied
ataque (el) . . . . .attack
atento/a . . . . attentive
aterrizar . . . . to land
atestado/a . . . . crowded
atlético/a . . . . athletic
atraer . . . . to attract
atrás . . . . behind
atreverse a . . . . .to dare to
atrevido/a . . . . .bold, daring
aumentar . . . . .to increase
aunque . . . . although
autobús (el) . . . . .bus
autógrafo (el) . . . . autograph
autopista (la) (autovía)
. . . . highway, freeway
autoridad (la) . . . . authority
avanzado/a . . . . .advanced
avaricioso/a . . . . greedy
averiguar . . . . to find out
avión (el) . . . . airplane
avisar . . . . to notify, to let know
ayer .yesterday
ayuda (la) . . . . help
ayudar . . . . .to help
ayunar . . . . to fast
ayuntamiento (el) . . . . .city hall
azúcar (el, la) . . . . sugar
azul . . . . blue

B

bailar . . . . .to dance
bailarín (el), bailarina (la) . . . . . . dancer
bajar . . . . to go down, to get off
(a train, etc.)
bajo . . . . .under
bajo/a . . . . short
baloncesto (el) . . . . basketball
balcón (el) . . . . balcony
ballena (la) . . . . .whale
banco (el) . . . . bench, pew, bank
banda (la) . . . . band
bandeja (la) . . . . tray
bandera (la) . . . . flag
banquero/a (el/la) . . . . banker
bañador (el) . . . . bathing suit
bañarse . . . . to take a bath
bañera (la) . . . . .tub
baño (el) . . . . .bathroom
banquete (el) . . . . banquet
barato/a . . . . .cheap
barba (la) . . . . beard
barco (el) . . . . boat
barrio (el) . . . . .neighborhood,
section, quarter
barrote (el) . . . . bar (of a window
or a prison cell)
bastante . . . . enough, quite

basura (la) . . . . garbage
basurero/a (el/la) . . . . garbage collector
bata (la) . . . . bathrobe
batalla (la) . . . . battle
batidor/a (el/la) . . . . beater
batir . . . . to beat
bebé (el) . . . . baby
beber . . . . to drink
bebida (la) . . . . drink
beca (la) . . . . scholarship
béisbol (el) . . . . .baseball
belleza (la) . . . . beauty
bello/a . . . . beautiful
bendecir . . . . to bless
besar . . . . to kiss
beso (el) . . . . kiss
biblioteca (la) . . . . library
bibliotecario/a (el/la) . . . . .librarian
bicicleta (la) . . . . .bicycle
bien . . . . .fine, well
bienes . . . . possessions, property
bigote (el) . . . . .mustache
bilingüe . . . . bilingual
billete (el) . . . . ticket (for bus, train, etc.)
billetera (la) . . . . wallet
biología (la) . . . . biology
bisabuela (la) . . . . . . great-grandmother
bisabuelo (el) . . . . . . great-grandfather
bistec (el) . . . . steak
blanco/a . . . . white
blando/a . . . . soft
blusa (la) . . . . blouse
boca (la) . . . . mouth
bocadillo (el) . . . . .sandwich
boda (la) . . . . wedding
boleto (el) . . . . ticket
bolígrafo (el) . . . . pen
bolsa (la) . . . . bag, purse
bombero/a (el/la) . . . . firefighter
bombones (los) . . . . chocolates
bonito/a . . . . .pretty
borracho/a . . . . .drunk
borrar . . . . to erase
bosque (el) . . . . .forest, woods
bosque de lluvia (el) . . . . rain forest
bota (la) . . . . .boot
botas (las) . . . . boots
botella (la) . . . . .bottle
boleto (el) . . . . ticket
bravo/a . . . . brave, fierce, angry
brazo (el) . . . . arm
brillar . . . . to shine
brindar . . . . to toast (drink)
brújula (la) . . . . compass
brusco/a . . . . .abrupt, sudden
buenas noches . . . . good evening,
. . . . .good night
buenas tardes . . . . good afternoon
bueno/a . . . . good
buenos días . . . . good morning
buey (el) . . . . ox

bufanda (la) . . . . scarf
buitre (el) . . . . .vulture
bullicioso/a . . . .noisy, rowdy, boisterous
buscar . . . . .to look for
buzón (el) . . . . .mailbox

C

caballo (el) . . . . horse
cabello (el) . . . . hair
caber . . . . to fit
cabeza (la) . . . . .head
cada . . . . each, every
caer .to fall
caerle bien (mal) . . . . .to get along
well (poorly)
café (el) . . . . coffee
cafetera (la) . . . . coffee maker
caja (la) . . . . box
cajón (el) . . . . .drawer
calcetines (los) . . . . socks
calendario (el) . . . . .calendar
calentamiento global (el) global warming
calentar (ie) . . . . to heat
caliente . . . . warm, hot
callarse . . . . to be quiet
calle (la) . . . . street
caluroso/a . . . . .hot
calvo/a . . . . bald
calzoncillos (los) . . . . . men's underwear
cama (la) . . . . bed
cámara (la) . . . . .camera
camarero/a (el/la) (mesero/a) . . . . waiter
cambiar . . . . .to change
cambio (el) . . . . .change
caminar . . . . to walk
caminata (la) . . . . stroll, walk
camión (el) . . . . truck
camisa (la) . . . . .shirt
camiseta (la) . . . . .T-shirt
campamento (el) . . . . camp
campana (la) . . . . bell
campaña (la) . . . . .campaign
campeón (el), campeona (la)
. . . . champion
campeonato (el) . . . . championship
campista (el/la) . . . . camper
campo (el) . . . . field, country(side)
cancelado/a . . . . .cancelled
cancha (la) . . . . court
canción (la) . . . . .song
candidato/a (el/la) . . . . .candidate
canela (la) . . . . cinnamon
cansado/a . . . . .tired
cansancio (el) . . . . . . .tiredness, fatigue
cantante (el/la) . . . . singer
cantar . . . . to sing
cañón (el) . . . . canyon, cannon
caoba (la) . . . . mahogany
capaz . . . . capable
capitán . . . . .captain

cara (la) . . . . face
caracola (la) . . . . seashell
carbón (el) . . . . coal
caries (la) . . . . cavity
cárcel (la) . . . . jail
cariño (el) . . . . affection
cariñoso/a . . . . affectionate
carnaval (el) . . . . carnival
carne (la) . . . . meat
carnicero/a (el/la) . . . . butcher
caro/a . . . . expensive
carpintero/a (el/la) . . . . carpenter
carrera (la) . . . . race, career
carretera (la) . . . . road, highway
carta (la) . . . . letter
cartel (el) . . . . poster
cartero/a (el/la) . . . . mail carrier
casa (la) . . . . house
casarse . . . . to get married
casarse con . . . . to get married to
casco (el) . . . . helmet
casi . . . . almost
castaño/a . . . . chesnut
castigar . . . . to punish
castigo (el) . . . . punishment
castillo (el) . . . . castle
catarata (la) . . . . waterfall
catedral (la) . . . . cathedral
causar . . . . to cause
cauteloso/a . . . . . cautious, careful, wary
caza (la) . . . . hunting
celda (la) . . . . cell
célebre . . . . celebrated, famous
celoso/a . . . . jealous
cementerio (el) . . . . cemetery
cenar . . . . to have supper
centro (el) . . . . center, downtown
centro comercial (el) . . . . mall
cepillarse . . . . to brush one's (hair, teeth)
cerca . . . . near(by)
cerca (de) . . . . near
cercano/a . . . . nearby, neighboring
ceremonia (la) . . . . ceremony
cero . . . . zero
cerrado/a . . . . closed
cerradura (la) . . . . lock
cerrar (ie) . . . . to close
césped (el) . . . . lawn
chaleco (el) . . . . vest
champaña (la), (el champán) . champagne
chaqueta (la) . . . . jacket
charlar . . . . to chat
chica (la) . . . . girl
chicle (el) . . . . gum
chico (el) . . . . boy
chico/a . . . . little, small
chimenea (la) . . . . . . chimney, fireplace
chiste (el) . . . . joke
chófer (el) . . . . chauffeur
ciclismo (el) . . . . cycling
ciego/a . . . . blind

cielo (el) . . . . sky, heaven
ciencia (la) . . . . science
científico/a (el/la) . . . . scientist
cierto/a . . . . certain
cigarrillo (el) . . . . cigarette
cine (el) . . . . cinema, movie theater
cinturón (el) . . . . belt
cinturón de seguridad (el) . . . . . seatbelt
circo (el) . . . . circus
circular . . . . round, circular
cita (la) . . . . date
ciudad (la) . . . . city
ciudadano/a (el/la) . . . . citizen
clarinete (el) . . . . clarinet
claro/a . . . . clear
clase (la) . . . . class
cliente/clienta (el/la) . . . client, customer
clima (el) . . . . climate
clínica (la) . . . . clinic, hospital
cloro (el) . . . . chlorine
coche (el) . . . . car
cochinillo (el) . . . . baby pig
cocina (la) . . . . kitchen
cocinar . . . . to cook
cocinero/a (el/la) . . . . cook
coco (el) . . . . coconut
código postal (el) . . . . zip code
coger . . . . to take, to catch
cola (la) . . . . line, tail
colección (la) . . . . collection
coleccionar . . . . to collect
colega (el/la) . . . . colleague
colegio (el) . . . . high school
colgar (ue) . . . . to hang (up)
collar (el) . . . . necklace
colocar . . . . to place, to arrange
combinar . . . . to combine
comedor (el) . . . . dining room
comenzar (ie) . . . . to begin
comer . . . . to eat
comida (la) . . . . food
comisaría (la) . . . . police station
como . . . . as, since, like
¿cómo? . . . . how?
cómodo/a . . . . comfortable
compañero/a de cuarto (el/la)
. . . . roommate
compasión (la) . . . . compassion
competición (la) . . . . competition
competir (i) . . . . to compete
competitivo/a . . . . competitive
comportarse . . . . to behave
comprar . . . . to buy
comprender . . . . to understand
computadora (la) . . . . computer
común . . . . common
con . . . . with
concierto (el) . . . . concert
concurso (el) . . . . contest
conducir . . . . to drive
conferencia de prensa (la)

. . . . press conference
confesar (ie) . . . . to confess
confianza (la) . . . . . confidence, trust (in)
confiar en . . . . to trust
confundido/a . . . . confused
confundir . . . . to confuse
confuso/a . . . . confused, confusing
congelador (el) . . . . freezer
conocer . . . . to know (a person)
conocido/a . . . . well-known
consecutivo/a . . . . consecutive
conseguir (i) . . . . to get, to obtain
consejo (el) . . . . advice
conservar . . . . to conserve
constante . . . . constant
constelación (la) . . . . constellation
construir . . . . to build, to construct
contaminado/a . . . . contaminated
contar (ue) . . . . to count, to tell
contar (ue) chismes . . . . to gossip
contar con . . . . to count on
contento/a . . . . content, happy
contestador automático (el)
. . . . answering machine
contestar . . . . to answer
continente (el) . . . . continent
contra . . . . against
contraseña (la) . . . . password
contrato (el) . . . . contract
convencer . . . . to convince
convertir (ie) . . . . to convert
corazón (el) . . . . heart
corbata (la) . . . . tie
cordero (el) . . . . lamb
cordial . . . . cordial, polite
cordialidad (la) . . . . cordiality
cordones (los) . . . . shoelaces
corpulento/a . . . . stout, heavy-set, burly
corregir (i) . . . . to correct
correo (el) . . . . mail
correo electrónico (el) . . . . e-mail
correr . . . . to run
corriente . . . . current, present
corrupto/a . . . . corrupt
cortacésped (el) . . . . lawn mower
cortar . . . . to cut
corte (la) . . . . court
cortés . . . . courteous, polite
cortesía (la) . . . . courtesy
cortinas (las) . . . . curtains
corto/a . . . . short
cosa (la) . . . . thing
cosecha (la) . . . . crop
costa (la) . . . . coast
costar (ue) . . . . to cost
costurera (la) . . . seamstress, dressmaker
crema (la) . . . . cream
crimen (el) . . . . crime
cotidiano/a . . . . daily, everyday
crear . . . . to create, to make
crecer . . . . to grow, to increase

creer . . . . to believe
cremallera (la) . . . . zipper
criada (la) . . . . maid
cristal (el) . . . . glass (the material)
cristiano/a . . . . Christian
crucero (el) . . . . cruise (ship)
cruel . . . . cruel, mean
cuaderno (el) . . . . notebook
cuadrado/a . . . . square
cuadro (el) . . . . painting
¿cuál? . . . . which?, what?
¿cuál(es)? . . . . which one(s)?
cualquier . . . . any
cualquiera . . . . anybody
¿cuándo? . . . . when?
¿cuánto/a(s)? . . . . . . how much?/many?
cuarto (el) . . . . room, quarter, fourth
(cuarto de) baño (el) . . . . bathroom
cubiertos (los) . . . . silverware
cubrir . . . . to cover
cuchara (la) . . . . .spoon
cuchillo (el) . . . . knife
cuenta (la) . . . . .bill
cuento (el) . . . . story, tale
cuero (el) . . . . leather
cuidadoso/a . . . . careful, cautious
cuidar . . . . to care for
culpa (la) . . . . fault, guilt
culpable . . . . .guilty
cumbre (la) . . . . .summit, peak
cumplir . . . . to complete, fulfill
cumpleaños (el) . . . . .birthday
cuñada (la) . . . . sister-in-law
cuñado (el) . . . . brother-in-law
cura (el) . . . . priest
curso (el) . . . . course

D

dama (la) . . . . lady
dama de honor (la) . . . . . . maid of honor
dar . . . . to give
dar una vuelta . . . . . to take a walk/drive
darle asco a . . . . to be loathsome to,
                          to be sickened by
darse cuenta de . . . . to realize
                  (i.e., come to awareness of)
de . . . . .of, from
de flores . . . . flowered
de la mañana . . . . . A.M. (in the morning)
de la noche . . . . P.M. (in the evening)
de la tarde . . . . . . .P.M. (in the afternoon)
de lunares . . . . .polka-dot
de nuevo, otra vez . . . . again
de rayas . . . . striped
de repente . . . . suddenly
debajo . . . . underneath
debajo de . . . . below, under
deber . . . . to owe, ought to
débil . . . . weak
década (la) . . . . decade

decidir . . . . to decide
décimo/a . . . . tenth
declarar . . . . to declare
defecto (el) . . . . defect
dejar . . . . to leave (behind), to allow
dejar de (+ infinitive)
. . . . to stop doing something
delante de . . . . in front of
deletrear . . . . to spell
demás (los/las) . . . . (the) others
demasiado/a (adv.) . . . . too much
demasiado/a (adj.) . . . . too much,
                          (pl. too many)
dentista (el/la) . . . . dentist
dentro de . . . . inside of
dependienta (la) . . . . salesclerk
dependiente (el) . . . . salesclerk
deporte (el) . . . . sport
deportes (los) . . . . .sports
deportivos (los) . . . . .tennis shoes
deprimido/a . . . . depressed
deprimir . . . . to depress
derecha (la) . . . . .right
derecho (el) . . . . right, privilege
derecho/a (adj.) . . . . .right
derramar . . . . .to spill
derrota (la) . . . . defeat
desafortunadamente . . . . .unfortunately
desaparecer . . . . .to disappear
desarrollar . . . . to develop
desastre (el) . . . . disaster
desayunar . . . . .to have breakfast
descansar . . . . to rest, to relax
descubrir . . . . to discover
desde . . . . since, from
desear . . . . to desire
desesperar . . . . . . to despair, to lose hope
desfile (el) . . . . parade
desgraciadamente . . . . . . .unfortunately
desierto (el) . . . . .desert
desordenado/a . . . . messy, not neat
despacho (el) . . . . .office
despacio . . . . slowly
despedida (la) . . . . farewell, parting
despedirse (i) (de) . . . . to say goodbye to
despertador (el) . . . . alarm clock
despertarse (ie) . . . . to wake up
después (de) . . . . .after
destino (el) . . . . .destiny, fate, destination
destruir . . . . to destroy
detrás . . . . behind
desván (el) . . . . attic
desvestirse (i) . . . . to undress
detalle (el) . . . . detail
detener . . . . to detain, to stop
detrás, detrás de . . . . behind
deuda (la) . . . . debt
devolver (ue) . . . . . to return (an object)
día (el) . . . . day
diadema (la) . . . . .headband
diamante (el) . . . . diamond

dibujo (el) . . . . sketch, painting, drawing
dichoso/a . . . . . . lucky, happy, fortunate
diciembre . . . . December
diente (el) . . . . tooth
diestro/a . . . . right-handed
dieta (la) . . . . diet
difícil .difficult
difunto/a . . . . .dead
dinero (el) . . . . money
dios (el) . . . . god
diosa (la) . . . . goddess
dirigir . . . . .to direct
disciplina (la) . . . . .discipline
disco (el) . . . . record
disco compacto (el) . . compact disc (CD)
discoteca (la) . . . . discotheque, nightclub
discreto/a . . . . discreet
discurso (el) . . . . speech
diseñar . . . . to design
disfraz (el) . . . . disguise, costume
disfrutar de . . . . to enjoy
disparar . . . . to shoot
distinto/a . . . . .different, distinct
divertirse (ie) . . . . to enjoy oneself,
                          to have a good time
divino/a . . . . divine
divorcio (el) . . . . divorce
doblar . . . . to fold
doble . . . . double
doler (ue) . . . . to hurt
docena (la) . . . . .dozen
doler (ue) . . . . to ache, to hurt
dolor (el) . . . . pain, grief
dominar . . . . .to dominate
domingo . . . . Sunday
¿dónde? . . . . .where?
dorado/a . . . . golden
dormir (ue) . . . . to sleep
dos veces . . . . twice
droga (la) . . . . .drug
ducha (la) . . . . .shower
ducharse . . . . to take a shower
duda (la) . . . . doubt
dudoso/a . . . . .doubtful
dueño/a (el/la) . . . . owner
dulce .sweet
durante . . . . during
durar . . . . to last
durazno (el) . . . . .peach
duro/a .hard

E

echar . . . . to throw, to throw away
echar de menos . . . . . . to miss someone,
                          something
echar(le) la culpa a . . to blame(someone)
economía (la) . . . . economy
edad (la) . . . . .age
edificio (el) . . . . .building
ejercicio (el) . . . . .exercise

él . . . . he, him
electricista (el/la) . . . . electrician
eléctrico/a . . . . electric
elegancia (la) . . . . elegance
elegir (i) . . . . to choose, to elect
ella . . . . she ,her
ellas/os . . . . they, them
embajador (el) . . . . ambassador
embarazoso/a . . . . embarrassing
emocionado/a, ilusionado/a . . . . .excited
empatado/a . . . . tied
empezar (ie) . . . . .to begin
empleado/a (el/la) . . . . .employee
empleo (el) . . . . .job
empresa (la) . . . . company
en . . . . .in, on
en absoluto . . . . in no way
en casa . . . . at home
en seguida (enseguida) . . . . .at once
en vez de . . . . instead of
en voz alta . . . . aloud
enamorarse de . . . . . to fall in love with
encender (ie) . . . . . . to light (e.g., a fire),
                    to turn on (e.g., a light)
enchufar . . . . .to plug in
encima de . . . . on top of
encontrar (ue) . . . . to find, to meet
enemigo (el) . . . . enemy
energía nuclear (la) . . . . nuclear energy
enero . . . . January
enfadar(se) . . . . to become angry
enfermero/a (el/la) . . . . nurse
enfermo/a . . . . sick
enfrente de . . . . in front of
engañado/a . . . . .tricked
engañar . . . . to deceive, to cheat
engordar . . . . to get fat
enojarse . . . . to become angry
enojo (el) . . . . anger
enorme . . . . enormous
ensalada (la) . . . . salad
ensayo (el) . . . . essay
enseñanza (la) . . . . .teaching
enseñar . . . . to teach
entender (ie) . . . . to understand
entero/a . . . . whole, entire
enterrar (ie) . . . . .to bury
entrada (la) . . . . admission, ticket,
                                     entrance
entrar . . . . to enter
entre . . . . between, among
entregar . . . . . . to deliver, to hand over,
                                   to turn in
entrenador (el), entrenadora (la)
. . . . .coach
entrenamiento (el) . . . . training
entrevista (la) . . . . .interview
entrevistar . . . . .to interview
enviar . . . . .to send
envidioso/a . . . . envious, jealous
episodio (el) . . . . episode

época (la) . . . . era
equipaje (el) . . . . luggage
equipo (el) . . . . team
equivocado/a . . . . mistaken
equivocarse . . . . .to make a mistake
escalar una montaña . to scale a mountain
escalera (la) . . . . ladder, stair
escaleras (las) . . . . stairs
escapar . . . . to escape
escena (la) . . . . scene
escoba (la) . . . . broom
escoger . . . . to choose, to select
esconder . . . . .to hide
escribir . . . . to write
escritor (el), escritora (la) . . . . . . .writer
escritorio (el) . . . . .desk
escuchar . . . . to listen to
escudo (el) . . . . .shield, coat of arms
escuela (la) . . . . school
escupir . . . . to spit
escurrir . . . . to strain (e.g., pasta)
ese/a . . . . that
esencial . . . . essential
esfuerzo (el) . . . . .effort
esmalte de uñas (el) . . . . nail polish
espacio (el) . . . . space
espaguetis (los) . . . . spaghetti
espárrago (el) . . . . asparagus
especial . . . . .special
espectáculo (el) . . . . show, performance
espejo (el) . . . . mirror
esperar . . . . .to hope, to wait
espeso/a . . . . thick, dense
espiar . . . . to spy
esposa (la) . . . . wife
esposo (el) . . . . .husband
esquí (el) . . . . skiing
esquina (la) . . . . corner (of a street)
esta mañana . . . . this morning
esta noche . . . . .tonight
esta tarde . . . . this afternoon
estación de tren (la) . . . . . . .train station
estacionamiento (el) . . . . . . .parking lot
                                     (garage)
estacionar . . . . .to park
estadio (el) . . . . stadium
estampilla (la) . . . . .stamp
estante (el) . . . . shelf
estar . . . . to be
estar de acuerdo . . . . .to agree
estar de moda . . . . to be in style
estatua (la) . . . . .statue
este . . . . east
este/a . . . . this
estilo (el) . . . . .style
estómago (el) . . . . .stomach
estornudar . . . . to sneeze
estrecho/a . . . . .narrow
estrella (la) . . . . star
estreno (el) . . . . .debut, premiere
estudiante (el/la) . . . . .student

estudiar . . . . to study
estúpido/a, tonto/a . . . . stupid
eterno/a . . . . .eternal
evitar . . . . .to avoid
examen (el) . . . . .test
excursión (la) . . . . .excursion, trip
exigir . . . . to demand, to require
éxito (el) . . . . success
exitoso/a . . . . successful
exótico/a . . . . exotic
explicar . . . . to explain
explorador(a) (el/la) . . . . .explorer
exposición (la) . . . . art show, fair,
                                   exhibition
extranjero/a . . . . .foreign
extraño/a (raro/rara) . . . . .strange
extraordinario/a . . . . .extraordinary
extraterrestre . . . . .extraterrestrial

F

fábrica (la) . . . . .factory
fabricar . . . . to manufacture
fácil .easy
falda (la) . . . . .skirt
falsificado/a . . . . .fake
falta (la) . . . . .lack, absence
fama (la) . . . . fame
fantástico/a . . . . .fantastic
fascinar . . . . to fascinate
fastidiar . . . . to annoy
fe (la) .faith
febrero . . . . February
fecha (la) . . . . date
felicidad (la) . . . . happiness
felicidades (las) . . . . congratulations
felicitar . . . . to congratulate
feliz . . . . happy
fenomenal . . . . .phenomenal
feo/a . . . . .ugly
feroz . . . . fierce, ferocious
fiarse de . . . . .to trust
fideo (el) . . . . .noodle
fiel . . . . faithful
fiesta (la) . . . . party
fijarse en . . . . to notice
fijo/a . . . . .fixed, firm
fila (la) . . . . row
filosofía (la) . . . . philosophy
fin de semana (el) . . . . weekend
final (el) . . . . .final, end
finca (la) . . . . .farm
fingir . . . . .to pretend, to fake
fino/a . . . . fine, delicate
firmar . . . . to sign
firmeza (la) . . . . firmness
física (la) . . . . physics
flaco/a . . . . thin, skinny
flauta (la) . . . . .flute
flecha (la) . . . . .arrow
flor (la) . . . . flower

folleto (el) . . . . brochure
formidable . . . . wonderful, terrific
fortuna (la) . . . . fortune
foto (la) . . . . photo
foto(grafía) (la) . . . . photo(graph)
francés (el) . . . . French (language)
franco/a . . . . frank
frasco (el) . . . . bottle
frase (la) . . . . sentence
frecuentemente . . . . frequently
fregadero (el) . . . . sink (in kitchen)
fregar (ie) . . . . to scour, to scrub
freír (i) . . . . to fry
frente (la) . . . . forehead
fresco/a . . . . fresh, cool
frío/a . . . . cold
frontera (la) . . . . border, frontier
frustrado/a . . . . frustrated
fuego (el) . . . . fire
fuente (la) . . . . fountain
fuerte . . . . strong
fumar . . . . to smoke
funcionar . . . . to work, to function
fundar . . . . to found, to establish
furioso/a . . . . furious, very mad
fútbol (el) . . . . soccer
fútbol americano (el) . . . . football

G

gafas (las) . . . . glasses
galería de arte (la) . . . . art gallery
galleta (la) . . . . cookie
gallina (la) . . . . hen
ganar . . . . to win, to earn
ganso (el) . . . . goose
garaje (el) . . . . garage
garganta (la) . . . . throat
gasolinera (la) . . . . gas station
gastar . . . . to spend, to waste
gato (el) . . . . cat
generoso/a . . . . generous
genial . . . . . smart, original, exceptional
gente (la) . . . . people
geranio (el) . . . . geranium
gerente (el) . . . . manager
gesto (el) . . . . gesture
gira (la) . . . . tour
girar . . . . . . to revolve, to rotate, to turn
globo (el) . . . . balloon
gobernador/a (el/la) . . . . governor
gobernar (ie) . . . . to govern
gobierno (el) . . . . government
gol (el) . . . . . goal (e.g., soccer, hockey)
golpear . . . . to beat, to hit, to punch
gordo/a . . . . fat
gorra (la) . . . . hat, cap
gota (la) . . . . drop (of liquid)
gozar de . . . . to enjoy
gracias . . . . thanks
grabadora (la) . . . . tape recorder

grabar . . . . to engrave, to record
graduarse . . . . to graduate
gran . . . . great
grande . . . . big
graniza . . . . it is hailing
granizar . . . . to hail
granja (la) . . . . farm
gratis . . . . free
grave . . . . serious
grifo (el) . . . . faucet
gris . . . . grey
gritar . . . . to shout
grosero/a . . . . rude, crude
guante (el) . . . . glove
guantes (los) . . . . gloves
guapo/a . . . . good-looking
guardar . . . . to guard, to keep
guardar silencio . . . . to keep silent
guerra (la) . . . . war
guerrero/a (el/la) . . . . warrior
guerrillero/a (el/la) . . . . guerrilla
guía (el/la) . . . . tour guide
guitarra (la) . . . . guitar
gusto (el) . . . . taste

H

había . . . . there was, there were
hábil . . . . clever, intelligent
habitación doble (la) . . . . . double room
hablar . . . . to talk, to speak
hacer . . . . to do, to make
hacer caso . . . . to pay attention to
hacer cola . . . . to wait in line
hacer la maleta . . . . to pack
hacer un viaje . . . . to take a trip
hacer una pregunta . . . . to ask a question
hacia . . . . towards
hallar . . . . to find
hamburguesa (la) . . . . hamburger
harina (la) . . . . flour
harto/a . . . . fed up, enough
hasta . . . . until
hasta luego . . . . see you later
hay . . . . there is, there are
hecho (el) . . . . fact
hecho/a a mano . . . . handmade
heladería (la) . . . . ice cream store
helado (el) . . . . ice cream
helar (ie) . . . . to freeze
helicóptero (el) . . . . helicopter
hemisferio (el) . . . . hemisphere
heredar . . . . to inherit
herida (la) . . . . wound, injury
herido/a . . . . wounded
herir (ie) . . . . to wound
hermana (la) . . . . sister
hermano (el) . . . . brother
héroe (el) . . . . hero
heroína (la) . . . . heroine
herramienta (la) . . . . tool

hervir (ie) . . . . to boil
hielo (el) . . . . ice
hierba (la) . . . . grass
higiene (la) . . . . hygiene
hija (la) . . . . daughter
hijo (el) . . . . son
himno (el) . . . . hymn
historia (la) . . . . history, story
hockey sobre hielo (el) . . . . . . ice hockey
hogar (el) . . . . home, hearth
hoja (la) . . . . leaf
hombre (el) . . . . man
hondo/a . . . . deep
hora (la) . . . . hour
horario (el) . . . . schedule
(horno de) microondas (el)
. . . . microwave (oven)
hotel (el) . . . . hotel
hoy . . . . today
huelga (la) . . . . strike
huevo (el) . . . . egg
humilde . . . . humble
huracán (el) . . . . hurricane

I

idéntico/a . . . . identical
idioma (el) . . . . language
iglesia (la) . . . . church
ilegal . . . . illegal
ilustre . . . . illustrious
imagen (la) . . . . image
imbécil . . . . imbecile
impedir (i) . . . . to prevent
impermeable (el) . . . . raincoat
impresionante . . . . impressive
impreso/a . . . . printed
imprimir . . . . to print
impuesto (el) . . . . tax
incendio (el) . . . . fire
incluso . . . . including, even (adv.)
incómodo/a . . . . uncomfortable
increíble . . . . incredible
infancia (la) . . . . childhood
infeliz . . . . unhappy
inferior . . . . inferior, lower
informe (el) . . . . report
ingeniero/a (el/la) . . . . engineer
ingenuo/a . . . . naive
inglés (el) . . . . English
ingrediente (el) . . . . ingredient
inmortal . . . . immortal
insistir en . . . . to insist on
insoportable . . . . unbearable, intolerable
inspiración (la) . . . . inspiration
instalar . . . . to install
instinto (el) . . . . instinct
instrucciones (las) . . . . instructions
insultar . . . . to insult
integridad (la) . . . . integrity
intenso/a . . . . intense

intentar . . . . to try, to attempt
interés (el) . . . . interest
interesante . . . . interesting
internacional . . . . international
interrumpir . . . . to interrupt
íntimo/a . . . . intimate, close
inútil . . . . useless
invertir (ie) . . . . to invest (money)
invierno (el) . . . . winter
invitado/a (el/la) . . . . guest
invitar . . . . to invite
ir . . . . to go
ir de camping . . . . to go camping
ir de compras . . . . to go shopping
ir de viaje . . . . to travel
irritar . . . . to irritate
isla (la) . . . . island
izquierdo/a . . . . left

J

jabón (el) . . . . soap
jamón (el) . . . . ham
japonés (el) . . . . Japanese
jardín (el) . . . . garden
jardín botánico (el) . . . . botanical garden
jardín (parque) zoológico (el) . . . . . zoo
jardinero/a (el/la) . . . . gardener
jaula (la) . . . . cage
jefa (la) . . . . boss
jefe (el) . . . . boss
jirafa (la) . . . . giraffe
jonrón (el) . . . . homerun
jóvenes (los) . . . . youth, youngsters
joyería (la) . . . . jewelry
jubilado/a . . . . retired
judío/a . . . . Jewish
jueves . . . . Thursday
juez/jueza (el/la) . . . . judge
jugador/a (el/la) . . . . player
jugar (ue) . . . . to play
jugo (el) . . . . juice
juicio (el) . . . . judgement, trial
julio . . . . July
junio . . . . June
juntos/as . . . . together
jurar . . . . to swear
justo/a . . . . just, fair, appropriate
juventud (la) . . . . youth
juzgar . . . . to judge

L

lacio/a . . . . straight (e.g., hair)
lado (el) . . . . side
ladrar . . . . to bark
ladrón (el) . . . . robber
ladrona (la) . . . . robber
lago (el) . . . . lake
lágrima (la) . . . . tear
lamentar . . . . to regret

lámpara (la) . . . . lamp, light
langosta (la) . . . . lobster
lanzador (el) . . . . pitcher
lanzar . . . . to throw, to hurl, to pitch
lápiz (el) . . . . pencil
lápiz de labios (el pintalabios) . . lipstick
largo/a . . . . long
lata (la) . . . . can
lavabo (el) . . . . sink (in bathroom)
lavadora (la) . . . . washer
lavaplatos (el) . . . . dishwasher
lavar . . . . to wash
lavarse . . . . to wash oneself
leal . . . . loyal
lección (la) . . . . lesson
leche (la) . . . . milk
lector/a (el/la) . . . . reader
leer . . . . to read
lejano/a . . . . distant
lejos . . . . far (away)
lejos de . . . . far from
lengua (la) . . . . tongue, language
lentes de contacto (los, las)
. . . . contact lenses
lentilla (la) . . . . contact lens
lentillas (las) . . . . contact lenses
lento/a . . . . slow
leña (la) . . . . firewood
león (el) . . . . lion
lesión (la) . . . . injury
lesionado/a . . . . injured
letra (la) . . . . lyrics, letter
levantarse . . . . to get up
leve . . . . slight, light
leyenda (la) . . . . legend
libertad (la) . . . . liberty
libra (la) . . . . pound
libre . . . . free, available
libro (el) . . . . book
licencia (la) . . . . license
líder (el) . . . . leader
ligero/a . . . . light
limón (el) . . . . lemon
limonada (la) . . . . lemonade
limpiar . . . . to clean
limpio/a . . . . clean
lindo/a . . . . pretty
liso/a . . . . smooth, flat
listo/a . . . . ready, clever, smart
loco/a . . . . crazy
locura (la) . . . . . madness, insanity, folly
lograr . . . . to obtain, to succeed in
loro (el) . . . . parrot
lotería (la) . . . . lottery
luchador (el) . . . . wrestler
luchar . . . . to fight, to struggle
lucir . . . . to shine
luego . . . . later
luminoso/a . . . . bright, brilliant
luna (la) . . . . moon
luna de miel (la) . . . . honeymoon

lunes . . . . Monday
lupa (la) . . . . magnifying glass
luz (la) . . . . light

LL

llama (la) . . . . llama
llamar . . . . to call
llave (la) . . . . key
llegada (la) . . . . arrival
llegar . . . . to arrive
llenar . . . . to fill
lleno/a . . . . full
llevar . . . . to take, to carry
llevarse bien (mal) con
. . . . . . to get along well (badly) with
llorar . . . . to cry
llover (ue) . . . . to rain
lluvia (la) . . . . rain

M

madera (la) . . . . wood
madrastra (la) . . . . stepmother
madre (la) . . . . mother
madrina (la) . . . . godmother
madrugada (la) . . . . dawn
maduro/a . . . . mature, ripe
maestría (la) . . . . master's degree
maestro/a (el/la) . . . . teacher
mal . . . . bad, poorly
malcriado/a . . . . . ill-bred, bad-mannered
maldito/a . . . . accursed, damned
maleducado/a . . . . rude
maleta (la) . . . . suitcase
malo/a . . . . bad
mancha (la) . . . . stain
manchado/a . . . . stained
mandar . . . . to order, to send
mandón (m.) . . . . bossy
mandona (f.) . . . . bossy
mano (la) . . . . hand
manta (la) . . . . blanket
mantel (el) . . . . tablecloth
mantener . . . . to maintain, to keep
mantequilla (la) . . . . butter
manzana (la) . . . . apple
mañana . . . . tomorrow
mapa (el) . . . . map
máquina (la) . . . . machine
mar (el) . . . . sea
maravilla (la) . . . . marvel
maravilloso/a . . . . wonderful, marvelous
marcharse . . . . to go away
marciano (el) . . . . Martian
marido (el) . . . . husband
marinero/a (el/la) . . . . sailor
marisco (el) . . . . seafood, shellfish
martillo (el) . . . . hammer
marrón . . . . brown
martes . . . . Tuesday

marzo . . . . March	monja (la) . . . . nun	niñez (la) . español-inglés . childhood
más . . . . more	monje (el) . . . . monk	niño (el) . . . . boy
masticar . . . . to chew	montaña (la) . . . . mountain	no . . . . no
matar .to kill	montar en bicicleta . . . . .to ride a bicycle	noche (la) . . . . night
matemáticas (las) . . . . math	montar un negocio . . . to start a business	nombrar . . . . to name
matrícula (la) . . . . tuition	montón (el) . . . . .heap, pile	noreste (el) . . . . northeast
maullar . . . . to meow (like a cat)	morado/a . . . . purple	noroeste (el) . . . . northwest
mayo . . . . .May	morder (ue) . . . . to bite	norte . . . . north
mayor . . . . older	moreno/a . . . . .brunette, brown	nosotros/as . . . . we
medalla (la) . . . . medal	morir (ue) . . . . .to die	noticias (las) . . . . news
mediano/a . . . . .medium, average	mosca (la) . . . . fly	novela (la) . . . . novel
medianoche (la) . . . . midnight	mostrar (ue) . . . . to show	novia (la) . . . . . bride, fiancée, girlfriend
médico/a (el/la) . . . . doctor	moto(cicleta) (la) . . . . motorcycle	noviazgo (el) . . . . .engagement
mediodía (el) . . . . noon	mover (ue) . . . . .to move	noviembre . . . . November
medir (i) . . . . .to measure	móvil (el) . . . . .cellphone	novio (el) . . . . . groom, fiancé, boyfriend
mejor . . . . .better, best	mucho .a lot	nublado/a . . . . cloudy
melancólico/a . . . . . gloomy, melancholy	muchos/as . . . . many	nuevo/a . . . . new
melocotón (el) . . . . .peach	mudarse . . . . .to move (relocate)	nunca . . . . never
melodía (la) . . . . melody	mudo/a . . . . .mute, dumb	
mencionar . . . . .to mention	mujer (la) . . . . woman	
menor . . . . younger	mula (la) . . . . mule	**O**
menos . . . . less	multa (la) . . . . fine	
mensaje (el) . . . . message	mundo(el) . . . . .world	obra (la) . . . . work
mentir (ie) . . . . to lie, to fib	muñeca (la) . . . . doll, wrist	obrero/a (el/la) . . . . .worker
mentira (la) . . . . lie	museo (el) . . . . .museum	o(b)scuro/a . . . . .dark, obscure
mentiroso/a . . . . lying, untruthful	música (la) . . . . .music	obstinado/a (terco) . . stubborn, obstinate
mercado (el) . . . . .market	músico/a (el/la) . . . . musician	occidental . . . . western
merecer . . . . .to deserve, to merit	musulmán . . . . Muslim	océano (el) . . . . .ocean
mes (el) . . . . month	mutuo/a . . . . .mutual	octubre . . . . .October
mesa (la) . . . . table	muy . . . . .very	ocultar . . . . .to hide
meta (la) . . . . .goal (objective)		ocupado/a . . . . .busy
meteorólogo (el) . . . . meteorologist		ocurrir . . . . to occur, to happen
meter . . . . to put into	**N**	odiar . . . . to hate
método (el) . . . . method		oeste .west
metro (el) . . . . .metro, subway	nacer . . . . to be born	ofender . . . . to offend
mezclado/a . . . . mixed	nada . . . . nothing	oficina (la) . . . . .office
mezclar . . . . to mix	nadar . . . . to swim	ofrecer . . . . to offer
mezquita (la) . . . . mosque	nadie . . . . no one	oír . . . . to hear
mientras . . . . while	naranja (la) . . . . orange	ojalá . . . . if only
miércoles . . . . Wednesday	nariz (la) . . . . .nose	ojo (el) . . . . .eye
miga (la) . . . . crumb	nata (batida) (la) . . . . . .(whipped) cream	ola (la) . . . . wave
mil . . . . thousand	natación (la) . . . . swimming	oler (ue) . . . . to smell
milagro (el) . . . . miracle	naturaleza (la) . . . . nature	olla (la) . . . . .pot
milla (la) . . . . .mile	nave (la) . . . . ship	optimista (el/la) . . . . optimist
millón . . . . .million	navegar . . . . to sail	opuesto (el) (n.) . . . . .opposite
mimado/a . . . . .spoiled	necesitar . . . . to need	opuesto/a (adj.) . . . . .opposite
ministro (el) . . . . .minister	necio/a . . . . stupid, foolish	ordenador (el) . . . . . . computer (Spain)
mirar . . . . .to look at	negar (ie) . . . . to deny	ordinario/a . . . . .ordinary
misa (la) . . . . mass (church)	negocio (el) . . . . .business	organizar . . . . to organize
mismo/a . . . . same	negro/a . . . . black	órgano (el) . . . . organ
misterio (el) . . . . mystery	nevar (ie) . . . . to snow	orgullo (el) . . . . pride
misterioso/a . . . . .mysterious	nevera (la) . . . . refrigerator	orgulloso/a . . . . .proud
mochila (la) . . . . .backpack	ni . . . . neither, nor	oriental . . . . .eastern
moda (la) . . . . .style, fashion	niebla (la) . . . . .fog	original . . . . original
modesto/a . . . . .modest	nieta (la) . . . . granddaughter	orilla (la) . . bank, shore (of river, ocean)
mofeta (la) (el zorrillo) . . . . .skunk	nieto (el) . . . . grandson	oro (el) . . . . .gold
mojado/a . . . . wet	nieve (la) . . . . snow	orquesta (la) . . . . orchestra
mojar . . . . to wet, to moisten	ninguno/a . . . . none	oscuridad (la) . . . . darkness
molestar . . . . to bother	nivel (el) . . . . level	oscuro/a . . . . .dark
monasterio (el) . . . . monastery	niña (la) . . . . .girl	oso (el) . . . . bear
moneda (la) . . . . coin	niñero/a (el, la) . . . . babysitter	ostra (la) . . . . oyster

otoñal . . . . autumnal
otoño (el) . . . . fall
otra vez, de nuevo . . . . again
otro/a . . . . another, other
oveja (la) . . . . sheep

P

padre (el) . . . . father
padrino (el) . . . . godfather
padrino de boda (el) . . . . best man
pagar . . . . to pay
país (el) . . . . country
paisaje (el) . . . . landscape, scenery
pájaro (el) . . . . bird
pala (la) . . . . shovel
palabra (la) . . . . word
palacio (el) . . . . palace
pálido/a . . . . pale
palomitas (las) . . . . popcorn
pampas (las) . . . . plains
pan (el) . . . . bread
panadero/a (el/la) . . . . baker
pantalla (la) . . . . screen
pantalones (los) . . . . pants
pantalones cortos (los) . . . . .shorts
pañuelo (el) . . . . handkerchief, scarf
papa (la) . . . . potato
papel (el) . . . . paper
paquete (el) . . . . package
par . . . . pair
para . . . . by, for, in order to
para que . . . . in order that
para siempre . . . . .forever
parabrisas (el) . . . . windshield
paraguas (el) . . . . umbrella
parar . . . . to stop
parecer . . . . to seem, to appear
parecerse a . . . . to resemble
pared (la) . . . . wall
pareja (la) . . . . pair, couple
pariente (el) . . . . relative
parrilla (la) . . . . grill
parque (el) . . . . park
parque de atracciones (el)
. . . . amusement park
partido (el) . . . . game
pasado/a . . . . past, last
pasajero/a (e/la) . . . . passenger
pasaporte (el) . . . . passport
pasar . . . . to pass
pasar (tiempo) . . . . to spend (time)
pasar la aspiradora . . . . to vacuum
pasárselo bien/mal . . . . . to have a great/
bad time
pasear . . . . to take a stroll
paseo (el) . . . . stroll, trip
pasillo (el) . . . . hallway
pastel (el) . . . . .cake
pastilla (la) . . . . .pill
patata (la) . . . . potato

patinador (el) . . . . .skater
patinaje (el) . . . . .skating
patinar . . . . to skate
patines (los) . . . . skates
patria (la) . . . . country, homeland
payaso (el) . . . . clown
pecado (el) . . . . sin
pedazo (el) . . . . piece
pedir (i) . . . . . . to ask for, to order (food)
pedir (i) prestado . . . . to borrow
pegar . . . . to hit
peinado (el) . . . . hairdo, hairstyle
peinado/a . . . . combed
peinar . . . . .to comb
peinarse . . . . to comb one's hair
pelea (la) . . . . .fight
pelear . . . . to fight
película (la) . . . . .film (used in a
camera), movie
peligro (el) . . . . danger
pelirrojo/a . . . . red-headed
pelo (el) . . . . hair
pelota (la) . . . . ball
pelotero (el) . . . . ballplayer
peluquero/a (el/la) . . barber, hairdresser
pena (la) . . . . pain
pendiente (el) . . . . .earring
pendientes (los) . . . . earrings
penoso/a . . . . .painful
pensar (ie) . . . . to think
pensar en . . . . to think about
peor . . . . worse, worst
pequeño/a . . . . small
pera (la) . . . . pear
percha (la) . . . . hanger
perder (ie) . . . . to lose
perder (tiempo) . . . . to waste (time)
perdonar . . . . .to pardon
perezoso/a . . . . lazy
periódico (el) . . . . newspaper
permiso (el) . . . . .permission
permitir . . . . to permit, to allow
perro (el) . . . . dog
perrito caliente (el) . . . . hot dog
perseguir (i) . . . . to pursue, to persecute
pertenecer a . . . . .to belong to
pesado/a . . . . heavy, annoying
pescado (el) . . . . fish
pesas (las) . . . . weights
pescar . . . . to fish
pesimista (el/la) . . . . pessimist
peso (el) . . . . .weight
petróleo (el) . . . . oil, petroleum
pez (el) . . . . fish
piano (el) . . . . piano
picadura (la) (de mosquito)
. . . . (mosquito) bite
pícaro/a . . . . roguish, rascally
pie (el) . . . . foot
piedra (la) . . . . .stone, rock
piel (la) . . . . skin

pierna (la) . . . . leg
pimienta (la) . . . . pepper
pino (el) . . . . pine tree
(el) pintalabios (lápiz de labios) . lipstick
pintar . . . . to paint
pintor/a (el/la) . . . . .painter
pintoresco/a . . . . picturesque
pintura (la) . . . . painting
piscina (la) . . . . swimming pool
piso (el) . . . . floor
pizarra (la) . . . . blackboard
placer . . . . to please
planchar . . . . to iron
planeta (el) . . . . planet
plástico (el) . . . . plastic
plátano (el) . . . . plantain, banana
plato (el) . . . . plate, dish
playa (la) . . . . .beach
plazo (el) . . . . period of time
pluma (la) . . . . pen
pobre . . . . .poor
poco . . . . a little
poder (ue) . . . . to be able to
poderoso/a . . . . powerful
poesía (la) . . . . poetry
poetisa (la) . . . . poet
poliéster (el) . . . . polyester
política (la) . . . . politics
político/a . . . . .political
pollo (el) . . . . chicken
poner . . . . .to put
poner la mesa . . . . .to set the table
ponerse . . . . to put on
por . . . . by, for, through
por consiguiente . . . . consequently
por desgracia . . . . .unfortunately
por ejemplo . . . . .for example
por eso . . . . therefore, so
por fin . . . . finally
por qué . . . . why?
por supuesto . . . . of course
porcentaje . . . . .percentage
porque . . . . because
portada (la) . . . . cover
portal cibernético (el) . . . . website
portarse bien/mal . . . . .to behave
well/poorly
portero/a (el/la) . . . . goalie
porvenir (el) . . . . .future
postal . . . . .postcard
postizo/a . . . . false, fake
postre (el) . . . . dessert
precio (el) . . . . price
precioso/a . . . . precious, cute
preciso/a . . . . . . necessary, precise, clear
preferir (ie) . . . . to prefer
premiar . . . . .to reward
premio (el) . . . . prize
prender . . . . to turn on (lights, etc.)
prensa (la) . . . . press (media)
preocupado/a . . . . worried, upset

preocuparse . . . . to worry
preparar . . . . to prepare
presentación (la) . . . . .presentation
prestar .to lend
prestar atención . . . . . . to pay attention
pretender . . . . to aspire to, to seek,
to claim to be
primavera (la) . . . . spring
primero/a . . . . first
primo/a (el/la) . . . . cousin
principio (el) . . . . beginning
prisa . . . . hurry
probar (ue) . . . . to try, to taste
problema (el) . . . . .problem
producir . . . . to produce
profesor (el) . . . . .teacher
profesora (la) . . . . .teacher
profundo/a . . . . .deep
prohibir . . . . to prohibit
prometer . . . . to promise
pronto . . . . .soon
propina (la) . . tip (e.g., given to a waiter)
propio/a . . . . .own, proper
proteger . . . . .to protect
protegido/a . . . . protected
próximo/a . . . . next
proyecto (el) . . . . project
prueba (la) . . . . .proof, quiz, test
pueblo (el) . . . . town, village
puerta (la) . . . . .door
pues . . . . well, so
puesta del sol (la) . . . . sunset
pulido/a . . . . .polished
pulir . . . . to polish
pulmón (el) . . . . .lung
pulsera (la) . . . . bracelet
punto (el) . . . . point
puntualmente . . . . punctually
pupitre (el) . . . . student desk

Q

que . . . . that, which
¿qué? . . . . .what?, which?
qué . . . . what
quebrado/a . . . . broken
quebrarse . . . . to break
quedar . . . . .to remain
queja (la) . . . . complaint
quejarse de . . . . . . to complain (about)
quemado/a . . . . burnt
quemar . . . . .to burn
querer (ie) . . . . . to wish, to want, to like
querido/a . . . . dear
queso (el) . . . . cheese
¿quién? . . . . who?
química (la) . . . . chemistry
quiosco (el) . . . . newspaper stand
quitarse . . . . to take off

R

rabino (el) . . . . rabbi
radio (el/la) . . . . radio
raíz (la) . . . . root
rana (la) . . . . frog
rápidamente . . . . quickly
raqueta (la) . . . . racquet
raro/a . . . . rare, strange
rascacielos (el) . . . . skyscraper
rastrillo (el) . . . . .rake
ratón (el) . . . . mouse
rayas (las) . . . . stripes
real . . . . real, royal
realidad (la) . . . . reality
realizar . . . . to realize
(e.g., a dream, a goal)
receta (la) . . . . recipe, prescription
recibir . . . . to receive
recibo (el) . . . . receipt
recién . . . . recent, recently
reciente . . . . recent
recoger . . . . to collect
recomendar (ie) . . . . . . .to recommend
recordar (ue) . . . . to remember
recuperar . . . . to recover
red (la) . . . . net, network
redondo/a . . . . .round
referir (ie) . . . . to refer
reflejar . . . . to reflect
reflexionar . . . . . .to think over, to reflect
refrigerador (el) . . . . refrigerator
regalar . . . . to give a present, gift
regalo (el) . . . . .present
regar (ie) . . . . .to water
regresar . . . . to return
reina (la) . . . . .queen
reinar . . . . to reign
reír (i) . . . . .to laugh
relación (la) . . . . relationship
relámpago (el) . . . . lightning
relajarse . . . . to relax
reloj (el) . . . . clock, watch
remo (el) . . . . rowing
remoto/a . . . . .remote
reñir (i) . . . . to scold
renovar (ue) . . . . to renovate
renunciar . . . . to resign, to quit
repaso (el) . . . . review
repetir (i) . . . . to repeat
reportero/a (el/la) . . . . reporter
representante (el) . . . . . . representative
requesón . . . . .cottage cheese
resbaladizo/a . . . . slippery
reservación (la) . . . . reservation
residencia (la) . . . . . residence, dormitory
resolver (ue) . . . . to resolve, to solve
a problem
respetar . . . . .to respect
respirar . . . . to breathe
respuesta (la) . . . . .answer, reply

restaurante (el) . . . . restaurant
restaurar . . . . .to restore
resultado (el) . . . . result
resumen (el) . . . . summary
retrato (el) . . . . picture, portrait
reunión (la) . . . . .meeting, reunion
revelar . . . . to reveal
revista (la) . . . . .magazine
rey (el) .king
rezar .to pray
rincón (el) . . . . corner
rico/a . . . . rich
riesgo (el) . . . . risk
rígido/a . . . . .rigid
río (el) .river
risa (la) . . . . laugh, laughter
risueño/a . . . . .smiling, cheerful
ritmo (el) . . . . .rhythm
rizado/a . . . . curly
roble (el) . . . . oak
rodear . . . . to surround
rogar (ue) . . . . to beg
rojo/a . . . . .red
romper . . . . .to break
roncar . . . . to snore
ropa (la) . . . . .clothes
ropa interior (la) . . . . underwear
rosa (la) . . . . rose
rosado/a . . . . .pink
roto/a . . . . broken
rubio/a . . . . .blond(e)
ruido (el) . . . . noise
ruidoso/a . . . . noisy
ruinas (las) . . . . ruins
rumbo (el) . . . . .direction, road
ruta (la) . . . . route

S

sábado (el) . . . . Saturday
saber . . . . to know (a fact)
saber de memoria . . . . . to know by heart
sabiduría (la) . . . . .knowledge
sabio/a . . . . .wise, learned
sabroso/a . . . . tasty, delicious
sacacorchos (el) . . . . corkscrew
sacapuntas (el) . . . . pencil sharpener
sacar .to take out
sacar (fotos) . . . . .to take (pictures)
sacar (prestado) un libro
. . . . to check out a book
saco de dormir . . . . sleeping bag
sacrificio (el) . . . . .sacrifice
sagrado/a . . . . sacred
sal (la) .salt
sala (de estar) (la) . . . . living room
salado/a . . . . .salty
salchicha (la) . . . . sausage
salida (la) . . . . exit
salida del sol (la) . . . . sunrise
salir . . . . to leave

salirse con la suya . . .to have one's way
saludo (el). . . . . greeting
salvo/a. safe
sano/a . . . . healthy
santo (el). . . . . .saint
sargento (el) . . . . .sargent
sartén (el/la) . . . . frying pan
satisfacer. . . . . to satisfy
satisfecho/a . . . . .satisfied
saxofón (el) . . . . saxophone
secadora (la). . . . . dryer
secadora de pelo (la) . . . . . . hair dryer
seco/a .dry
secretario/a (el/la) . . . . secretary
secreto (el) . . . . .secret
seda (la) . . . . silk
seguir (i) . . . . to follow
según . . . . according to
segundo/a . . . . second
seguridad (la) . . . . . . security, certainty
seguro/a. . . . . sure, secure
selva (la) . . . . jungle
semáforo(el) . . . . traffic light
semana (la) . . . . week
semanal. . . . . .weekly
semejante. . . . . similar
senador/a (el/la) . . . . .senator
sencillo/a. . . . . simple
sentar (ie) . . . . to seat (someone)
sentarse (ie). . . . . to sit down
sentimiento (el) . . . . . feeling, sentiment
sentir (ie). . . . . to feel, to regret
separado/a. . . . . separate
separar . . . . .to separate
septiembre. . . . . September
ser . . . . to be
ser humano (el). . . . . human being
serie (la) . . . . series
serio/a . . . . .serious
serpiente (la). . . . . serpent, snake
servilleta (la). . . . . napkin
servir (i) . . . . to serve
si . . . . if
sí . . . . .yes
siempre . . . . .always
siglo (el) . . . . century
siguiente . . . . following, next
silbar. . . . . to whistle
silla (la). . . . . seat, chair
sillón (el). . . . . armchair
símbolo (el). . . . . symbol
simpático/a . . . . .likeable, nice
sin . . . . without
sinfonía (la). . . . . symphony
sinagoga (la). . . . . synagogue
sistema (el) . . . . system
sitio (el). . . . . site, place
soberbio/a . . . . proud, haughty
sobrar . . . . . . to remain, to be left over
sobre . . . . about, over, on top of
sobrevivir . . . . to survive

sobrina (la). . . . . niece
sobrino (el) . . . . nephew
sofá (el). . . . . sofa
soldado (el). . . . . soldier
soledad (la). . . . . . . solitude, loneliness
sólo . . . . only
solo/a. . . . . alone
sombrero (el). . . . . hat
sonar (ue) . . . . to ring
soñar (ue) con. . . . . to dream about
sonido (el). . . . . .sound
sonreír (i) . . . . to smile
sopa (la) . . . . .soup
soplar . . . . to blow
sordo/a . . . . deaf
sorprendido/a . . . . surprised
sorpresa (la) . . . . surprise
soso/a . . . . .lacking salt, bland
sospechar . . . . to suspect
sótano (el) . . . . .basement
suave . . . . soft, smooth
suavemente . . . . suavely, smoothly
subir . . . .to go up, to get on (a bus, etc.)
subrayar . . . . .to underline
suceder . . . . to happen
sucio/a. . . . . .dirty
sucursal (la) . . . . branch (office)
sudar. . . . . .to sweat
suegra (la). . . . . mother-in-law
suegro (el) . . . . father-in-law
sueldo (el) . . . . .salary
suelo (el) . . . . floor
suelto/a . . . . loose
suerte (la) . . . . .luck
suéter (el) . . . . sweater
sugerir (ie) . . . . to suggest
superior. . . . . superior, upper
supermercado (el). . . . . . . supermarket
suponer . . . . .to suppose
sur . . . . south
sureste (el). . . . . southeast
suroeste (el). . . . . southwest
susurrar . . . . to whisper
susurro (el) . . . . whisper

T

tacaño/a. . . . . stingy
tailandés/a. . . . . .Thai
tal vez . . . . perhaps
talento (el). . . . . talent
tamaño (el) . . . . size
también . . . . also
tambores (los). . . . . drums
tan . . . . .so
tanto (adv.). . . . . .so much
tantos/as . . . . .so many
tapar . . . . .to cover
tarde . . . . late
tarea (la) . . . . .task, assignment,
homework

tarjeta (la). . . . . card, postcard
tarjeta postal (la) . . . . .postcard
tatuaje (el). . . . . .tattoo
taxi (el) . . . . taxi
taza (la). . . . . cup
té (el). . . . . tea
teatro (el) . . . . theater
tejado (el) . . . . roof
tejer . . . . to knit
tela (la) . . . . .cloth, material
telaraña (la) . . . . .spider web
teléfono (el). . . . . .telephone
teléfono celular (el). . . . . .cellphone
telenovela (la) . . . . .soap opera
telescopio (el) . . . . telescope
televisión (la) . . . . .television
televisor (el) . . . . .television set
tema (el) . . . . theme
temer. . . . . to fear
tempestad (la) . . . . .storm
templo (el) . . . . temple
temporada (la)
. . . . .season (e.g., sports season)
temprano. . . . . early
tenedor (el) . . . . fork
tener . . . . to have
tener en cuenta . . . . to take into
consideration
tener éxito . . . . .to be successful
tener lugar. . . . . to take place
tener prisa. . . . . .to be in a hurry
tener que ver con . . . .to have to do with
tener razón . . . . to be right
tener vergüenza. . . . . .to be ashamed
teñir (i) . . . . to dye
tenis (el) . . . . .tennis
tercero/a . . . . .third
terco/a. . . . . stubborn
terminar. . . . . .to finish
terremoto (el) . . . . .earthquake
tesorero/a (el/la). . . . . treasurer
tesoro (el) . . . . treasure
testigo (el) . . . . witness
texto (el) . . . . text
tía (la) . . . . aunt
tiburón (el) . . . . shark
tiempo (el). . . . . time
tienda (la) . . . . store
tienda de campaña (la). . . . . tent
tierra (la). . . . . soil, earth
tigre (el) . . . . .tiger
tijeras (las) . . . . scissors
timbre (el) . . . . bell
tío (el) . . . . uncle
tipo (el) . . . . type
típico/a . . . . typical
tirano (el) . . . . .tyrant
tiroteo (el). . . . . shooting
título (el) . . . . title
tiza (la) . . . . chalk
toalla (la) . . . . .towel

tocadiscos (el). . . . . record player
tocador (el). . . . . dresser
tocar . . to play (an instrument), to touch
tocino (el) . . . . bacon
todavía. still
todavía no . . . . not yet
todo . . . . all
tomar apuntes . . . . to take notes
tomar el pelo. . to tease, to pull one's leg
tomar una decisión . . .to make a decision
tomate (el). . . . . tomato
tonto/a. . . . . foolish
torcer (ue). . . . . to twist, to bend
torero/a (el/la). . . . . bullfighter
tormenta (la). . . . . storm
torneo (el) . . . . tournament
torre (la) . . . . tower
torta (la) . . . . .cake
tortuga (la) . . . . turtle
toser. . . . . to cough
tostador (el). . . . . toaster
trabajar . . . . to work
traducir . . . . to translate
traer. . . . . to bring
tragar . . . . .to swallow
traje (el) . . . . suit
traje de baño (el) . . . . swimsuit
trama (la) . . . . .plot (of a story)
tranquilamente . . . . calmly
tranquilo/a. . . . . calm
tras . . . . behind, after
trasero/a . . . . back, rear (adj)
tratar (de) . . . . to try
tren (el). . . . . .train
trigo (el) . . . . .wheat
trineo (el) . . . . sled, sleigh
triste . . . . .sad
triunfar . . . . to triumph
trofeo (el) . . . . trophy
trombón (el) . . . . .trombone
trompeta (la). . . . . trumpet
tropezar (ie) . . . . to trip
tropical . . . . tropical
trozo (el) . . . . bit, piece, selection
trueno (el). . . . . thunder
tú . . . . you (familiar)
tulipán (el). . . . . .tulip
tumba (la) . . . . tomb
túnel (el) . . . . tunnel

U

último/a. . . . . last (of a group)
una vez . . . . .once
único/a. . . . . only, unique
universidad (la). . . . . university
universo (el) . . . . .universe
uno/a. . . . . .a, an
unos/as . . . . some
uña (la) . . . . fingernail, toenail
urgente . . . . urgent

usted (Ud.) . . . . you (formal)
ustedes (Uds.). . . . . .you all (formal)
uva (la) . . . . grape

V

vaca (la) . . . . cow
vacaciones (las) . . . . .vacation
vacío/a. . . . . empty
vagón (el) . . . . car (of train)
valer . . . . to be worth
valer (no) la pena . . . . to (not) be
worth the trouble
valle (el) . . . . valley
vaqueros (los) . . . . jeans
varios/as . . . . several, various
vaso (el). . . . . glass
vecino/a (el/la) . . . . neighbor
vegetal (el) . . . . .vegetable
vela (la). . . . . .candle, sailing
velocidad (la) . . . . .speed
vejez (la) . . . . old age
vencer . . . . to defeat, to expire
vencimiento (el). . . . . expiration
vender . . . . to sell
veneno (el). . . . . poison
venganza (la). . . . . . .revenge, vengeance
venir . . . . to come
ventaja (la) . . . . advantage
ventana (la). . . . . window
ventilador (el) . . . . .fan
ver. .to see
verano (el). . . . . summer
verdad (la). . . . . .truth
¿verdad? . . . . isn't that so?
verdadero/a. . . . . true, real
verde . . . . green
verdura (la). . . . . .vegetable
vergüenza (la) . . . . embarrassment,
shame
vestido (el). . . . . dress
veterinario/a (el/la). . . . . . . .veterinarian
viajar. . . . . .to travel
viaje (el) . . . . .trip
víctima (la) . . . . victim
vídeo (el), video (el) . . . . . . .VCR, video
viejo/a . . . . old
viento (el) . . . . wind
viernes (el) . . . . Friday
vino (el). . . . . wine
violencia (la). . . . . .violence
violín (el). . . . . .violin
virtud (la) . . . . virtue
viudo/a (el/la) . . . . widower, widow
vivir. . . . . to live
volar (ue). . . . . to fly
volcán (el) . . . . volcano
volver (ue). . . . . to return
volverse loco/a . . . . to go crazy
vosotros/as . . . . .you all (familiar)
voto (el) . . . . vote

vuelo (el). . . . . .flight
vulgar . . . . .common, ordinary

Y

y. . . . . and
ya. . . . . already
ya no . . . . .no longer, anymore
yo. I

Z

zanahoria (la). . . . . .carrot
zapatero/a (el/la) . . . .cobbler, shoemaker
zapato (el). . . . . .shoe
zoológico (el) . . . . zoo
zorrillo (el) (la mofeta). . . . . .skunk
zorro (el) . . . . .fox
zurdo/a . . . . left-handed

DICCIONARIO INGLÉS-ESPAÑOL

A

a, an . . . . *uno/a*
abandon (to) . . . . *abandonar*
able (to be) (to) . . . . *poder (ue)*
abnormal . . . . *anormal*
about, over, on top of . . . . *sobre*
abrupt, sudden . . . . *brusco/a*
absence, lack . . . . *(la) falta*
accident . . . . *(el) accidente*
accompany (to) . . . . *acompañar*
according to . . . . *según*
accordion . . . . *(el) acordeón*
accursed, damned . . . . *maldito/a*
accuse (to) . . . . *acusar*
ache (to), to hurt . . . . *doler (ue)*
acquire (to) . . . . *adquirir (ie)*
action . . . . *(la) acción*
actor . . . . *(el) actor*
actress . . . . *(la) actriz*
add (to) . . . . *añadir*
additional . . . . *adicional*
admission, entrance, ticket

. . . . *(la) entrada*
admit (to) . . . . *admitir*
adorable, beautiful . . . . *precioso/a*
advanced . . . . *avanzado/a*
advantage . . . . *(la) ventaja*
advice . . . . *(el) consejo*
advise (to) . . . . *aconsejar*
advertisement, announcement

. . . . *(el) anuncio*
affection . . . . *(el) cariño*
affectionate . . . . *cariñoso/a*
after . . . . *después (de)*
after, behind . . . . *tras*
afternoon (this) . . . . *esta tarde*
again . . . . *de nuevo, otra vez*
against . . . . *contra*
age . . . . *(la) edad*
agree (to) . . . . *estar de acuerdo*
ahead, forward . . . . *adelante*
aid (to), to support . . . . *apoyar*
air conditioner

. . . . *(el) acondicionador de aire*
airplane . . . . *(el) avión*
airport . . . . *(el) aeropuerto*
alarm . . . . *(la) alarma*
alarm clock . . . . *(el) despertador*
all . . . . *todo*
allow (to), to leave behind . . . . . . *dejar*
allow (to), to permit . . . . *permitir*
almost . . . . *casi*
alone . . . . *solo/a*
along . . . . *a lo largo*
aloud . . . . *en voz alta*
alphabet . . . . *(el) alfabeto*

already . . . . *ya*
also . . . . *también*
although . . . . *aunque*
always . . . . *siempre*
A.M. (in the morning) . . . . *de la mañana*
ambassador . . . . *(el) embajador*
among, between . . . . *entre*
amusement park

. . . . *(el) parque de atracciones*
an, a . . . . *uno/a*
analysis . . . . *(el) análisis*
anchovy . . . . *(la) anchoa*
and . . . . *y*
anger . . . . *(el) enojo*
angry, brave, fierce . . . . *bravo/a*
angry (to become) . . . . *enfadar(se),*
enojarse
announcement, advertisement

. . . . *(el) anuncio*
annoy (to) . . . . *fastidiar*
annoying, heavy . . . . *pesado/a*
another, other . . . . *otro/a*
answer (to) . . . . *contestar*
answering machine

. . . . *(el) contestador automático*
anxious, eager . . . . *ansioso/a*
any . . . . *cualquier*
anybody . . . . *cualquiera*
appeal to (to) . . . . *apetecer*
appear (to) . . . . *aparecer*
appear (to), to seem . . . . *parecer*
applaud (to) . . . . *aplaudir*
apple . . . . *(la) manzana*
applied, dedicated, industrious

. . . . *aplicado/a*
appropriate, just, fair . . . . *justo/a*
April . . . . *abril*
Arabic . . . . *(el) árabe*
architect . . . . *(el/la) arquitecto/a*
arm . . . . *(el) brazo*
armchair . . . . *(el) sillón*
around . . . . *alrededor*
arrange (to), to fix . . . . *arreglar*
arrange (to), to place . . . . *colocar*
arrival . . . . *(la) llegada*
arrive (to) . . . . *llegar*
arrow . . . . *(la) flecha*
art . . . . *(el) arte (f.)*
art gallery . . . . *(la) galería de arte*
art show, exhibition,

fair . . . . *(la) exposición*
as, since, like . . . . *como*
ashamed (to be) . . . . . . *tener vergüenza*
ask (a question) (to)

. . . . *hacer una pregunta*
ask (for) (to), to order (food) . . . *pedir (i)*
asparagus . . . . *(el) espárrago*

aspire to (to), to seek,
to claim to be . . . . *pretender*
assignment, task, homework

. . . . *(la) tarea*
astute . . . . *astuto/a*
astute, sharp . . . . *agudo/a*
at, to . . . . *a*
at approximately . . . . *a eso de*
at once . . . . *en seguida (enseguida)*
at times, sometimes . . . . *a veces*
athletic . . . . *atlético/a*
attack . . . . *(el) ataque*
attack (to) . . . . *atacar*
attempt (to), to try . . . . *intentar*
attend (to) . . . . *asistir*
attention (to pay) . . . . . *prestar atención*
attention (to pay) to . . . . . . *hacer caso a*
attentive . . . . *atento/a*
attic . . . . *(el) desván*
attitude . . . . *(la) actitud*
attract (to) . . . . *atraer*
August . . . . *agosto*
aunt . . . . *(la) tía*
authority . . . . *(la) autoridad*
autograph . . . . *(el) autógrafo*
autumnal . . . . *otoñal*
available, free . . . . *libre*
average, medium . . . . *mediano/a*
avoid (to) . . . . *evitar*

B

baby . . . . *(el) bebé*
baby pig . . . . *(el) cochinillo*
babysitter . . . . *(el, la) niñero/a*
backpack . . . . *(la) mochila*
bacon . . . . *(el) tocino*
bad . . . . *malo/a*
bad, poorly . . . . *mal*
bad-mannered, ill-bred . . . . *malcriado/a*
bag, purse . . . . *(la) bolsa*
baker . . . . *(el/la) panadero/a*
balcony . . . . *(el) balcón*
bald . . . . *calvo/a*
ball . . . . *(la) pelota*
balloon . . . . *(el) globo*
ballplayer . . . . *(el) pelotero*
banana . . . . . . *(la) banana, (el) plátano*
band . . . . *(la) banda*
bank, bench, pew . . . . *(el) banco*
bank, shore (of river, ocean)

. . . . *(la) orilla*
banker . . . . *(el/la) banquero/a*
banquet . . . . *(el) banquete*
bar (of a window or a prison cell)

. . . . *(el) barrote*
barber, hairdresser . . . *(el/la) peluquero/a*
bark (to) . . . . *ladrar*

baseball . . . . (el) béisbol
basement . . . . (el) sótano
basketball . . . . (el) baloncesto
bath (to take a) . . . . bañarse
bathing suit . . . . (el) bañador
bathrobe . . . . (la) bata
bathroom . . . . (el) (cuarto de) baño
battle . . . . (la) batalla
be (to) . . . . estar, ser
be able to (to) . . . . poder (ue)
be born (to) . . . . nacer
be happy about (to) . . . . . . alegrarse de
be worth (to) . . . . valer
beach . . . . (la) playa
bear . . . . (el) oso
beard . . . . (la) barba
beat (to) . . . . batir
beat (to), to hit . . . . golpear
beater . . . . (el/la) batidor/a
beautiful . . . . bello/a
beautiful, adorable . . . . precioso/a
beauty . . . . (la) belleza
because . . . . porque
become night (to) . . . . anochecer
bed . . . . (la) cama
bed (to go to) . . . . acostarse (ue)
bedroom . . . (el) dormitorio, (la) alcoba
bee . . . . (la) abeja
before . . . . antes (de)
beg (to) . . . . suplicar, rogar (ue)
begin (to) . . . comenzar (ie), empezar (ie)
beginning . . . (el) comienzo, (el) principio
behave (to) . . . . comportarse
behave well/poorly (to)
. . . . portarse bien/mal
behind . . . . atrás, detrás, detrás de
behind, after . . . . tras
believe (to) . . . . creer
bell . . . . (la) campana, (el) timbre
belong to (to) . . . . pertenecer a
below . . . . abajo
below, under . . . . debajo de
belt . . . . (el) cinturón
bench, pew, bank . . . . (el) banco
bend (to), to twist . . . . torcer (ue)
best man . . . . (el) padrino de boda
bet (to) . . . . apostar (ue)
better, best . . . . mejor
between, among . . . . entre
bicycle . . . . (la) bicicleta
bicycle (to ride a) . . montar en bicicleta
big . . . . grande
bilingual . . . . bilingüe
bill . . . . (la) factura, (la) cuenta
biology . . . . (la) biología
bird . . . . (el) pájaro
birthday . . . . (el) cumpleaños
bit, piece, selection . . . . (el) trozo
bite (to) . . . . morder (ue)
bite (mosquito)
. . . . (la) picadura (de mosquito)

bitter, sour . . . . agrio/a, (amargo/a)
black . . . . negro/a
blackboard . . . . (la) pizarra
blame (to) . . . . echarle la culpa a
blame (someone) (to)
. . . . culpar a, echar(le) la culpa
blanket . . . . (la) manta
bland, lacking salt . . . . soso/a
bless (to) . . . . bendecir
blind . . . . ciego/a
blond(e) . . . . rubio/a
blouse . . . . (la) blusa
blow (to) . . . . soplar
blue . . . . azul
board (to) . . . . abordar
boat . . . . (el) barco
boil (to) . . . . hervir (ie)
boisterous, rowdy, noisy . . . . bullicioso/a
bold, daring . . . . atrevido/a
book . . . . (el) libro
boot . . . . (la) bota
border, frontier . . . . (la) frontera
bored, boring . . . . aburrido/a
bored (to become [get]) . . . . . aburrirse
borrow (to) . . . . pedir (i) prestado
boss . . . . (la) jefa, (el) jefe
bossy . . . . . . mandón (m.), mandona (f.)
botanical garden . . . . (el) jardín botánico
both . . . . ambos/as
bother (to) . . . . molestar
bottle . . . . (la) botella, (el) frasco
box . . . . (la) caja
boy . . . . (el) chico, (el) niño
boyfriend, fiancé, groom . . . . . (el) novio
bracelet . . . . (la) pulsera
branch (office) . . . . (la) sucursal
brave, fierce, angry . . . . bravo/a
bread . . . . (el) pan
break (to) . . . . . quebrar(se), romper(se)
breakfast (to have) . . . . desayunar
breathe (to) . . . . respirar
bride, fiancée, girlfriend . . . . (la) novia
bright, brilliant . . . . luminoso/a
bring (to) . . . . traer
brochure . . . . (el) folleto
broken . . . . quebrado/a, roto/a
broom . . . . (la) escoba
brother . . . . (el) hermano
brother-in-law . . . . (el) cuñado
brown . . . . marrón
brunette, brown . . . . moreno/a
brush one's (hair, teeth) (to) . . cepillarse
build (to), to construct . . . . . . construir
building . . . . (el) edificio
bullfighter . . . . (el/la) torero/a
burly, stout, heavy-set . . . . corpulento/a
burn (to) . . . . quemar
burning, passionate . . . . ardiente
burnt . . . . quemado/a
bury (to) . . . . enterrar (ie)
bus . . . . (el) autobús

bush . . . . (el) arbusto
business . . . . (el) negocio
busy . . . . ocupado/a
butcher . . . . (el/la) carnicero/a
butter . . . . (la) mantequilla
buy (to) . . . . comprar
by, for, in order to . . . . para
by, for, through . . . . por

C

cage . . . . (la) jaula
cake . . . . (la) torta, (el) pastel
calendar . . . . (el) calendario
call (to) . . . . llamar
calm . . . . tranquilo/a
calmly . . . . tranquilamente
camera . . . . (la) cámara
camp . . . . (el) campamento
campaign . . . . (la) campaña
camper . . . . (el/la) campista
can . . . . (la) lata
can opener . . . . (el) abrelatas
cancelled . . . . cancelado/a
candidate . . . . (el/la) candidato/a
candle, sailing . . . . (la) vela
canyon . . . . (el) cañón
capable . . . . capaz
captain . . . . capitán
car . . . . (el) carro, (el) coche
car (of train) . . . . (el) vagón
care for (to) . . . . cuidar (de)
career, race . . . . (la) carrera
careful, cautious . . . . cuidadoso/a
careful, cautious, wary . . . . cauteloso/a
carnival . . . . (el) carnaval
carpenter . . . . (el/la) carpintero/a
carpet, rug . . . . (la) alfombra
carrot . . . . (la) zanahoria
carry (to), to take . . . . llevar
castle . . . . (el) castillo
cat . . . . (el) gato
catch (to), to take . . . . coger
cathedral . . . . (la) catedral
cause (to) . . . . causar
cautious, careful . . . . cuidadoso/a
cautious, careful, wary . . . . cauteloso/a
cavity . . . . (la) caries
celebrated, famous . . . . célebre
cell . . . . (la) celda
cellphone . . (el) teléfono celular, (el) móvil
cemetery . . . . (el) cementerio
center, downtown . . . . (el) centro
century . . . . (el) siglo
ceremony . . . . (la) ceremonia
certain . . . . cierto/a
certainty, security . . . . . (la) seguridad
chair, seat . . . . (la) silla
chalk . . . . (la) tiza
champagne . . . . (el) champán,
. . . . (el) champaña

champion . . . *(el) campeón, (la) campeona*
championship . . . . *(el) campeonato*
change . . . . *(el) cambio*
change (to) . . . . *cambiar*
chat (to) . . . . *charlar*
chauffeur . . . . *(el) chófer*
cheap . . . . *barato/a*
cheat (to), to deceive . . . . *engañar*
check out a book (to)
. . . . *sacar (prestado) un libro*
cheerful, smiling . . . . *risueño/a*
cheese . . . . *(el) queso*
chemistry . . . . *(la) química*
chess . . . . *(el) ajedrez*
chestnut . . . . *castaño/a*
chew (to) . . . . *masticar*
chicken . . . . *(el) pollo*
childhood . . . . . . *(la) niñez, (la) infancia*
chimney, fireplace . . . . *(la) chimenea*
chlorine . . . . *(el) cloro*
chocolates . . . . *(los) bombones,*
. . . . *(los) chocolates*
choose (to), to elect . . . . *elegir (i)*
choose (to), to select . . . . *escoger*
Christian . . . . *cristiano/a*
church . . . . *(la) iglesia*
church service, mass . . . . *(la) misa*
cigarette . . . . *(el) cigarrillo*
cinnamon . . . . *(la) canela*
circular, round . . . . *circular*
circus . . . . *(el) circo*
citizen . . . . *(el/la) ciudadano/a*
city . . . . *(la) ciudad*
city hall . . . . *(el) ayuntamiento*
claim to be (to), to aspire to,
to seek . . . . *pretender*
clarinet . . . . *(el) clarinete*
class . . . . *(la) clase*
clean . . . . *limpio/a*
clean (to) . . . . *limpiar*
clear . . . . *claro/a*
clear, necessary, precise . . . . . . *preciso/a*
clever, skillful . . . . *hábil*
clever, ready, smart . . . . *listo/a*
client . . . . *(el) cliente, (la) clienta*
climate . . . . *(el) clima*
clinic, hospital . . . . *(la) clínica*
clock, watch . . . . *(el) reloj*
close (to) . . . . *cerrar (ie)*
close, intimate . . . . *íntimo/a*
closed . . . . *cerrado/a*
closet . . . . *(el) armario*
cloth, material . . . . *(la) tela*
clothes . . . . *(la) ropa*
cloudy . . . . *nublado/a*
clown . . . . *(el) payaso*
coach . . *(el) entrenador, (la) entrenadora*
coal . . . . *(el) carbón*
coast . . . . *(la) costa*
coat, overcoat . . . . *(el) abrigo*
cobbler, shoemaker . . *(el/la) zapatero/a*

coconut . . . . *(el) coco*
corkscrew . . . . *(el) sacacorchos*
coffee . . . . *(el) café*
coffee maker . . . . *(la) cafetera*
coin . . . . *(la) moneda*
cold . . . . *frío/a*
colleague . . . . *(el/la) colega*
collect (to) . . . . *coleccionar, recoger*
collection . . . . *(la) colección*
comb (to) . . . . *peinar*
comb one's hair (to) . . . . *peinarse*
combed . . . . *peinado/a*
combine (to) . . . . *combinar*
come (to) . . . . *venir*
comfortable . . . . *cómodo/a*
common . . . . *común*
common, ordinary . . . . *vulgar*
compact disc (CD) . . . *(el) disco compacto*
company . . . . *(la) empresa*
compartment (of train) . . . . . . *(el) vagón*
compass . . . . *(la) brújula*
compassion . . . . *(la) compasión*
compete (to) . . . . *competir (i)*
competition . . . . *(la) competición*
competitive . . . . *competitivo/a*
complain (about) (to) . . . . . . *quejarse de*
complaint . . . . *(la) queja*
complete (to), to finish . . . . *cumplir*
computer . . . . *(la) computadora*
computer (Spain) . . . . *(el) ordenador*
concert . . . . *(el) concierto*
confess (to) . . . . *confesar (ie)*
confidence, trust (in) . . . . . *(la) confianza*
confuse (to) . . . . *confundir*
confused . . . . *confundido/a*
confused, confusing . . . . *confuso/a*
congratulate (to) . . . . *felicitar*
congratulations . . . . . . *(las) felicidades*
conquer (to), to defeat . . . . *vencer*
consecutive . . . . *consecutivo/a*
consequently . . . . *por consiguiente*
conserve (to) . . . . *conservar*
constellation . . . . *(la) constelación*
construct (to), to build . . . . *construir*
contact lens . . . . *(la) lentilla*
contact lenses . . . . *(las) lentillas,*
. . . . *(los) lentes de contacto*
contaminated . . . . *contaminado/a*
content, happy . . . . *contento/a*
contest . . . . *(el) concurso*
continent . . . . *(el) continente*
contract . . . . *(el) contrato*
convert (to) . . . . *convertir (ie)*
convince (to) . . . . *convencer*
cook . . . . *(el/la) cocinero/a*
cook (to) . . . . *cocinar*
cookie . . . . *(la) galleta*
cool, fresh . . . . *fresco/a*
cordial, polite . . . . *cordial*
cordiality . . . . *(la) cordialidad*
corkscrew . . . . *(el) sacacorchos*

corner . . . . *(el) rincón*
corner (of a street) . . . . *(la) esquina*
correct (to) . . . . *corregir (i)*
cost (to) . . . . *costar (ue)*
costume, disguise . . . . *(el) disfraz*
cottage cheese . . . . *requesón*
cotton . . . . *(el) algodón*
cough (to) . . . . *toser*
count (to), to tell . . . . *contar (ue)*
count on (to) . . . . *contar con*
country . . . . *(el) país*
country, homeland . . . . *(la) patria*
couple, pair . . . . *(la) pareja*
course . . . . *(el) curso*
course, direction . . . . *(el) rumbo*
court . . . . *(la) cancha*
court . . . . *(la) corte*
courteous, polite . . . . *cortés*
courtesy . . . . *(la) cortesía*
cousin . . . . *(el/la) primo/a*
cover . . . . *(la) portada*
cover (to) . . . . *cubrir, tapar*
cow . . . . *(la) vaca*
cranberry . . . . *(el) arándano (rojo)*
crazy . . . . *loco/a*
crazy (to go) . . . . *volverse loco/a*
cream . . . . *(la) crema*
cream (whipped) . . . . *(la) nata*
create (to), to make . . . . *crear*
crime . . . . *(el) crimen*
crop . . . . *(la) cosecha*
crowded . . . . *atestado/a*
crude, rude . . . . *grosero/a*
cruel, mean . . . . *cruel*
cruise ship . . . . *(el) crucero*
crumb . . . . *(la) miga*
cry (to) . . . . *llorar*
cup . . . . *(la) taza*
curly . . . . *rizado/a*
current, present . . . . *corriente*
current, present day . . . . *actual*
curtain(s) . . . . *(la) cortina, (las) cortinas*
cut (to) . . . . *cortar*
cute, precious . . . . *precioso/a*
cycling . . . . *(el) ciclismo*

D

daily, everyday . . . . *cotidiano/a*
damned, accursed . . . . *maldito/a*
dance (to) . . . . *bailar*
dancer . . . . . . *(el) bailarín, (la) bailarina*
danger . . . . *(el) peligro*
dare to (to) . . . . *atreverse a*
daring, bold . . . . *atrevido/a*
dark . . . . *oscuro/a*
dark, brunette . . . . *moreno/a*
dark, obscure . . . . *o(b)scuro/a*
darkness . . . . *(la) oscuridad*
date . . . . *(la) fecha, (la) cita*
daughter . . . . *(la) hija*

dawn . . . . . (el) alba (f.), (la) madrugada
day . . . . (el) día
day before yesterday (the) . . . . . anteayer
dead . . . . muerto/a, difunto/a
deaf . . . . sordo/a
dear . . . . querido/a
debt . . . . (la) deuda
debut, premiére . . . . (el) estreno
decade . . . . (la) década
deceive (to), to cheat . . . . engañar
December . . . . diciembre
decide (to) . . . . .decidir
declare (to) . . . . declarar
dedicated, applied, industrious
. . . . aplicado/a
deep . . . . hondo/a, profundo/a
defeat . . . .(la) derrota
defeat (to), to conquer . . . . vencer
defect . . . . (el) defecto
delicate, fine . . . . fino/a
delicious, tasty . . . . sabroso/a
deliver (to), to hand over,
   to turn in . . . . entregar
demand (to), to require . . . . .exigir
dense, thick . . . . espeso/a
dentist . . . .(el/la) dentista
deny (to) . . . . negar (ie)
department store . . . . (el) almacén
depress (to) . . . . deprimir
depressed . . . . .deprimido/a
desert . . . .(el) desierto
deserve (to), to merit . . . . merecer
design (to) . . . . diseñar
desire (to) . . . . desear
desk . . . . (el) escritorio
despair (to), to lose hope . . . .desesperar
dessert . . . . (el) postre
destiny, fate, destination . . . . (el) destino
destroy (to) . . . . destruir
detail . . . .(el) detalle
detain (to), to stop . . . . detener
develop (to) . . . . desarrollar
die (to) . . . . morir (ue)
diet . . . .(la) dieta
different, distinct . . . . distinto/a
difficult . . . . .difícil
dining room . . . . (el) comedor
direct (to) . . . . dirigir
direction, course . . . .(el) rumbo
dirty . . . . .sucio/a
disappear (to) . . . . desaparecer
disaster . . . . (el) desastre
discipline . . . .(la) disciplina
discotheque, nightclub . . . (la) discoteca
discover (to) . . . . descubrir
discreet . . . . discreto/a
disguise, costume . . . .(el) disfraz
dish, plate . . . .(el) plato
dishwasher . . . .(el) lavaplatos
distant . . . . .lejano/a
distinct, different . . . . .distinto/a

divine . . . . .divino/a
divorce . . . . (el) divorcio
do (to), to make . . . . .hacer
doctor . . . .(el/la) médico/a
dog . . . .(el) perro
doll, wrist . . . .(la) muñeca
dominate (to) . . . . .dominar
door . . . .(la) puerta
dormitory, residence . . . . (la) residencia
double . . . . .doble
double room . . . . . (la) habitación doble
doubt . . . . (la) duda
doubtful . . . . .dudoso/a
down (to go), to get off
   (a train, etc.) . . . . bajar
downtown, center . . . . (el) centro
dozen . . . . (la) docena
drain (to) (e.g., pasta) . . . . escurrir
drawer . . . .(el) cajón
drawing, sketch, painting
. . . . (el) dibujo
dream about (to) . . . . . . .soñar (ue) con
dress . . . . (el) vestido
dresser . . . .(el) tocador
dressmaker, seamstress . . . (la) costurera
drink . . . . (la) bebida
drink (to) . . . . .beber
drive (to) . . . . conducir
drop (of liquid) . . . . (la) gota
drug . . . . (la) droga
drums . . . .(los) tambores
drunk . . . . borracho/a
dry . . . . seco/a
dryer . . . .(la) secadora
dumb, mute . . . . mudo/a
during . . . . durante
dye (to) . . . . teñir (i)

E

each, every . . . . cada
eager, anxious . . . . .ansioso/a
eagle . . . . (el) águila (f.)
early . . . . .temprano
earn (to), to win . . . . .ganar
earring . . . . (el) arete, (el) pendiente
earthquake . . . . (el) terremoto
east . . . . este
eastern . . . . oriental
easy .fácil
eat (to) . . . . comer
eat lunch (to) . . . . almorzar (ue)
economy . . . . (la) economía
effort . . . . (el) esfuerzo
egg . . . . (el) huevo
elect (to), to choose . . . . .elegir (i)
electric . . . . eléctrico/a
electrician . . . . (el/la) electricista
elegance . . . . (la) elegancia
elevator . . . . (el) ascensor
e-mail . . . . (el) correo electrónico

embarrassing . . . . embarazoso/a
embarrassment, shame . . . .(la) vergüenza
embrace . . . . (el) abrazo
embrace (to), to hug . . . . abrazar
employee . . . .(el/la) empleado/a
empty . . . . vacío/a
end, final . . . . (el) final
enemy . . . .(el/la) enemigo/a
engagement . . . . (el) noviazgo
engagement ring
. . . . (el) anillo de compromiso
engineer . . . .(el/la) ingeniero/a
English . . . . (el) inglés
engrave (to), to record . . . . .grabar
enjoy (to) . . . . disfrutar de, gozar de
enjoy (to) oneself, to have
   a good time . . . . divertirse (ie)
end . . . . (el) final
enormous . . . . enorme
enough . . . . .suficiente, bastante
enter (to) . . . . entrar
entire, whole . . . . .entero/a
entrance, admission, ticket
. . . .(la) entrada
envious, jealous . . . . envidioso/a
episode . . . . (el) episodio
era . . . . (la) época
erase (to) . . . . borrar
escape (to) . . . . escapar
essay . . . . (el) ensayo
essential . . . . .esencial
establish (to), to found . . . . .fundar
eternal . . . . .eterno/a
every, each . . . . cada
everyday, daily . . . . cotidiano/a
exceptional, original, smart . . . . . genial
excited . . . . emocionado/a
excursion, trip . . . . (la) excursión
exercise . . . .(el) ejercicio
exhausted . . . . agotado/a
exhibition, show, fair . . . (la) exposición
exit . . . . (la) salida
exotic . . . . exótico/a
expensive . . . . caro/a
expiration . . . . vencimiento (el)
explain (to) . . . . .explicar
explorer . . . . (el/la) explorador/a
extraordinary . . . . extraordinario/a
extraterrestrial . . . . extraterrestre
eye . . . . (el) ojo

F

face . . . . (la) cara
fact . . . . (el) hecho
factory . . . . (la) fábrica
fair, exhibition, show . . . (la) exposición
fair, appropriate, just . . . . .justo/a
faithful .fiel
fake . . . . falsificado/a
fake, false . . . . postizo/a

fake (to), to pretend, to feign
. . . . *fingir*
fall . . . . *(el) otoño*
fall (to) . . . . *caer*
fall in love with (to) . . . . *enamorarse de*
fame . . . .*(la) fama*
famous, celebrated . . . . *célebre*
fan . . . . *(el/la) aficionado/a*
fan . . . . *(el) ventilador*
fantastic . . . .*fantástico/a*
far (away) . . . .*lejos*
far from . . . . *lejos de*
farewell, parting . . . . *(la) despedida*
farm . . . . *(la) finca, (la) granja*
fascinate (to) . . . .*fascinar*
fashion, style, ... *(la) moda*
fast (to) . . . .*ayunar*
fat . . . .*gordo/a*
fate, destiny, destination
. . . . *(el) destino*
father . . . . *(el) padre*
father-in-law . . . .*(el) suegro*
fatigue, tiredness . . . . *(el) cansancio*
faucet . . . .*(la) llave, (el) grifo*
fault, guilt . . . . *(la) culpa*
fear (to) . . . .*temer*
February . . . . *febrero*
fed up . . . . *harto/a*
feel (to), to regret . . . . *sentir (ie)*
feeling, sentiment . . . . . .*(el) sentimiento*
feign (to), to fake . . . .*fingir*
ferocious, fierce . . . . *feroz*
fiancé, boyfriend, groom . . . . .*(el) novio*
fiancée, girlfriend, bride . . . . *(la) novia*
fib (to), to lie . . . .*mentir (ie)*
field . . . .*(el) campo*
fierce, ferocious . . . . *feroz*
fierce, angry, brave . . . . *bravo/a*
fight . . . .*(la) pelea*
fight (to) . . . . *pelear*
fight (to), to struggle . . . .*luchar*
fill (to) . . . .*llenar*
film (used in a camera), movie
. . . . *(la) película*
final, end . . . . *(el) final*
finally . . . . *por fin*
find (to) . . . . *hallar*
find out (to) . . . . *averiguar*
find (to), to meet . . . .*encontrar (ue)*
fine . . . . *(la) multa*
fine, delicate . . . .*fino/a*
fine, well . . . . *bien*
finger . . . . *(el) dedo*
fingernail, toenail . . . . *(la) uña*
finish (to) . . . . *terminar*
finish (to), to complete . . . . *cumplir*
fire . . . . *(el) incendio, (el) fuego*
firefighter . . . . *(el/la) bombero/a*
fireplace, chimney . . . . *(la) chimenea*
firewood . . . . *(la) leña*
firmness . . . .*(la) firmeza*

first . . . . *primero/a*
fish . . . . *(el) pescado, (el) pez*
fish (to) . . . . *pescar*
fit (to) . . . . *caber*
fix (to), to arrange . . . .*arreglar*
fixed, firm . . . . *fijo/a*
flag . . . . (la) bandera
flat, smooth . . . . *liso/a*
flight . . . .*(el) vuelo*
flight attendant
. . . . . *(el/la) auxiliar (asistente) de vuelo*
floor . . . . *(el) suelo, (el) piso*
flour . . . .*(la) harina*
flower . . . . *(la) flor*
flute . . . . *(la) flauta*
fly . . . .*(la) mosca*
fly (to) . . . . *volar (ue)*
fog . . . .*(la) niebla*
fold (to) . . . . *doblar*
follow (to) . . . . *seguir (i)*
following, next . . . . *siguiente*
folly, madness, insanity . . . . . .*(la) locura*
food . . . .*(la) comida*
foolish, silly, stupid . . . .*tonto/a*
foolish, stupid . . . . *necio/a*
foot . . . .*(el) pie*
football . . . . *(el) fútbol americano*
for, by, in order to . . . .*para*
for, by, through . . . .*por*
for example . . . . *por ejemplo*
forehead . . . . *(la) frente*
foreign . . . . *extranjero/a*
forest, woods . . . . *(el) bosque*
forever . . . . *para siempre*
fork . . . . *(el) tenedor*
fortunate, happy, lucky . . . . . .*dichoso/a*
fortune . . . .*(la) fortuna*
forward, ahead . . . . *adelante*
found (to), to establish . . . . *fundar*
fountain . . . . *(la) fuente*
fourth, quarter, room . . . . *(el) cuarto*
fox . . . .*(el) zorro*
frank . . . .*franco/a*
free . . . .*libre, gratis*
freeway, highway
. . . . *autopista (la), (autovía)*
freeze (to) . . . . *helar (ie)*
freezer . . . .*(el) congelador*
French (language) . . . .*(el) francés*
frequently . . . . *frecuentemente*
fresh, cool . . . .*fresco/a*
Friday . . . . *(el) viernes*
friend . . . . *(la) amiga, (el) amigo*
friendly, kind . . . . *amable*
frighten (to), to scare . . . .*asustar*
frog . . . . *(la) rana*
from, of . . . .*de*
from, since . . . .*desde*
frontier, border . . . .*(la) frontera*
frustrated . . . .*frustrado/a*
fry (to) . . . . *freír (i)*

frying pan . . . . *(el/la) sartén*
full . . . .*lleno/a*
function (to), to work . . . .*funcionar*
furious, very mad . . . .*furioso/a*
future . . . .*(el) porvenir*

G

game . . . . *(el) juego, (el) partido*
garage . . . .*(el) garaje*
garbage collector . . . . . *(el/la) basurero/a*
garden . . . . *(el) jardín*
gardener . . . .*(el/la) jardinero/a*
garlic . . . . *(el) ajo*
gas station . . . . *(la) gasolinera*
generous . . . . *generoso/a*
geranium . . . .*(el) geranio*
German . . . . *(el) alemán*
gesture . . . .*(el) gesto*
get (to), to obtain . . . . *conseguir (i)*
get along well (badly) with (to)
. . . .*llevarse bien (mal) con*
get along well (poorly) (to)
. . . . *caerle bien (mal)*
get angry (to) . . . . . .*enojarse, enfadarse*
get fat (to) . . . . *engordar*
get mad (to) . . . . *enfadarse*
get married to (to) . . . .*casarse con*
get off (a train, etc.) (to),
to go down . . . . *bajar*
get on (a bus, etc.) (to),
to go up . . . . *subir*
get up (to) . . . . *levantarse*
get used to (to) . . . .*acostumbrarse a*
get wet (to) . . . .*mojar*
giraffe . . . . *(la) jirafa*
girl . . . .*(la) chica, (la) niña*
girlfriend, fiancée, bride . . . . . *(la) novia*
give (to) . . . .*dar*
give a present (to),
to give a gift . . . . *regalar*
glass . . . . *(el) vaso*
glass (the material)
. . . .*(el) vidrio, (el) cristal*
glasses . . . .*(las) gafas, (los) anteojos*
global warming
. . . . *(el) calentamiento global*
gloomy, melancholy . . . . . . *melancólico/a*
glove . . . .*(el) guante*
go (to) . . . .*ir*
go away (to) . . . .*irse, marcharse*
go camping (to) . . . . *ir de camping*
go down (to) . . . . *bajar*
go to bed (to) . . . .*acostarse (ue)*
goal (objective) . . . . *(la) meta*
goal (e.g., soccer, hockey) . . . . . *(el) gol*
goalie
. . . . . .*(el/la) arquero/a, (el/la) portero/a*
god . . . .*(el) dios*
goddess . . . .*(la) diosa*
godfather . . . .*(el) padrino*

godmother . . . . (la) madrina
gold . . . . (el) oro
golden . . . . dorado/a
good . . . . bueno/a
good afternoon . . . . buenas tardes
good evening . . . . buenas noches
good morning . . . . buenos días
good time (to have a),
    to enjoy oneself . . . . divertirse (ie)
good-looking . . . . guapo/a
goodbye to (to say)
    . . . . despedirse (i) (de)
goose . . . . (el) ganso
gossip (to) . . . . contar (ue) chismes
govern (to) . . . . gobernar (ie)
governor . . . . (el/la) gobernador/a
government . . . . (el) gobierno
graduate (to) . . . . graduarse
granddaughter . . . . (la) nieta
grandmother . . . . (la) abuela
grandfather . . . . (el) abuelo
grandson . . . . (el) nieto
grape . . . . (la) uva
grass . . . . (la) hierba
grateful . . . . agradecido/a
grateful for (to be), to thank
    . . . . agradecer
great . . . . gran
great-grandfather . . . . (el) bisabuelo
great-grandmother . . . . (la) bisabuela
greedy . . . . avaricioso/a
green . . . . verde
greeting . . . . (el) saludo
grey . . . . gris
grief, pain . . . . (el) dolor
grill . . . . (la) parrilla
groom, fiancé, boyfriend . . . . . (el) novio
grow dark (to) . . . . anochecer
grow (to), to increase . . . . crecer
guard (to), to keep . . . . guardar
guerrilla . . . . (el/la) guerrillero/a
guest . . . . (el/la) invitado/a
guitar . . . . (la) guitarra
guilt, fault . . . . (la) culpa
guilty . . . . culpable
gum (chewing) . . . . (el) chicle

H

hail (to) . . . . granizar
hair . . . . (el) cabello, (el) pelo
hair dryer . . . . (la) secadora de pelo
hairdresser, barber
    . . . . (el/la) peluquero/a
hallway . . . . (el) pasillo
ham . . . . (el) jamón
hamburger . . . . (la) hamburguesa
hammer . . . . (el) martillo
hand . . . . (la) mano
hand over (to), to deliver,
    to turn in . . . . entregar

handmade . . . . hecho/a a mano
hang (up) (to) . . . . colgar (ue)
hanger . . . . (el) gancho, (la) percha
happen (to) . . . . suceder
happen (to), to occur . . . . ocurrir
happiness . . . . (la) felicidad
happiness, joy . . . . (la) alegría
happy . . . . alegre, feliz
happy, content . . . . contento/a
happy, fortunate, lucky . . . . . . dichoso/a
hard . . . . duro/a
harmony . . . . (la) armonía
hat . . . . (el) sombrero
hate (to) . . . . odiar
haughty, proud . . . . soberbio/a
have (to) . . . . tener
have breakfast (to) . . . . desayunar
have a great/bad time (to)
    . . . . pasárselo bien/mal
have just (to) (done
    something) . . . . acabar de
have lunch (to) . . . . almorzar (ue)
have one's way (to)
    . . . . salirse con la suya
have supper (to) . . . . cenar
he, him . . . . él
head . . . . (la) cabeza
healthy . . . . sano/a
heap, pile . . . . (el) montón
hear (to) . . . . oír
heart . . . . (el) corazón
hearth, home . . . . (el) hogar
heat (to) . . . . calentar (ie)
heavy, annoying . . . . pesado/a
heavy-set, stout, burly . . . . . corpulento/a
helicopter . . . . (el) helicóptero
helmet . . . . (el) casco
help . . . . (la) ayuda
help (to) . . . . ayudar
hemisphere . . . . (el) hemisferio
hen . . . . (la) gallina
her, she . . . . ella
here . . . . aquí
hero . . . . (el) héroe
heroine . . . . (la) heroína
hide (to) . . . . esconder, ocultar
high school
    . . . . (el) colegio, (la) escuela secundaria
highway . . . . (la) carretera
highway, freeway
    . . . . (la) autopista (autovía)
him, he . . . . él
history . . . . (la) historia
hit (to) . . . . pegar
hit (to), to beat, to punch . . . . . . golpear
home, hearth . . . . (el) hogar
home (at) . . . . en casa
homeland, country . . . . (la) patria
homerun . . . . (el) jonrón
homework, task. assignment
    . . . . (la) tarea

honeymoon . . . . (la) luna de miel
hope (to), to wait . . . . esperar
horse . . . . (el) caballo
hospital, clinic . . . . (la) clínica
hot . . . . caluroso/a
hot, warm . . . . caliente
hot dog . . . . (el) perrito caliente
hotel . . . . (el) hotel
hour . . . . (la) hora
house . . . . (la) casa
how? . . . . ¿cómo?
how much? . . . . ¿cuánto?
how many? . . . . ¿cuánto/a(s)?
hug (to), to embrace . . . . abrazar
human being . . . . (el) ser humano
humble . . . . humilde
hunting . . . . (la) caza
hurricane . . . . (el) huracán
hurl (to), to throw, to pitch . . . . . lanzar
hurt (to), to ache . . . . doler (ue)
hurry . . . . prisa
hurry (in a), rushed . . . . apurado/a
hurry (to be in a)
    . . . . tener prisa, estar apurado/a
husband . . . . . . (el) marido, (el) esposo
hygiene . . . . (la) higiene
hymn . . . . (el) himno

I

I . . . . yo
ice . . . . (el) hielo
ice cream . . . . (el) helado
ice cream store . . . . (la) heladería
ice hockey . . . . . . (el) hockey sobre hielo
identical . . . . idéntico/a
if . . . . si
if only . . . . ojalá
ill-bred, bad-mannered . . . . . malcriado/a
illegal . . . . ilegal
illustrious . . . . ilustre
image . . . . (la) imagen
imbecile . . . . imbécil
immortal . . . . inmortal
impressive . . . . impresionante
in, on . . . . en
in front of . . . . . . delante de, enfrente de
in no way . . . . en absoluto
in order that . . . . para que
in order to, by, for . . . . para
in spite of . . . . a pesar de
in style (to be) . . . . estar de moda
in this way . . . . así
including . . . . incluso
increase (to) . . . . aumentar
increase (to), to grow . . . . crecer
incredible . . . . increíble
industrious, applied, dedicated
    . . . . aplicado/a
inferior, lower . . . . inferior
ingredient . . . . (el) ingrediente

inherit (to) . . . . heredar
injured (sports) . . . . lesionado/a
injury . . . . (la) lesión
injury, wound . . . . la herida
insanity, folly, madness . . . . . . (la) locura
inside of . . . . .dentro de
insist on (to) . . . . insistir en
inspiration . . . .(la) inspiración
install (to) . . . . instalar
instead of . . . . en vez de
instinct . . . . (el) instinto
instructions . . . . (las) instrucciones
insult (to) . . . . insultar
integrity . . . .(la) integridad
intense . . . . intenso/a
interest . . . .(el) interés
interesting . . . . interesante
international . . . . .internacional
interrupt (to) . . . . interrumpir
interview . . . . (la) entrevista
interview (to) . . . . .entrevistar
intimate, close . . . . íntimo/a
intolerable, unbearable . . . . insoportable
invest (to) (money) . . . . invertir (ie)
invite (to) . . . . invitar
iron (to) . . . . planchar
irritate (to) . . . . irritar
island . . . . (la) isla
isn't that so? . . . .¿verdad?
it is hailing . . . . graniza

J

jacket . . . .(la) chaqueta
jail . . . . (la) cárcel
January . . . . .enero
Japanese . . . .(el) japonés
jealous .celoso/a
jealous, envious . . . . envidioso/a
jewelry . . . . (la) joyería
Jewish . . . . .judío/a
job . . . . (el) trabajo, (el) empleo
joke . . . . (el) chiste
joy, happiness . . . . (la) alegría
judge . . . . (el/la) juez/jueza
judge (to) . . . . juzgar
judgement, trial . . . . (el) juicio
juice . . . . (el) jugo
July . . . . .julio
June . . . . junio
jungle . . . . (la) selva, (la) jungla
just, fair, appropriate . . . . .justo/a

K

keep (to), to guard . . . . .guardar
keep silent (to) . . . . . . guardar silencio
key . . . . (la) llave
kill (to) . . . . .matar
kindly, friendly, nice . . . . amable
king . . . . (el) rey
kiss . . . . (el) beso

kiss (to) . . . . besar
kitchen . . . .(la) cocina
knife . . . .(el) cuchillo
knit (to) . . . . .tejer
know (a fact) (to) . . . . saber
know (a person) (to) . . . . .conocer
know (by heart) (to) . . saber de memoria
knowledge
. . . . . . (el) conocimiento, (la) sabiduría

L

lack, absence . . . . (la) falta
lacking salt, bland . . . . soso/a
ladder, stair . . . . (la) escalera
lady . . . .(la) dama
lake . . . . (el) lago
lamb . . . .(el) cordero
lamp, light . . . . (la) lámpara
land (to) . . . . aterrizar
landscape, scenery . . . . (el) paisaje
language . . . . (el) idioma
language, tongue . . . . (la) lengua
last (of a group) . . . . .último/a
last, past . . . . pasado/a
last (to) . . . . durar
last night . . . . .anoche
late . . . . tarde
later . . . . luego
laugh, laughter . . . .(la) risa
laugh (to) . . . . reír (i)
lawn . . . .(el) césped
lawn mower . . . . (el) cortacésped
lawyer . . . . (el/la) abogado/a
lazy . . . . .perezoso/a
leader . . . .(el/la) líder
leaf . . . . (la) hoja
learn (to) . . . . aprender
learn by heart (to)
. . . . aprender de memoria
learned, wise . . . . sabio/a
leather . . . . (el) cuero
leave (to) . . . . .irse, salir
leave behind (to), to allow . . . . dejar
left . . . . izquierdo/a
left (to the) . . . . a la izquierda
left over (to be), to remain . . . . . sobrar
left-handed . . . . zurdo/a
leg . . . .(la) pierna
legend . . . .(la) leyenda
lemon . . . . (el) limón
lemonade . . . . (la) limonada
lend (to) . . . . .prestar
less . . . . menos
lesson . . . . (la) lección
let know (to), to notify . . . . avisar
letter . . . .(la) carta
letter, lyrics . . . . (la) letra
level . . . . (el) nivel
liberty . . . .(la) libertad
librarian . . . . (el/la) bibliotecario/a
library . . . . (la) biblioteca

license . . . .(la) licencia
lie . . . .(la) mentira
lie (to), to fib . . . . .mentir (ie)
light (adj.) . . . . ligero/a
light, lamp . . . . (la) lámpara, (la) luz
light, slight . . . . leve
light (to) (e.g., a fire), to turn
on (e.g., a light)
. . . . encender (ie), prender
lightning . . . . (el) relámpago
like, as, since . . . . .como
like (to), to wish, to want . . . .querer (ie)
line, tail . . . . (la) cola
lion . . . .(el) león
lipstick
. . . . . (el) lápiz de labios, (el) pintalabios
listen to (to) . . . . escuchar
little, small . . . . pequeño/a, chico/a
little (a) . . . . poco
live (to) . . . . .vivir
living room . . . . (la) sala (de estar)
llama . . . . (la) llama
loathsome to (to be),
to be sickened by . . . . darle asco a
lobster . . . . (la) langosta
lock . . . .(la) cerradura
loneliness, solitude . . . .(la) soledad
long . . . . largo/a
look at (to) . . . . mirar
look for (to) . . . . buscar
lose (to) . . . . .perder (ie)
lose hope (to), to despair . . . .desesperar
loose . . . . suelto/a
lot (a) . . . . mucho
lottery . . . .(la) lotería
love . . . . (el) amor
love (to) . . . . amar
lover . . . . (el/la) amante
loving . . . . .amoroso/a
lower, inferior . . . . inferior
loyal . . . . leal
luck . . . . (la) suerte
lucky, happy, fortunate . . . . . . .dichoso/a
luggage . . . . (el) equipaje
lung . . . . (el) pulmón
lying, untruthful . . . . .mentiroso/a
lyrics, letter . . . . (la) letra

M

machine . . . .(la) máquina
mad (very), furious . . . . furioso/a
madness, insanity, folly . . . . . .(la) locura
magazine . . . . (la) revista
magnifying glass . . . . (la) lupa
maid . . . .(la) criada
maid of honor . . . . . .(la) dama de honor
mail . . . .(el) correo
mail carrier . . . . (el/la) cartero/a
mailbox . . . . (el) buzón
maintain (to) . . . . .mantener
make (to), to do . . . . hacer

make (to), to create . . . . *crear*
make a decision (to)
. . . . *tomar una decisión*
make a mistake (to) . . . . *equivocarse*
mall . . . . *(el) centro comercial*
man . . . . *(el) hombre*
manager . . . . *(el) gerente*
manufacture (to) . . . . *fabricar*
many . . . . *muchos/as*
map . . . .*(el) mapa*
March . . . . *marzo*
market . . . . *(el) mercado*
married (to get) . . . . *casarse*
Martian . . . . *(el) marciano*
marvel . . . . *(la) maravilla*
marvelous, wonderful . . . . *maravilloso/a*
mass (church) . . . . *(la) misa*
master's degree . . . .*(la) maestría*
material, cloth . . . .*(la) tela*
math . . . . *(las) matemáticas*
matter, subject . . . .*(el) asunto*
mature, ripe . . . .*maduro/a*
May . . . . *mayo*
mayor . . . . *(el) alcalde*
mean, cruel . . . . *cruel*
measure (to) . . . . *medir (i)*
meat . . . . *(la) carne*
meatball . . . .*(la) albóndiga*
medal . . . . *(la) medalla*
medium, average . . . . *mediano/a*
meet (to), to find . . . . . . *encontrar (ue)*
meeting, reunion . . . .*(la) reunión*
melancholy, gloomy . . . . . *melancólico/a*
melody . . . . *(la) melodía*
mention (to) . . . .*mencionar*
merit (to), to deserve . . . .*merecer*
meteorologist . . . . *(el) meteorólogo*
meow (like a cat) (to) . . . . *maullar*
message . . . . *(el) mensaje*
messy, not neat . . . . *desordenado/a*
method . . . . *(el) método*
metro, subway . . . . *(el) metro*
microwave oven
. . . .*(el) horno de microondas*
midnight . . . . *(la) medianoche*
mile . . . . *(la) milla*
milk . . . .*(la) leche*
million . . . .*(el) millón*
minister . . . . *(el) ministro*
miracle . . . .*(el) milagro*
mirror . . . .*(el) espejo*
miss someone (to),
something . . . . *echar de menos*
mistaken . . . .*equivocado/a*
mix (to) . . . . *mezclar*
mixed . . . . *mezclado/a*
modest . . . . *modesto/a*
moisten (to), to wet . . . . *mojar*
monastery . . . . *(el) monasterio*
Monday . . . . *lunes*
money . . . .*(el) dinero*

monk . . . . *(el) monje*
month . . . . *(el) mes*
moon . . . . *(la) luna*
more . . . . *más*
mosque . . . .*(la) mezquita*
mother . . . .*(la) madre*
mother-in-law . . . . *(la) suegra*
motorcycle . . . . *(la) moto(cicleta)*
mountain . . . . *(la) montaña*
mouse . . . .*(el) ratón*
mouth . . . . *(la) boca*
move (to) . . . .*mover (ue)*
move (to) (location) . . . . *mudarse*
movie . . . . *(la) película*
movie, film (used in
a camera) . . . . *(la) película*
movie theater . . . .*(el) cine*
much (too), (pl. too many)
. . . .*demasiado/a (adj.)*
mule . . . .*(la) mula*
museum . . . . *(el) museo*
music . . . . *(la) música*
musician . . . .*(el/la) músico/a*
Muslim . . . . *musulmán*
mustache . . . . *(el) bigote*
mute, dumb . . . . *mudo/a*
mutual . . . .*mutuo/a*
mysterious . . . . *misterioso/a*
mystery . . . . *(el) misterio*

N

nail polish . . . . *(el) esmalte de uñas*
naive . . . . *ingenuo/a*
name (to) . . . . *nombrar*
napkin . . . . *(la) servilleta*
narrow . . . . *angosto/a, estrecho/a*
nature . . . . *(la) naturaleza*
near . . . . *cerca (de)*
near(by) . . . . *cerca*
nearby, neighboring . . . . *cercano/a*
necessary, precise, clear . . . . . *preciso/a*
need (to) . . . . *necesitar*
neighbor . . . . *(el/la) vecino/a*
neighborhood, section,
quarter . . . . *(el) barrio*
neighboring, nearby . . . . *cercano/a*
neither, nor . . . .*ni*
nephew . . . .*(el) sobrino*
net, network . . . . *(la)*
red . . . .
never . . . . *nunca*
new . . . . *nuevo/a*
news . . . .*(las) noticias*
newspaper . . . . *(el) periódico*
newspaper stand . . . .*(el) quiosco*
next . . . . *próximo/a*
next, following . . . . *siguiente*
nice . . . . *amable, simpático/a*
niece . . . .*(la) sobrina*
night . . . . *(la) noche*

nightclub, discotheque . . . *(la) discoteca*
no . . . . *no*
no longer . . . . *ya no*
no one . . . . *nadie*
noise . . . .*(el) ruido*
noisy . . . .*ruidoso/a*
noisy, rowdy, boisterous . . . . *bullicioso/a*
none . . . . *ninguno/a*
noodle . . . .*(el) fideo*
noon . . . .*(el) mediodía*
nor, neither . . . .*ni*
north . . . . *norte*
northeast . . . .*(el) noreste*
northwest . . . . *(el) noroeste*
not neat, messy . . . . . . *desordenado/a*
not yet . . . .*todavía no*
note . . . .*(el) apunte*
notebook . . . . *(el) cuaderno*
nothing . . . . *nada*
notice (to) . . . .*fijarse en*
notify (to), to let know . . . . *avisar*
nose . . . .*(la) nariz*
novel . . . .*(la) novela*
November . . . . *noviembre*
now . . . . *ahora*
nuclear energy . . . . . *(la) energía nuclear*
nun . . . . *(la) monja*
nurse . . . . *(el/la) enfermero/a*

O

oak . . . .*(el) roble*
obscure, dark . . . .*o(b)scuro/a*
obstinate, stubborn . . . . *obstinado/a*
obtain (to), to get . . . . *conseguir (i)*
obtain (to), to succeed in . . . . *lograr*
occur (to), to happen . . . .*ocurrir*
ocean . . . . *(el) océano*
October . . . . *octubre*
of, from . . . . *de*
of course . . . . *por supuesto*
offend (to) . . . . *ofender*
offer (to) . . . .*ofrecer*
office . . . . *(el) despacho, (la) oficina*
often . . . . *a menudo*
oil . . . . *(el) aceite*
oil, petroleum . . . . *(el) petróleo*
old . . . . *viejo/a*
old age . . . . *(la) vejez*
older . . . . *mayor*
on, in . . . . *en*
on top of . . . . *encima de*
on top of, about, over . . . .*sobre*
once . . . . *una vez*
only, unique . . . . *único/a*
only . . . . *sólo*
open . . . . *abierto/a*
open (to) . . . . *abrir*
opponent . . . .*(el/la) adversario/a*
opposite (n.) . . . . *(el) opuesto*
opposite (adj.) . . . .*opuesto/a*

optimist . . . . (el/la) optimista
orange . . . . anaranjado/a
orange . . . .(la) naranja
orchestra . . . . (la) orquesta
order (to), to send . . . . mandar
order (to) (food), to ask for. . . . pedir (i)
ordinary. . . . . ordinario/a
ordinary, common. . . . . vulgar
organ . . . . (el) órgano
organize (to) . . . . organizar
original . . . . original
original, exceptional, smart. . . . . genial
other, another . . . . otro/a
others (the) . . . . (los/las) demás
ought to. . . . . deber
outside. . . . . afuera
oven. . . . . (el) horno
over, about, on top of . . . . sobre
overcoat, coat . . . .(el) abrigo
owe (to). . . . . deber
own, proper. . . . . propio/a
owner. . . . . (el/la) dueño/a
ox. . . . . (el) buey
oyster. . . . .(la) ostra

P

pack (to) . . . . .hacer la maleta
package . . . .(el) paquete
pain . . . . (la) pena
pain, grief . . . .(el) dolor
painful. . . . . penoso/a
paint (to) . . . . pintar
painter . . . . (el/la) pintor/a
painting . . . . (la) pintura, (el) cuadro
painting, sketch, drawing . . . .(el) dibujo
pair . . . . .par
pair, couple . . . . (la) pareja
palace . . . . (el) palacio
pale . . . . .pálido/a
pants . . . . (los) pantalones
paper . . . .(el) papel
parade . . . .(el) desfile
pardon (to). . . . . .perdonar
park . . . . (el) parque
park (to). . . . . .estacionar
parking lot (garage)
. . . .(el) estacionamiento
parrot. . . . .(el) loro
parting, farewell . . . .(la) despedida
party . . . .(la) fiesta
pass (to). . . . . .pasar
passenger. . . . .(el/la) pasajero/a
passionate, burning. . . . . .ardiente
passionately. . . . . apasionadamente
passport. . . . . (el) pasaporte
password . . . . (la) contraseña
past, last . . . . pasado/a
pay (to) . . . . .pagar
peach. . . . . (el) durazno
peach . . . .(el) melocotón

peak, summit . . . .(la) cumbre
pear . . . . (la) pera
pen. . . . . (el) bolígrafo, (la) pluma
pencil . . . . (el) lápiz
pencil sharpener . . . . (el) sacapuntas
people . . . .(la) gente
pepper . . . . (la) pimienta
percentage . . . . .porcentaje
performance, show . . . . .(el) espectáculo
perhaps . . . . tal vez
period of time . . . .(el) plazo
permission . . . .(el) permiso
permit (to), to allow . . . . . . .permitir
persecute (to), to pursue
. . . . perseguir (i)
pessimist . . . . (el/la) pesimista
petroleum, oil . . . . (el) petróleo
pew, bench, bank . . . . (el) banco
phenomenal . . . . .fenomenal
philosophy. . . . . (la) filosofía
photo . . . .(la) foto
photo(graph) . . . .(la) foto(grafía)
physics. . . . .(la) física
piano . . . . (el) piano
picture, portrait . . . . (el) retrato
picturesque . . . . pintoresco/a
piece . . . . (el) pedazo
piece, bit, selection, portion . . .(el) trozo
pile, heap. . . . . (el) montón
pill. . . . .(la) pastilla
pillow . . . .(la) almohada
pine tree. . . . . (el) pino
pink . . . . rosado/a
pitch (to), to throw, to hurl . . . . . lanzar
pitcher . . . .(el) lanzador
place, site . . . .(el) sitio
place (to), to arrange. . . . . colocar
plains. . . . . (las) pampas
planet. . . . . (el) planeta
plant. . . . .(la) planta
plastic . . . .(el) plástico
plate, dish . . . . (el) plato
platform. . . . . (el) andén
play (to). . . . . jugar (ue)
play (to) (an instrument),
to touch . . . . tocar
player. . . . .(el/la) jugador/a
please (to) . . . . placer
plot (of a story). . . . . (la) trama
plug in (to) . . . . enchufar
P.M. (in the afternoon). . . . . . .de la tarde
P.M. (in the evening) . . . . de la noche
poet . . . . (el) poeta, (la) poetisa
poetry . . . .(la) poesía
point . . . . (el) punto
poison . . . . (el) veneno
police station . . . .(la) comisaría
polish (to) . . . . pulir
polished. . . . . .pulido/a
polite, cordial . . . . .cordial
polite, courteous . . . . cortés

political . . . . .político/a
politics. . . . .(la) política
polka-dot. . . . . de lunares
polyester . . . .(el) poliéster
poor. . . . . .pobre
poorly, bad . . . . mal
popcorn . . . . (las) palomitas
portion, piece, bit, selection . . .(el) trozo
possessions, property . . . . bienes
postcard. . . . . (la) (tarjeta) postal
poster. . . . . (el) cartel
postpone (to) . . . . aplazar
pot . . . .(la) olla
potato. . . . . (la) papa, (la) patata
pound. . . . . (la) libra
powerful . . . . poderoso/a
praise (to) . . . . alabar
pray (to). . . . . rezar
precious, cute . . . . precioso/a
precise, necessary, clear . . . . . preciso/a
prefer (to) . . . . .preferir (ie)
premiere, debut. . . . . (el) estreno
prepare (to) . . . . preparar
prescription, recipe . . . . (la) receta
present. . . . .(el) regalo
present, current . . . . corriente
present day . . . . actual
presentation . . . .(la) presentación
press conference
. . . . (la) conferencia de prensa
press (media). . . . . (la) prensa
pretend (to), to fake . . . . .fingir
pretty. . . . . bonito/a, lindo/a
prevent (to) . . . . evitar, impedir (i)
price. . . . . (el) precio
pride . . . . (el) orgullo
priest . . . . (el) cura
print (to) . . . . imprimir
printed. . . . . impreso/a
privilege, right. . . . .(el) derecho
prize. . . . . (el) premio
problem . . . . (el) problema
produce (to). . . . . producir
prohibit (to). . . . . .prohibir
project . . . .(el) proyecto
promise (to). . . . . prometer
proof, quiz, test . . . . (la) prueba
proper, own. . . . . propio/a
property, possessions . . . . bienes
protect (to). . . . . proteger
protected . . . . .protegido/a
proud. . . . . orgulloso/a
proud, haughty . . . . soberbio/a
pull one's leg (to), to tease
. . . . .tomar el pelo
punch (to), to hit . . . . golpear
punctually . . . . puntualmente
punish (to). . . . . .castigar
punishment . . . . (el) castigo
purple . . . . .morado/a
purse, bag . . . .(la) bolsa

pursue (to), to persecute. . . . *perseguir (i)*
put (to). *poner*
put into (to) . . . . *meter*
put on (to) . . . . *ponerse*

Q

quarter, fourth, room. . . . . . . *(el) cuarto*
quarter, neighborhood,
   section . . . . *(el) barrio*
queen. . . . .*(la) reina*
quickly. . . . . *rápidamente*
quit (to), to resign . . . .*demitir, renunciar*
quiz, proof, test. . . . . *(la) prueba*

R

rabbi . . . .*(el) rabino*
race, career . . . .*(la) carrera*
racquet. . . . .*(la) raqueta*
radio . . . .*(el/la) radio*
rain . . . . *(la) lluvia*
rain (to) . . . .*llover (ue)*
rain forest . . . . *(el) bosque de lluvia*
raincoat . . . .*(el) impermeable*
raise (to) (up) . . . .*levantar, alzar*
rake . . . . *(el) rastrillo*
rare, strange. . . . . *raro/a*
rascally, roguish . . . .*pícaro/a*
read (to). . . . . *leer*
reader. . . . .*(el/la) lector/a*
ready, clever, smart. . . . . *listo/a*
real, royal . . . . *real*
real, true . . . .*verdadero/a*
reality . . . . *(la) realidad*
realize (to) (i.e., come to
   awareness of). . . . . . .*darse cuenta de*
realize (to) (e.g., a dream,
   a goal) . . . . *realizar*
receipt . . . . *(el) recibo*
receive (to) . . . .*recibir*
recent. . . . . *reciente*
recent/recently. . . . . *recién*
recipe, prescription . . . . *(la) receta*
record (to), to engrave . . . .*grabar*
recommend (to). . . . . . .*recomendar (ie)*
record . . . .*(el) disco*
record (to), to engrave . . . .*grabar*
record player. . . . .*(el) tocadiscos*
recover (to) . . . . *recuperar*
red . . . . *rojo/a*
red-headed. . . . .*pelirrojo/a*
refer (to) . . . . *referir (ie)*
referee. . . . . *(el) árbitro*
reflect (to) . . . . *reflejar*
reflect (to), to think over. . . . *reflexionar*
refrigerator *(el) refrigerador, (la) nevera*
regret (to) . . . . *lamentar, sentir (ie),*
                    arrepentirse (ie) de
reign (to). . . . . *reinar*
relationship . . . . *(la) relación*
relative. . . . . *(el) pariente*

relax (to) . . . . *relajarse*
relax (to), to rest . . . . *descansar*
remain (to). . . . .*quedar*
remain (to), to be left over . . . . . *sobrar*
remember (to) . . . . *recordar (ue)*
remote . . . . *remoto/a*
renovate (to) . . . . *renovar (ue)*
rent (to) . . . .*alquilar*
rented. . . . .*alquilado/a*
repeat (to) . . . .*repetir (i)*
reply . . . . *(la) respuesta*
report . . . .*(el) informe*
reporter . . . . *(el/la) reportero/a*
representative . . . . *(el) representante*
require (to), to demand . . . .*exigir*
resemble (to) . . . .*parecerse a*
reservation. . . . .*(la) reservación*
residence, dormitory . . . .*(la) residencia*
resign (to), to quit . . . .*dimitir, renunciar*
resolve (to), to solve
   a problem. . . . .*resolver (ue)*
respect (to) . . . .*respetar*
rest (to), to relax . . . . *descansar*
restaurant. . . . .*(el) restaurante*
restore (to). . . . . *restaurar*
result . . . . *(el) resultado*
retired . . . .*jubilado/a*
return (to) . . . .*regresar, volver (ue)*
return (to) (an object). . . . . *devolver (ue)*
reunion, meeting. . . . .*(la) reunión*
reveal (to) . . . .*revelar*
revenge, vengeance. . . . . . *(la) venganza*
review . . . .*(el) repaso*
revolve (to), to rotate, to turn . . . . *girar*
reward (to). . . . . *premiar*
rhythm. . . . .*(el) ritmo*
rice. . . . .*(el) arroz*
rich . . . .*rico/a*
right. . . . . *(la) derecha*
right. . . . . *derecho/a*
right, privilege. . . . .*(el) derecho*
right (to be). . . . . *tener razón*
right (to the) . . . . *a la derecha*
right-handed . . . . *diestro/a*
right now. . . . .*ahora mismo*
rigid. . . . . *rígido/a*
ring . . . . *(el) anillo*
ring (to). . . . . *sonar (ue)*
ripe, mature. . . . .*maduro/a*
risk. . . . . *(el) riesgo*
river. . . . .*(el) río*
roast (to) . . . .*asar*
roasted. . . . . *asado/a*
robber . . . . *(el) ladrón, (la) ladrona*
rock, stone. . . . .*(la) piedra*
roguish, rascally . . . .*pícaro/a*
roof . . . . *(el) tejado*
room, quarter, fourth. . . . . .*(el) cuarto*
roommate . . . . *(el/la) compañero/a*
                       de cuarto
root . . . .*(la) raíz*
rose . . . . *(la) rosa*

round. . . . . *redondo/a*
round, circular. . . . . *circular*
route . . . .*(la) ruta*
row . . . . *(la) fila*
rowdy, noisy, boisterous . . .*bullicioso/a*
rowing. . . . . *(el) remo*
royal, real . . . . *real*
rude . . . .*maleducado/a*
rude, crude . . . .*grosero/a*
rug, carpet . . . .*(la) alfombra*
ruins. . . . . *(las) ruinas*
run (to) . . . . *correr*
rushed, in a hurry . . . . *apurado/a*

S

sacred . . . . *sagrado/a*
sacrifice. . . . . *(el) sacrificio*
sad . . . . *triste*
safe . . . .*seguro/a, salvo/a*
sail (to) . . . .*navegar*
sailing, candle . . . .*(la) vela*
sailor . . . . *(el/la) marinero/a*
saint. . . . .*(el) santo*
salad . . . .*(la) ensalada*
salary. . . . .*(el) sueldo*
salesclerk. . . . . *el dependiente*
                        la dependienta
salt. . . . .*(la) sal*
salty. . . . . *salado/a*
same . . . .*mismo/a*
sand. . . . . *(la) arena*
sandwich . . . . *(el) bocadillo*
sargent. . . . . *(el) sargento*
satisfied. . . . . *satisfecho/a*
satisfy (to) . . . . *satisfacer*
Saturday . . . . *(el) sábado*
sausage . . . . *(la) salchicha*
save (to). . . . . *ahorrar*
saxophone . . . . *(el) saxofón*
say (to), to tell. . . . . *decir*
say goodbye to (to) . . .*despedirse (i) (de)*
scale a mountain (to)
        . . . . *escalar una montaña*
scare (to), to frighten . . . . *asustar*
scarf. . . . . *(la) bufanda*
scene . . . . *(la) escena*
scenery, landscape . . . . *(el) paisaje*
schedule. . . . . *(el) horario*
scholarship . . . . *(la) beca*
school . . . .*(el) colegio, (la) escuela*
science. . . . . *(la) ciencia*
scientist. . . . . *(el/la) científico/a*
scissors . . . . *(las) tijeras*
scold (to). . . . . *reñir (i)*
scour (to), to scrub . . . . *fregar (ie)*
screen . . . . *(la) pantalla*
sea . . . .*(el/la) mar*
seafood, shellfish . . . .*(el) marisco*
seamstress, dressmaker . . . *(la) costurera*
seashell . . . . *(la) caracola*
season (e.g., sports season)

. . . . *(la) temporada*	shower (to take a) . . . . *ducharse*	so, well . . . . *pues*
seat . . . . *(el) asiento*	sick . . . . *enfermo/a*	so many . . . . *tantos/as*
seat, chair . . . . *(la) silla*	sickened by (to be),	so much (adv.). . . . . *tanto*
seat (someone) (to) . . . . *sentar (ie)*	to be loathsome to . . . . . *darle asco a*	soap . . . . *(el) jabón*
seatbelt . . . . . *(el) cinturón de seguridad*	side . . . . *(el) lado*	soap opera . . . .*(la) telenovela*
second . . . . *segundo/a*	sidewalk . . . . *(la) acera*	soccer . . . . *(el) fútbol*
secret. . . . . *(el) secreto*	sign (to). . . . . *firmar*	socks . . . . *(los) calcetines*
secretary . . . . *(el/la) secretario/a*	silk. . . . . *(la) seda*	sofa . . . .*(el) sofá*
section, neighborhood,	silly, stupid, foolish. . . . .*tonto/a*	soft. . . . . *blando/a*
quarter . . . . *(el) barrio*	silverware . . . .*(los) cubiertos*	soft, smooth. . . . . *suave*
secure, sure . . . . *seguro/a*	similar . . . . *semejante*	soil, earth. . . . . *(la) tierra*
security, certainty . . . . *(la) seguridad*	simple . . . .*sencillo/a*	soldier . . . .*(el) soldado*
see (to). . . . . *ver*	sin . . . . *(el) pecado*	solitude, loneliness . . . .*(la) soledad*
see you later . . . . *hasta luego*	since, like, as . . . . *como*	solve a problem (to),
seek (to), to aspire to,	since, from . . . .*desde*	to resolve . . . . *resolver (ue)*
to claim to be. . . . .*pretender*	sing (to). . . . . *cantar*	some . . . . *alguno/a, unos/as*
seem (to), to appear . . . . *parecer*	singer. . . . .*(el/la) cantante*	someone . . . . *alguien*
select (to), to choose . . . . *escoger*	sink (in bathroom). . . . .*(el) lavabo*	something . . . .*algo*
selection, bit, piece . . . . *(el) trozo*	sink (in kitchen) . . . . *(el) fregadero*	sometimes, at times. . . . . *a veces*
sell (to) . . . . *vender*	sister . . . .*(la) hermana*	son. . . . .*(el) hijo*
senator. . . . . *(el/la) senador/a*	sister-in-law. . . . . *(la) cuñada*	song. . . . .*(la) canción*
send (to) . . . . *enviar, mandar*	sit (to) (down). . . . . *sentarse (ie)*	soon. . . . .*pronto*
sentence. . . . .*(la) frase*	site, place . . . .*(el) sitio*	sound. . . . .*(el) sonido*
sentiment, feeling . . . . . .*(el) sentimiento*	size . . . . *(el) tamaño*	soup. . . . . *(la) sopa*
separate . . . .*separado/a*	skate (to) . . . . *patinar*	sour, bitter. . . . . *agrio/a, (amargo/a)*
separate (to). . . . . *separar*	skates. . . . . *(los) patines*	south . . . . *sur*
September . . . .*septiembre*	skating. . . . . *(el) patinaje*	southeast . . . . *(el) sureste*
series . . . . *(la) serie*	sketch, drawing, painting . . . . *(el) dibujo*	southwest. . . . . *(el) suroeste*
serious. . . . . *grave,*	skiing. . . . .*(el) esquí*	space . . . .*(el) espacio*
serio/a	skillful, clever . . . . *hábil*	spaghetti . . . . *(el) espagueti*
serpent, snake . . . .*(la) serpiente*	skin . . . .*(la) piel*	speak (to), to talk . . . . *hablar*
serve (to) . . . . *servir (i)*	skinny, thin . . . .*flaco/a*	special . . . . *especial*
set the table (to) . . . . *poner la mesa*	skirt . . . .*(la) falda*	speech . . . . *(el) discurso*
shame, embarrassment . . .*(la) vergüenza*	skunk. . . . .*(el) zorrillo (la mofeta)*	speed . . . . *(la) velocidad*
share (to) . . . . *compartir*	sky. . . . . *(el) cielo*	spell (to) . . . . *deletrear*
shark . . . . *(el) tiburón*	skyscraper . . . . *(el) rascacielos*	spend (time) (to) . . . . . . *pasar (tiempo)*
sharp (e.g., knife) . . . . *afilado/a*	sled, sleigh . . . . *(el) trineo*	spend (to), to waste. . . . . *gastar*
sharp, astute . . . .*agudo/a*	sleep (to) . . . . *dormir (ue)*	spider. . . . . *(la) araña*
shave (to) (oneself) . . . . *afeitar(se)*	sleeping bag . . . . *saco de dormir*	spider web. . . . . *(la) telaraña*
she, her . . . . *ella*	slight, light . . . . *leve*	spill (to). . . . .*derramar*
sheep . . . .*(la) oveja*	slippery . . . . . *resbaloso/a, resbaladizo/a*	spit (to) . . . . *escupir*
shelf. . . . . *(el) estante*	slow. *lento/a*	spoiled. . . . . *mimado/a*
shellfish, seafood . . . .*(el) marisco*	slowly . . . . *despacio*	spoon. . . . .*(la) cuchara*
shield, coat of arms . . . . . . *(el) escudo*	small . . . . *pequeño/a*	sport(s) . . . . .*(el) deporte, (los) deportes*
shine (to). . . . . *brillar, lucir*	small, little . . . .*chico/a*	spring. . . . .*(la) primavera*
ship . . . . *(la) nave*	smart, original, exceptional. . . . . *genial*	spy (to) . . . . *espiar*
shirt. . . . .*(la) camisa*	smart, ready, clever. . . . . *listo/a*	square . . . . *cuadrado/a*
shoe. . . . .*(el) zapato*	smell (to). . . . . *oler (ue)*	squeeze (to), to tighten. . . . . *apretar (ie)*
shoelaces. . . . .*(los) cordones*	smile (to). . . . . *sonreír (i)*	stadium . . . . *(el) estadio*
shoemaker, cobbler. . . *(el/la) zapatero/a*	smiling, cheerful . . . . *risueño/a*	stain. . . . .*(la) mancha*
shoot (to) . . . . *disparar*	smoke (to). . . . .*fumar*	stained. . . . . *manchado/a*
shooting. . . . .*(el) tiroteo*	smooth, flat. . . . .*liso/a*	stair, ladder . . . . *(la) escalera*
shopping (to go) . . . . *ir de compras*	smooth, soft. . . . . *suave*	stairs . . . .*(las) escaleras*
shore, bank (of river, ocean). . *(la) orilla*	smoothly, suavely . . . . *suavemente*	stamp. . . . .*(la) estampilla*
short. . . . . *bajo/a, corto/a*	snake, serpent . . . .*(la) serpiente*	star. . . . .*(la) estrella*
shorts. . . . .*(los) pantalones cortos*	sneeze (to). . . . .*estornudar*	start a business (to)
shout (to). . . . .*gritar*	snore (to). . . . . *roncar*	. . . . *montar un negocio*
shovel . . . . *(la) pala*	snow . . . .*(la) nieve*	statue . . . .*(la) estatua*
show, performance . . . . *(el) espectáculo*	snow (to) . . . . *nevar (ie)*	steak . . . . *(el) bistec*
show (to). . . . . *mostrar (ue)*	so. . . . .*tan*	steel . . . . *(el) acero*
shower. . . . .*(la) ducha*	so, therefore . . . . *por eso*	still. . . . . *todavía*

stingy. . . . . *tacaño/a*
stomach. . . . . *(el) estómago*
stone, rock. . . . .*(la) piedra*
stop (to), to detain. . . . . *detener*
stop (to). . . . .*parar*
stop doing something (to)
. . . . *dejar de* (+ infinitive)
store. . . . . *(la) tienda*
storm . . . . . *(la) tempestad, (la) tormenta*
story, tale. . . . .*(el) cuento*
stout, heavy-set, burly. . . . . *corpulento/a*
straight (e.g., hair). . . . .*lacio/a*
strain (to) (e.g., pasta). . . . . *escurrir*
strange. . . . .*extraño/a*
strange, rare. . . . . *raro/a*
stream . . . .*(el) arroyo*
street . . . . *(la) calle*
strike . . . . *(la) huelga*
stripes . . . .*(las) rayas*
stroll, trip. . . . . *(el) paseo*
stroll, walk . . . . *(la) caminata*
strong. . . . .*fuerte*
struggle (to), to fight. . . . . *luchar*
stubborn. . . . . *obstinado/a (terco/a)*
stubborn, obstinate . . . . *obstinado/a*
student. . . . .*(el/la) alumno/a,*
(el/la) estudiante
student desk. . . . . *(el) pupitre*
study (to). . . . . *estudiar*
stupid. . . . .*estúpido/a*
stupid, foolish . . . . *necio/a*
stupid, silly, foolish. . . . .*tonto/a*
style . . . .*(el) estilo*
style, fashion . . . . *(la) moda*
suavely, smoothly . . . . *suavemente*
subject, matter. . . . .*(el) asunto*
suburbs . . . . *(las) afueras*
subway, metro. . . . . *(el) metro*
succeed in (to), to obtain . . . .*lograr*
success. . . . . *(el) éxito*
successful . . . . *exitoso/a*
successful (to be) . . . . *tener éxito*
sudden, abrupt. . . . . *brusco/a*
suddenly . . . . *de repente*
sugar . . . . *(el/la) azúcar*
suggest (to) . . . . *sugerir (ie)*
suit. . . . . *(el) traje*
suitcase . . . . *(la) maleta*
summary . . . . *(el) resumen*
summer . . . . *(el) verano*
summit, peak. . . . .*(la) cumbre*
Sunday. . . . . *domingo*
sunrise. . . . . *(la) salida del sol*
sunset. . . . . *(la) puesta del sol*
superior, upper . . . .*superior*
supermarket. . . . .*(el) supermercado*
support (to), to aid . . . .*apoyar*
suppose (to). . . . . *suponer*
supposed . . . . *supuesto/a*
sure, secure . . . . *seguro/a*
surprise . . . . *(la) sorpresa*
surprised . . . . *sorprendido/a*

surround (to) . . . . *rodear*
survive (to) . . . . *sobrevivir*
suspect (to) . . . . *sospechar*
swallow (to) . . . . *tragar*
swear (to) . . . . *jurar*
sweat (to). . . . . *sudar*
sweater . . . . *(el) suéter*
sweet . . . . *dulce*
swim (to). . . . .*nadar*
swimming . . . . *(la) natación*
swimming pool . . . . *(la) piscina*
swimsuit . . . . *(el) traje de baño*
symbol. . . . .*(el) símbolo*
symphony . . . . *(la) sinfonía*
synagogue . . . .*(la) sinagoga*
system . . . . *(el) sistema*

T

table. . . . .*(la) mesa*
tablecloth. . . . .*(el) mantel*
tail, line . . . . *(la) cola*
take (to), to catch . . . .*coger*
take a shower (to) . . . . *ducharse*
take a stroll (to). . . . . *pasear*
take a trip (to) . . . . *hacer un viaje*
take a walk/drive (to) . . . .*dar una vuelta*
take into consideration (to)
. . . . *tener en cuenta*
take notes (to) . . . . *tomar apuntes*
take off (to) . . . .*quitarse*
take out (to). . . . . *sacar*
take place (to) . . . . *tener lugar*
tale, story. . . . .*(el) cuento*
talent . . . . *(el) talento*
talk (to), to speak . . . . *hablar*
tall . . . .*alto/a*
tape recorder . . . . *(la) grabadora*
task, homework, assignment
. . . . *(la) tarea*
taste. . . . .*(el) gusto*
taste (to) . . . . *probar (ue)*
tasty, delicious . . . . *sabroso/a*
tax . . . .*(el) impuesto*
taxi. . . . . *(el) taxi*
tea . . . .*(el) té*
teach (to). . . . . *enseñar*
teacher. . . . .*(el/la) maestro/a*
teacher. . . . . *(el) profesor, (la) profesora*
teaching. . . . .*(la) enseñanza*
team. . . . . *(el) equipo*
tear. . . . .*(la) lágrima*
tease (to), to pull one's leg
. . . .*tomar el pelo*
telephone. . . . .*(el) teléfono*
telescope . . . .*(el) telescopio*
television . . . . *(la) televisión*
television set . . . . *(el) televisor*
tell (to), to count . . . . *contar (ue)*
tell (to), to say. . . . . *decir*
temple . . . .*(el) templo*
tennis. . . . . *(el) tenis*

tent. . . . .*(la) tienda de campaña*
tenth. . . . .*décimo/a*
terrific, wonderful. . . . .*formidable*
test. . . . . *(el) examen*
test, proof, quiz. . . . . *(la) prueba*
text. . . . . *(el) texto*
thank (to), to be grateful for
. . . . *agradecer*
thanks . . . . *gracias*
that. . . . . *ese/a*
that (over yonder) . . . .*aquel, aquella*
that, which. . . . . *que*
theater . . . . *(el) teatro*
them, they . . . . *ellas/os*
theme. . . . . *(el) tema*
there. . . . .*allí*
there are, there is. . . . . *hay*
there was, there were . . . .*había*
therefore, so . . . . *por eso*
they, them . . . . *ellas/os*
thick, dense . . . . *espeso/a*
thin, skinny . . . .*flaco/a*
thing . . . . *(la) cosa*
think (to) . . . .*pensar (ie)*
think over (to), to reflect. . . . *reflexionar*
third. . . . .*tercero/a*
this. . . . .*este/a*
this morning . . . . *esta mañana*
thousand . . . .*mil*
threaten (to). . . . . *amenazar*
throat . . . .*(la) garganta*
through, by, for . . . .*por*
throw (to) . . . . *arrojar*
throw (to), to throw away. . . . . . . *echar*
throw (to), to hurl, to pitch. . . . . *lanzar*
thunder . . . . *(el) trueno*
Thursday . . . . *jueves*
ticket, entrance, admission
. . . . *(la) entrada*
ticket . . . .*(el) billete, (el) boleto*
tie. . . . . *(la) corbata*
tied. . . . . *atado/a, empatado/a*
tiger . . . . *(el) tigre*
tighten (to), to squeeze. . . . . *apretar (ie)*
time . . . .*(el) tiempo*
tip (e.g., given to a waiter). . .*(la) propina*
tired. . . . . *cansado/a*
tiredness, fatigue. . . . . *(el) cansancio*
title . . . . *(el) título*
to, at . . . . *a*
toast (to) (drink) . . . . *brindar*
today . . . . *hoy*
toenail, fingernail . . . . *(la) uña*
together. . . . . *juntos/as*
tomato. . . . .*(el) tomate*
tomb . . . . *(la) tumba*
tomorrow. . . . . *mañana*
tongue, language . . . . *(la) lengua*
tonight. . . . . *esta noche*
too much . . . .*demasiado/a(s) (adv.)*
too much, (*pl.* too many)
. . . .*demasiado/a (adj.)*

tool . . . . (la) herramienta
tooth . . . . (el) diente
touch (to), to play (an instrument)
. . . . tocar
tour . . . .(la) gira
tour guide . . . . (el/la) guía
tournament . . . . (el) torneo
towards . . . . hacia
towel . . . . (la) toalla
tower . . . . (la) torre
town, village . . . .(el) pueblo
traffic light . . . .(el) semáforo
train. (el) tren
train station . . . . (la) estación de tren
training . . . . (el) entrenamiento
translate (to) . . . . traducir
travel (to). . . . . viajar, ir de viaje
travel agency. . . . . .(la) agencia de viajes
tray . . . . (la) bandeja
treasure . . . . (el) tesoro
treasurer. . . . .(el/la) tesorero/a
tree. . . . .(el) árbol
trial, judgement . .(el) proceso, (el) juicio
tricked . . . . engañado/a
trip . . . . (el) viaje
trip, excursion . . . . (la) excursión
trip, stroll. . . . . (el) paseo
trip (to) . . . . tropezar (ie)
triumph (to). . . . . triunfar
trombone. . . . . (el) trombón
trophy . . . . (el) trofeo
tropical . . . . tropical
truck . . . . (el) camión
true, real . . . . .verdadero/a
trumpet . . . .(la) trompeta
trust (in), confidence. . . . . (la) confianza
trust (to). . . . . confiar en, fiarse de
truth. . . . . (la) verdad
try (to) . . . . .tratar (de)
try (to), to attempt. . . . . intentar
T-shirt . . . .(la) camiseta
tub. . . . . (la) bañera
Tuesday. . . . . martes
tuition . . . . (la) matrícula
tulip. . . . . (el) tulipán
tunnel. . . . . (el) túnel
turn (to), to revolve, to rotate
. . . . girar
turn in (to), to deliver,
to hand over. . . . . entregar
turn off (to) . . . . .apagar
turn on (to) . . . . prender
turn on (to) (e.g., a light)
to light (e.g., a fire). . . . . .encender (ie)
turtle . . . . (la) tortuga
twice . . . . .dos veces
twist (to), to bend . . . . .torcer (ue)
type . . . . (el) tipo
typical . . . . típico/a
tyrant . . . . (el) tirano

U

ugly . . . . feo/a
umbrella . . . . (el) paraguas
unbearable, intolerable . . . . insoportable
uncle . . . .(el) tío
uncomfortable. . . . . incómodo/a
under. .bajo
under, below . . . . debajo de
underline (to). . . . . subrayar
underneath. . . . . debajo
understand (to) . . . . comprender,
entender (ie)
underwear . . . . (los) calzoncillos,
(la) ropa interior
undress (to) . . . . desvestirse (i)
unfortunately. . . . .desafortunadamente,
por desgracia
unhappy. . . . . .desdichado/a, infeliz
unique, only . . . . único/a
universe. . . . . (el) universo
university. . . . . (la) universidad
until. . . . . hasta
untruthful, lying . . . . . . .mentiroso/a
up. . . . . arriba
up (to go). . . . . subir
upper, superior . . . . .superior
upset . . . . preocupado/a
urgent . . . . urgente
useless. . . . . inútil

V

vacation. . . . . (las) vacaciones
vacuum cleaner. . . . . . . (la) aspiradora
vacuum (to). . . . . . . pasar la aspiradora
valley. . . . . (el) valle
various. . . . . varios/as
VCR, video. . . . . . (el) video, (el) vídeo
vegetable. . . . . (la) verdura, (el) vegetal
vengeance, revenge. . . . . . (la) venganza
very . . . . muy
vest . . . .(el) chaleco
veterinarian . . . . (el/la) veterinario/a
victim . . . . (la) víctima
video, VCR. . . . . . (el) video, (el) vídeo
violence. . . . .(la) violencia
violin . . . . (el) violín
virtue . . . . (la) virtud
volcano . . . .(el) volcán
vote . . . .(el) voto
vulture . . . . (el) buitre

W

wait (to), to hope. . . . . esperar
wait in line (to) . . . . .hacer cola
waiter. . . . (el/la) camarero/a (mesero/a)
wake (to) (up). . . . . . . .despertarse (ie)
walk, stroll . . . . (la) caminata
walk (to) . . . . .andar, caminar

wall . . . . (la) pared
wallet. . . . . (la) billetera
want (to), to wish, to like . . . .querer (ie)
war. . . . . (la) guerra
warm, hot . . . . caliente
warrior. . . . . (el/la) guerrero/a
wary, careful, cautious . . . . . cauteloso/a
wash (to) . . . . lavar
wash (oneself) (to) . . . . lavarse
washer. . . . .(la) lavadora
waste (to), to spend. . . . . gastar
waste (time) (to) . . . . .perder (tiempo)
watch, clock . . . . (el) reloj
water . . . . (el) agua (f.)
water (to). . . . . regar (ie)
waterfall . . . . (la) catarata
wave . . . . (la) ola
we . . . . nosotros/as
weak . . . . débil
website . . . .(el) portal cibernético
wedding. . . . .(la) boda
Wednesday . . . . .miércoles
week . . . .(la) semana
weekend . . . .(el) fin de semana
weekly. . . . . .semanal
weight . . . . (el) peso
weights . . . .(las) pesas
well, fine . . . . .bien
well, so . . . . .pues
well-known . . . . conocido/a
west. oeste
western . . . . occidental
wet. . . . . mojado/a
wet (to), to moisten. . . . . .mojar
whale. . . . . (la) ballena
what?. . . . .¿qué?
what?, which? . . . .¿qué?, ¿cuál?
wheat. . . . . (el) trigo
when? . . . . ¿cuándo?
where?. . . . .¿dónde?
which?, what? . . . .¿cuál?, ¿qué?
which one(s)? . . . .¿cuál(es)?
which, that. . . . . que
while . . . . mientras
whisper . . . .(el) susurro
whisper (to). . . . . susurrar
whistle. . . . . .silbar
white . . . . blanco/a
who? . . . .¿quién?
whole, entire . . . . entero/a
why? . . . . ¿por qué?
wide. . . . . ancho/a
widower/widow. . . . . . .(el/la) viudo/a
wife . . . . (la) esposa
win (to), to earn . . . . .ganar
wind. . . . . (el) viento
window . . . .(la) ventana
windshield. . . . . (el) parabrisas
wine. . . . .(el) vino
wing. . . . .(el) ala (f.)
winter . . . . (el) invierno

wise, learned . . . . *sabio/a*
wish (to), to want, to like

. . . . *querer (ie)*
with . . . . *con*
with *(to have to do)* . . . . *tener que ver con*
without . . . . *sin*
witness. . . . . *(el/la) testigo*
wonderful, marvelous . . . . *maravilloso/a*
wonderful, terrific . . . . *formidable*
woman. . . . . *(la) mujer*
wood . . . . *(la) madera*
woods, forest . . . . *(el) bosque*
word . . . . *(la) palabra*
work . . . . *(el) trabajo, (la) obra*
work (to) . . . . *trabajar*
work (to), to function . . . . *funcionar*
worker . . . . *(el/la) obrero/a*
world . . . . *(el) mundo*
worry (to) . . . . *preocuparse*
worse, worst . . . . *peor*
worth the trouble (to [not] be)

. . . . *(no) valer la pena*
wound, injury . . . . *la herida*
wound (to). . . . . *herir (ie)*
wounded . . . . *herido/a*
wrestler . . . . *(el) luchador*
wrist, doll . . . . *(la) muñeca*
write (to) . . . . *escribir*
writer . . . . *(el/la) escritor/a*

Y

year . . . . *(el) año*
yellow . . . . *amarillo/a*
yes . . . . *sí*
yesterday . . . . *ayer*
you (familiar) . . . . *tú*
you (formal) . . . . *usted (Ud.)*
you all (familiar) . . . . *vosotros/as*
you all (formal) . . . . *ustedes (Uds.)*
younger . . . . *menor*
youngsters, youth . . . . *(los) jóvenes*
youth . . . . *(la) juventud*
youth, youngsters . . . . *(los) jóvenes*

Z

zero . . . . *cero*
zip code . . . . *(el) código postal*
zipper . . . . *(la) cremallera*
zoo . . . . . . *(el) jardín (parque) zoológico,*
(el) zoológico

◿◤ INDEX ◿◤

INDEX